DE PROPRIETATIBUS LITTERARUM

edenda curat

C. H. VAN SCHOONEVELD

Indiana University

Series Practica, 96

ART AND THE ARTIST

IN THE WORKS OF SAMUEL BECKETT

by

HANNAH CASE COPELAND

Slippery Rock State College

1975

MOUTON

THE HAGUE · PARIS

ISBN 90 279 3331 6

Printed in The Netherlands by Mouton & Co., The Hague

For Tom and Owen

Un dévoilement sans fin, voile derrière voile, plan sur plan de transparences imparfaites, un dévoilement vers l'indévoilable, le rien, la chose à nouveau.

Beckett, "Peintres de l'empêchement"

ACKNOWLEDGMENTS

This book grew out of a seminar project under the direction of George H. Bauer, whose inspiration was essential to its development. I would also like to express my appreciation to William T. Starr for his help in preparing the original text. Special thanks go to Deborah Gunther McHattie for her typing of the manuscript. Finally, I wish to thank all the many friends who encouraged me in this study.

H. C. C.

PREFACE

The works of Samuel Beckett are dominated by an obsession with the creative act. Although many critics have noted the increasing spareness of his successive novels and plays and the recurrent image of the artist creating, none has yet stated the full significance of the evolution of his works or demonstrated the central importance of the author-hero. By tracing the development of the fiction and drama and by examining the protagonists in the novels, this study exposes the heart of the Beckettian vision: intense self-consciousness.

Like Montaigne, who often interrupts the course of an essay to comment upon his writing and upon himself as author, Beckett's author-heroes practice self-criticism and seek self-knowledge through their creative efforts. In this way, they inevitably create portraits of themselves in the act of creating. This is not to say that Beckett's art lacks the kind of self-consciousness or scrupulous craftsmanship which characterizes Flaubert's *Madame Bovary*. Rather, one can say that Beckett is doubly self-conscious, for he not only calculates the effect of every comma but also takes that very labor, the creative process, as his perennial subject; in his author-heroes' creative toil, we see Beckett himself weigh and measure his own words. It is this inwardness or introspection, embodied in the frequent image of the unblinking inner eye fixed upon the self, that distinguishes Beckett's works from those of equally careful artists. For Beckett's art, unlike Flaubert's, reflects not the world of objective reality but that of subjective experience.

So acute and so central to Beckett's art is this self-consciousness, this relentless self-reflection, that it determines even the evolution of his works. In each successive work there are more and more direct allusions to the work itself as novel or play; in each one, fewer traditional devices veil its fabricated nature. In the most recent works, in fact, fiction and drama are stripped to the bare bones of word and gesture. Uncompromising in its lucidity, Beckett's art presents the truth about itself – that it is artificial, not real, or rather, that it is a reality in its own right, distinct from any other reality – and at the same time it reveals the undeniable truth of the human condition, that man is mortal, that we are all in the process of dying.

The evolution of the protagonist in the novels illustrates clearly how Beckett's caustic lucidity burns away all exterior surfaces to reach the essence of the human condition. His early heroes, who resemble those of traditional fiction, are soon replaced by decrepit old men and ultimately by all but disembodied creatures, mere heads. All of these later protagonists are self-portraits, reflections and almost parodies of Beckett's own role, for all are artists busily telling tales or composing novels. Moreover, they are all self-conscious; they comment upon their creative efforts, often criticizing themselves severely, especially when they try to evade self-contemplation by inventing stories. In short, they acknowledge that self-consciousness, the search for self-knowledge, is the guiding principle of artistic endeavor. These personae are the result of Beckett's own self-discipline, no less rigorous than theirs. Denying himself distractions, he can write of nothing but himself. Indeed, he is compelled by his one essential faculty, self-awareness, to speak only of the self, to seek to capture its essence in the mirror of art. And his labor, like that of Sisyphus, is endless because the self is ever changing, and his few remaining tools, language and his personae, are masks which obscure it. The very nature of his search dooms it to failure.

This study is an investigation of the abiding theme of self-consciousness in Beckett's works. Part One examines the principles of lucidity and honesty as set forth in the novels, plays, and critical essays and illustrates the effect of their application in the evolution of the works and protagonists. Part Two investigates in greater depth the image of the artist and his dilemma, quest, and inevitable failure. Quotations from Beckett are extensive; all key passages, essential to any further research concerning the problem of self-consciousness, are quoted in full. Pertinent material taken from the most reliable critics is also included.

The scholar who wishes to pursue the question of self-consciousness and related topics in Beckett's works will find in the bibliography the most worthwhile works of criticism published before the summer of 1970, when the research for this study was completed. Many of the books listed in Part II of the bibliography contain helpful bibliographies for further reference.

CONTENTS

PART ONE:

A SELF-CONSCIOUS ART

1. THE CAUSTIC ART OF SAMUEL BECKETT

The art of Samuel Beckett, like that of many other contemporary writers, is extremely self-conscious, having art and the artist[1] as important concerns. Many critics have already made this observation. For example, Lawrence Harvey has published the articles "Art and the Existential in *Waiting for Godot*" and "Samuel Beckett on Life, Art, and Criticism". Similarly, the central Beckettian figure of the artist creating has been widely remarked, inspiring articles such as "Moran-Molloy: The Hero as Author" by Edith Kern. Ruby Cohn, perhaps the most outstanding American critic of Beckett's works, even chose for the title of the introductory chapter to her book *Samuel Beckett: The Comic Gamut* the phrase, "portrait of the artist as an old bum". However, as I have indicated above, the importance of self-consciousness in artistic creation is not unique to Samuel Beckett. Actually Beckett belongs to a literary tradition, including Proust and Joyce, in which art and the artist are the subjects of art: "It was the mind of Europe before the mind of Beckett that turned literature toward a more and more intricate self-consciousness, confronting a Joyce or Proust with an intellectual landscape whose most mysterious feature is himself performing the act of writing."[2] (Maurice Beebe, in his book *Ivory Towers and Sacred Founts: The Artist as Hero in Fiction from Goethe to Joyce*, has made a thorough study of this tradition from Goethe and Rousseau to Proust and Joyce.) Yet the obsession with art, as both creative act and created object, has unique significance in Beckett's works and merits special study. The end of this study is to define his concern with the role of the artist and the meaning of art.

An unusual intensity of self-consciousness distinguishes Beckett's works

---

[1] The term *artist* has a broad application in Beckett's works. In his essay "La Peinture des van Velde", 356, he includes in this category the poet, the musician, the painter, and the philosopher. His main concern in the novels is with the artist as writer. But when he refers to 'the artist', he usually seems to have no specific kind of artist in mind – simply man creating.

[2] Kenner, *Samuel Beckett: A Critical Study*, 67.

from others in the tradition. Shorn of nonessential trappings and traditional illusions, reduced to their fundamental elements, his novels and
plays are stripped of pretension. They present themselves as what they
are – novels and plays – and do not attempt to pose as alternatives to the
real world. Indeed, they are startling metaphors for reality. Moreover, the
narrator (often the central character in Beckett's fiction), rather than trying to hide behind his work, concentrates ever more intensely on his own
creative activity and can speak of nothing else. As Jean-Jacques Mayoux
observes regarding Beckett's art, "One almost never sees the dream, without at the same time seeing the dreamer playing with his dream, receiving
and evoking his images."[3] In effect, the Beckettian narrator (or actor)
underlines in his art the very aspect that traditional novelists (and playwrights) seek most diligently to efface from their work – the process of
fabrication. Thus Beckett lays bare both novel and novelist, play and
players, displaying a degree of self-consciousness which, to Mrs. Cohn,
seems unequalled: "no other modern writer... has integrated the act of
creation so consistently and ironically into his own creation."[4] It would
be difficult to overemphasize the importance of this artistic lucidity, for it
determines the entire course of Beckett's creative efforts. Self-consciousness grows from one work to the next, and, as it develops, the fictional
atmosphere and characters (especially the central figure of the artist creating) reflect its deep penetration in their increasing starkness. Taking note
of this movement in the works, critics have described it variously. One
writes: "C'est une ascèse tendue vers la nudité... de l'être et de l'écriture."[5]
Another envisions the author as "closing the lid and paring himself to the
bone"[6] in the course of his novels. Still another identifies and analyzes the
instrument of self-perception used to probe the nature of artistic creation:
"the paradox of art employing art to deny itself is rooted in the power of
human consciousness to view itself both as subject and object."[7] The
creating artist's self-awareness aware of itself gnaws inward to the core
of the work, uncovering what has so long lain hidden beneath layers of
fictional convention – the creative act itself.

For Beckett, it is the role of art, then, to make visible the traditionally
invisible; the role of the artist, to make others see[8] what their limited
vision does not reveal to them. As Proust writes in *Le Temps retrouvé*,

---

[3]   Mayoux, "Beckett and Expressionism", 239.
[4]   Cohn, *The Comic Gamut*, 296.
[5]   Gresset, "Création et cruauté", 64.
[6]   Steiner, "Of Nuance and Scruple", 170.
[7]   Hassan, *The Literature of Silence*, 13.
[8]   Harvey, "Life, Art, and Criticism", 552.

"L'ouvrage de l'écrivain n'est qu'une espèce d'instrument optique qu'il offre au lecteur afin de lui permettre de discerner ce que sans ce livre, il n'eût peut-être pas vu en soi-même." [9] The artist does not seek to please his reader by presenting him with images that correspond to generally accepted notions or preconceptions. Rather he aims to inspire new insights. "Art does not reproduce the visible, it makes visible",[10] says Paul Klee; Beckett (and Proust) would undoubtedly agree. But to make visible is not an easy task for the artist. Beckett describes it as "un travail d'une complexité diabolique".[11] Bram van Velde, a Dutch painter whose works Beckett admires, speaks of the difficulty involved in making the creative act: "Je ne fais pas de la peinture. Je tâche de rendre visible des phénomènes de notre époque; ils sont nombreux, et je perds souvent la trace."[12] For him, the artistic imperative is: "Attraper la bête, ne pas la laisser échapper."[13] The artist must seize upon the inspired vision and transform it into an image or metaphor before it escapes him. Referring to the painting of Geer van Velde (Bram's younger brother), Beckett provides perhaps the most illustrative description of this demanding creative process: "Un dévoilement sans fin, voile derrière voile, plan sur plan de transparences imparfaites, un dévoilement vers l'indévoilable, le rien, la chose à nouveau."[14]

Such a ceaseless unveiling appears everywhere in Beckett's own work. Dissatisfied with anything less than pure lucidity in thought and style, he develops insight keen enough to pierce the densest of conceptual veils and to perceive the most nearly transparent ones. For this reason, he discerns and rejects metaphors that convey only an imperfect impression of his ideas. Indeed, he creates one work after another in the renewed attempt to penetrate still more layers of illusory surface material that separate the outward image in his work from his inner vision of the essential nature of that work and of its creation. But perfection can never be achieved, for, as long as the writer pursues precise correspondence between insight and image, the literary and cogitative medium itself – language – will prevent his realization of that goal. An obstacle to the effective representation of his vision, language also bars the way to self-knowledge, dulling self-per-

---

[9]   M. Proust, *Le Temps retrouvé*, *Œuvres complètes*, 7, pt. 2 (Paris: Nouvelle Revue Française, 1932), 68.
[10] Klee quoted by Jean Genêt, "Letter from Paris", *The New Yorker*, 27 December 1969, 42.
[11] "La Peinture des van Velde", 354.
[12] "Paroles de Bram van Velde", *Derrière le Miroir*, 11-12, 13.
[13] "Paroles de Bram van Velde", 13.
[14] "Peintres de l'empêchement", 7.

ception, veiling the essential impossibility of the artist's obligation, and
masking the utter inadequacy of his efforts. As Mrs. Cohn writes, Beckett
"seeks ignorance, impotence, nakedness. He comes as close to them as
literature can, but he cannot achieve them",[15] "that is his curse, as it is
ours – that man is, as Descartes defined him, 'a thing that thinks'".[16]
Conception blocks the spontaneous expression of perception, rendering
impossible the artist's task to make visible his fleeting insight. Language
distorts his spare vision with its connotative padding. Still, undaunted in
the face of impossibility, Beckett persists in creating. As a result, his works
present "an endless development towards the unachievable absence of intervening veil".[17] Carried out with determination and marked by perseverance even in the face of insurmountable obstacles, this consistent development follows a course (possibly plotted, consciously or unconsciously,
as early as the second full-length novel *Watt*) which is analogous to the
movement up a hierarchy of laughs – the bitter, the hollow, and the mirthless – explained by Watt's predecessor at Knott's Arsene: "They [the
laughs] correspond to successive, how shall I say... successive excoriations
of the understanding, and the passage from the one to the other is the
passage from the lesser to the greater, from the lower to the higher, from
the outer to the inner, from the gross to the fine, from the matter to the
form."[18] Just as this hierarchy culminates in the mirthless laugh, "the
risus purus, the laugh laughing at the laugh" (*Watt*, p. 48), so does Beckett's
art culminate in rigorously self-conscious and, hence, self-reflective works,
works in which the creator and the act of creation are of ultimate importance in the thing created.

But the nature of art and the mind of the artist are not Beckett's sole
concerns. Finding man's fate as inescapable as his own artistic obsessions,
Beckett treats the human condition in the same lucid way he does art.
With unwavering gaze he beholds our earthly plight and maintains his
firm grasp of the horror throughout his works. As Onimus describes it,
"Le regard bleu et glacial de Beckett ne se laisse pas divertir: il soutient
la vue du réel."[19] Intent on truth above all, Beckett reveals in his works an
"uncompromising determination to face the stark reality of the human
situation and to confront the worst without even being in danger of yielding to any of the superficial consolations that have clouded man's self-

---

[15]   Cohn, *The Comic Gamut*, 290.
[16]   *Ibid.*
[17]   Beckett, *Bram van Velde*, 2.
[18]   *Watt*, 48; referred to hereafter in the text with the appropriate page number in
parentheses.
[19]   Onimus, *Beckett*, 15.

awareness in the past".[20] Just as the artist and the work of art must be as self-conscious, as true to self, as possible, so man must recognize his essential nature "in all its naked absurdity".[21] Beckett explores the human condition "with uncompromising honesty, ruthless integrity, and utter frankness";[22] and, even though his readers might prefer to be distracted from their misery rather than compelled to face it, he makes "no concessions... to his readers' comfort".[23] As George Steiner says, "There is no discernible waste motion [in Beckett's works], no public flourish, no concession... to the noise and imprecisions of life."[24] Art must make visible the hidden realities – both those concerning itself and those of human destiny. It must not divert our thoughts from ourselves, but rather make us increasingly perceptive to the true nature of our dilemma.

Aiming to make visible the human condition in all its pitifulness, Beckett differs greatly from conventional novelists. As Claude Mauriac writes of him, "Cet auteur est à l'opposé des écrivains qui édulcorent ou qui enjolivent la réalité"; and he goes on to say that Beckett refuses all "abusives consolations extérieures".[25] Moreover, like Joyce, he makes demands on his readers "for clear and relentless thought, and for moral courage sufficient to look directly at the complexities, the horrors, the absurdities of contemporary existence".[26] Acknowledging Joyce's influence in those even greater demands which he makes on himself, Beckett reveals the essential importance of that influence: "Joyce had a moral effect on me – he made me realize artistic integrity".[27] Interpreting Beckett's sentiments in the matter of integrity (which are fully expounded in the essay on Joyce),[28] Martin Esslin finds that it is "the artist's duty to express the totality and complexity of his experience regardless of the public's lazy demand for easy comprehensibility".[29] In short, to realize artistic integrity, the artist must be faithful to his vision. Beckett, according to Ihab Hassan, fulfills his artistic obligations and deserves to be known as "a profoundly responsible artist" both for "his relentless will toward truth and [for] his naked art, which strips itself to meet truth

[20]   Esslin, "Introduction", 14.
[21]   Esslin, "Samuel Beckett", 128.
[22]   *Ibid.*
[23]   Fletcher, *Samuel Beckett's Art*, 17.
[24]   Steiner, "Of Nuance and Scruple", 164.
[25]   Mauriac, "Samuel Beckett", 77.
[26]   Brick, "The Madman in His Cell", 42.
[27]   Beckett quoted by Gruen, "Nobel Prize Winner, 1969", 210.
[28]   "Dante . . . Bruno . Vico . . Joyce".
[29]   Esslin, *The Theatre of the Absurd*, 2.

bravely".[30] Still, the futility inherent in his efforts must not be overlooked, for it is because he demands the impossible relevation of the irreducible nature of reality that he continues to create. Each renewed attempt to remove the last veil only exposes yet one more veil to be removed. Thus, unable to abandon the struggle even in the face of endless frustration, Beckett earns the designation of "un chercheur d'absolu".[31]

His preoccupation with essences and the essential is everywhere present in his works. In *Murphy* (his first novel), the hero is anxious to overcome his preference for certain kinds of cookies, included with others in a package he buys for lunch, in order not "to violate the very essence of assortment"[32] by consuming them always according to a fixed pattern. He realizes that "he could not partake in their fullness [translated by Beckett as *l'essence* in the French edition][33] until he had learnt not to prefer any one to any other" (p. 97). Beckett's predilection for the essential reveals itself also by opposition in his frequent expressions of scorn for the superficial, for the surfaces that mask the essence. Comparing Murphy and any introspective fellows he might have to "rare birds", the author criticizes shallow vision: "It was not in order to obtain an obscene view of the surface that in days gone by the Great Auk dived under the ice, the Great Auk now no longer seen above it" (p. 193). Here he not only makes plain by contrast the worth of what lies beneath the surface but also suggests that the attempt to reach it is fraught with mystery and danger. For the solipsist and the artist too, the desire to plumb the depths could prove fatal. In *Molloy* even Moran, the bourgeois protagonist of Part II, takes exception to surfaces that disguise the truth. Speaking of the messenger Gaber, who, "lourdement, sombrement endimanché",[34] pays him a Sunday morning visit, Moran remarks: "Cette grossière observance de façade, alors que l'âme exulte en ses haillons, m'a toujours paru une chose abominable" (pp. 144-145). Malone, narrator-hero of *Malone meurt*, writes of "l'essentiel" as opposed to "le fortuit"[35] and then attempts to explain what he means by it: "et par l'essentiel je dois entendre cette minuscule tête de lard, enfouie quelque part dans ma vraie tête je crois"

---

[30] Hassan, *The Literature of Silence*, 198.
[31] Onimus, *Beckett*, 16.
[32] *Murphy*, 96; referred to hereafter in the text with the appropriate page number in parentheses.
[33] *Murphy* (Paris, 1965), 73.
[34] *Molloy*, 144-145; referred to hereafter in the text with the appropriate page number in parentheses.
[35] *Malone meurt*, 114; referred to hereafter in the text with the appropriate page number in parentheses.

(p. 114). With regard to himself the essential is his consciousness, that which perceives the fortuitous, the body. Applying the same kind of reductive vision to things, he speaks of "une compréhension du Bâton, débarrassé de tous ses accidents" (p. 151). But he achieves this kind of perception only after he has lost his stick and only with pain and effort. Still, delighted by his new understanding ("Voilà du coup ma conscience singulièrement élargie", p. 152), he reveals his own preference for "un monde néantisé, purifié de toute contingence".[36] As might be expected, Malone too distrusts surfaces, telling himself sometimes that the window beside him is nothing but "du trompe-l'oeil" (p. 114), a painted surface made to resemble a window. One can never tell about appearances, he seems to suggest. Distrust becomes outright disdain in L'Innommable. Thoroughly conscious of his pitiable fate, the author-hero, about to be hooked like a fish by a remote "they", admits frankly that he would perhaps accept the genuine article honestly proffered but that he will not be fooled or cajoled by deceptive surfaces: "Un hameçon rouillé et nu, je l'accepterais peut-être. Mais toutes ces friandises."[37] All is not so evident to the narrator of "Texte IV". Aware only of the extraneous, he assigns himself the task of discovering just what the essential might be: "à côté de quoi, c'est ça qu'il faut voir".[38] Yet in so saying, he clearly indicates the function of art and the duty of the artist "to get below the surface, to touch submerged reality via apparent unreality".[39]

The most striking image of this obligation appears in the second act of En attendant Godot where Estragon implores Vladimir: "Alors fous-moi la paix avec tes paysages! Parle-moi du sous-sol!"[40] In Beckett's English translation one finds: "You and your landscapes! Tell me about the worms!"[41] Here the contrast between paysages and sous-sol, landscapes and worms, brings to light the frequent use of art to entertain and to mask. Though Vladimir wants to make his companion remember the diversions of the day before, Estragon is too preoccupied with his present misery to recall anything. Furthermore, he seems to recognize the relative unimportance of nuances (paysages) in the static decor of his situation. It is his

[36] Lamont, "La Farce métaphysique de Samuel Beckett", 99.
[37] L'Innommable, 132; referred to hereafter in the text with the appropriate page number in parentheses.
[38] Nouvelles et Textes pour rien, 154; hereafter, reference to the Textes will be included in the text with the appropriate page number in parentheses.
[39] Reid, "Beckett and the Drama of Unknowing", 136.
[40] En attendant Godot, 103; referred to hereafter in the text with the appropriate page number in parentheses.
[41] Waiting for Godot, 39B.

awareness of this basic condition that makes it impossible for him to think of anything else. Thus, try as he may to conceal the emptiness of their common fate with memories, Vladimir does not succeed in engaging his friend in the game, for Estragon will hearken only to tales of man's condition (*sous-sol*, worms).[42] Similarly, Beckett rejects that art which seeks only to veil the ugly truth of existence by means of distracting surfaces. As noted above, it is the function of art, according to Beckett, to lay bare the truth, not to conceal or dissemble it.[43] Rather than concern itself with the creation of momentary diversions from our condition and destiny, art should espouse the truth of the *sous-sol* and the worms, revealing ever more clearly the dilemma of all. The arist himself must learn to create without the help of landscapes; he must be able to say, like Malone, "avec moi je n'ai plus besoin de pittoresque" (*Malone*, p. 8).

Against those who cannot do so, Beckett brings a strong indictment in his essay on Proust.[44] Here he qualifies the artist as one "who does not deal in surfaces" (p. 46), as one who is "active but negatively, shrinking from the nullity of extracircumferential phenomena" (p. 48). In fact, as Fletcher puts it, Beckett "makes it quite clear that he shares Proust's contempt for naturalistic writing"[45] when he speaks of "the grotesque fallacy of a realistic art – 'that miserable statement of line and surface,' and the penny-a-line vulgarity of a literature of notations" (p. 57).[46] Two pages later he refers again to Proust's scorn of "the literature that 'describes,' [of] the realists and naturalists worshipping the offal of experience, prostrate before the epidermis and the swift epilepsy, and content to transcribe the surface, the façade, behind which the Idea is prisoner" (p. 59). Proust himself writes of the *roman à thèse*: "L'art véritable n'a que faire de tant de proclamations et s'accomplit dans le silence"; "la grossière tentation pour l'écrivain d'écrire des oeuvres intellectuelles. Grande indélicatesse. Une oeuvre où il y a des théories est comme un objet sur lequel on laisse la marque du prix."[47] Later in the same volume he criticizes superficial vision once again: "seule la perception grossière et erronée

---

[42] In *Mercier et Camier*, 169-170, Camier, Estragon's predecessor, reveals similar obsessions when he replies to Mercier's remarks about the heather: "En dessous il y a la tourbe", and then queries: "Crois-tu qu'il y a des vers, ... comme dans la terre?"
[43] In the words of M. Conaire of *Mercier et Camier*, 79: "Bas les masques".
[44] *Proust*; referred to hereafter in the text with the appropriate page number in parentheses.
[45] Fletcher, *Samuel Beckett's Art*, 20.
[46] Beckett translates from *Le temps retrouvé*, *Œuvres complètes*, 7, pt. 2 (Paris: Nouvelle Revue Française, 1932), 27, "la fausseté même de l'art prétendu réaliste", and 33, "un misérable relevé de lignes et de surfaces".
[47] *Le Temps retrouvé*, 28-29.

place tout dans l'objet quand tout, au contraire, est dans l'esprit".[48] Certainly Proust himself did not create superficial art. In fact, as Beckett notes in his essay, "He was incapable of recording surface.... The copiable he does not see. He searches for a relation, a common factor, substrata" (p. 63). Like Beckett, Proust, then is an artist of the *sous-sol* (though one of his particular kind); and he, too, calls attention to the artist's concern with the essential, referring to artistic meditation as "cette contemplation de l'essence des choses".[49] Moreover, when he writes of wanting to make his experiences of involuntary memory clear "jusque dans leurs profondeurs",[50] his words recall Beckett's frequent references to the depths, another image for the domain of the essential (as illustrated earlier in the example of the Great Auk). Indicating that he inhabits some lower region, the Unnamable asks, "Y a-t-il d'autres fonds, plus bas? Auxquels on accède par celui-ci? Stupide hantise de la profondeur" (p. 11). With his question, "Ne serais-je après tout qu'au sous-sol?" (p. 63), he entertains the possibility that there are even deeper strata lying beyond those where one achieves the simple realization of man's mutability and inevitable death. Other of his statements such as "tourner vers le dedans" (p. 61) and "seul abandon possible, en dedans" (p. 212) suggest that the artist must seek within himself for the essence of his art. Indeed, there can be no doubt of this, for Beckett states clearly in his essay on Proust what direction the artist must take: "The only fertile research is excavatory, immersive, a contraction of the spirit, a descent" (p. 48).

The realm of surfaces, then, has nothing to offer the artist. Only the essential, which lies deep within his own private world, holds any meaning for his art. Thus, as "a creature of the depths",[51] Beckett himself scorns "the world of surfaces, itself a refuge of the faint-hearted or the unconscious from the terrors of the ultimate".[52] Attempting always "to maintain man in a state of awareness of his deepest nature – from which the *divertissements* (in the Pascalian sense) of the surface world... – turn him away",[53] Beckett seeks an essential reality described variously as "the bases of Being",[54] "the marrow of eternity",[55] "le silence",[56] and "l'au-

---

[48]   *Le Temps retrouvé*, 74.
[49]   *Le Temps retrouvé*, 20.
[50]   *Le Temps retrouvé*, 22.
[51]   Hassan, *The Literature of Silence*, xi.
[52]   Harvey, "Life, Art, and Criticism", 547.
[53]   Harvey, 550.
[54]   Harvey, 547.
[55]   Hassan, *The Literature of Silence*, 115.
[56]   Lamont, "La Farce métaphysique", 107.

thentique".[57] But perhaps a better description of the essence he aims for would be one that emphasizes the mystery and horror of what lies in the depths – our gratuitousness and the dreadful emptiness of self-consciousness. As Jean Onimus writes, "Beckett focalise l'attention sur ce qu'il faut bien appeler le Terrible ou le Néant et qui se situe au centre de l'existence consciente."[58]

To make the essence visible, he must eliminate all diverting surfaces; he must empty his form of all extraneous ornamentation, strip it down to its fundamental elements, and chisel it to a fine transparency. Indeed, since it is the absence, the nothingness at the center of being, that he wishes to reveal in his art, Beckett is wary of every detail that prevents our perceiving the central cavity behind it. This passion for perfectly transparent art, which appears first as a simple desire for purification (in *Murphy* the statue of Rima is "being cleaned of a copious pollution of red permanganate", p. 96), becomes a mania in the later works where to speak or write is to violate the silence or the blank page. As Molloy says, "on ferait mieux, enfin aussi bien, d'effacer les textes que de noircir les marges, de les boucher jusqu'à ce que tout soit blanc et lisse" (*Molloy*, p. 17). Later he expresses a similar taste for what has been wiped clean or purged when he speaks of winter's effect on the earth: "l'hiver la [la terre] débarrasserait de ces croûtes dérisoires" (*Molloy*, p. 73). Working as a gardener, Macmann, Malone's fictional creature, is handicapped by his predilection for soil made bare of plants: "le besoin de faire place nette et de ne plus avoir sous les yeux qu'un peu de terre marron débarrassée de ses parasites, c'était souvent plus fort que lui" (*Malone*, p. 131). The narrator-hero of *Premier amour* exhibits a similar passion for emptiness upon seeing the room where he is to stay in his mistress's apartment: "Je regardai la chambre avec horreur. Une telle densité de meubles dépasse les forces de l'imagination.... Je commençai à sortir les meubles par la porte qui donnait sur le couloir."[59] In *Mercier et Camier* too, there is the suggestion that things corrupt space and weigh one down by their superfluity. Camier, having disposed of his detective notes, declares: "M'être débarrassé de toute cette saleté m'a fait du bien. Je me sens plus léger."[60] The protagonist of *Comment c'est* considers his own presence in the mud a flaw and speaks of himself and his fellows sinking "sous cette boue noire

---

[57] Lamont, 109.
[58] Onimus, *Beckett*, 16.
[59] *Premier amour*, 41; referred to hereafter in the text with the appropriate page number in parentheses.
[60] *Mercier et Camier*, 92; referred to hereafter in the text with the appropriate page number in parentheses.

dont rien ne viendrait plus souiller la surface".[61] Feeling *de trop*, this author-hero thinks of himself as a distraction from the essential barrenness of
his fictional surroundings. But it is Moran who expresses with greatest
gusto the zeal for laying bare: "J'ai toujours aimé écorcher les branches et
mettre à nu la jolie stèle claire et lisse" (*Molloy*, p. 232). Later, after amus-
ing himself with "d'enfantins espoirs", he takes pleasure in the contemplation of his own inner emptiness: "puis je les [les espoirs] balayais, d'un
grand coup de balai dégoûté, je m'en nettoyais et je regardais avec satisfaction le vide qu'ils avaient pollué" (*Molloy*, p. 251). The mind itself,
then, is subject to pollution by extraneous material. For the Unnamable,
the fictional creatures which inhabit his inner world appear as a form of
dirt: "Impossible de m'en débarbouiller sans les nommer" (*L'Innommable*,
p. 79). Moreover, he is sensitive to the meaningless superfluity about him
and to what lies beneath it: "une vague idée de ce qu'il aurait fallu sous-
traire à ce décor pour que ce soit le vide et le silence" (p. 96). Here silence
and emptiness frame the gratuitousness of noisy being, as they do also
in Moran's words: "Se taire et écouter, pas un être sur cent n'en est capable, ne conçoit même ce que cela signifie. C'est pourtant alors qu'on dis-
tingue, au delà de l'absurde fracas, le silence dont l'univers est fait"
(*Molloy*, p. 188). Through these and other like statements, Beckett's creator-heroes call for an art that uncovers the essential absurdity of existence by purifying itself of illusory surfaces.

To describe the Beckettian technique of purification, critics often use
strong terms. Martin Gerard writes: "His work in fact in one of its aspects
is a simple and terrible cauterisation of the corruption of literary emotion,
the corruption of feeling.... It is a denial, a protest against the temptation
to falsify experience... [and against] the assumptions of extraneous and
more picturesque personality which are all too indigenous to the human
animal... his work asserts that most other writing... is a lie".[62] Comparing
Beckett's mental refinery to a crucible, [63]Claude Mauriac notes: "Situations et dialogues sortent de cet incandescent creuset réduits à un essentiel
à peine perceptible."[64] Hassan speaks in a similar way of Beckett's
poetry, though adopting the image of burning cold rather than that of
intense heat: "His poetry is like dry ice: it burns or freezes whatever it

---

[61] *Comment c'est*, 171; referred to hereafter in the text with the appropriate page number in parentheses.
[62] Gerard, "Molloy becomes Unnamable", 316.
[63] Compare Beckett's image for the mind of Marcel: "the tireless crucible of his mind",
Proust, 40.
[64] Mauriac, "Samuel Beckett", 92.

touches and leaves nothing superfluous in sight."[65] (Beckett himself uses
the metaphor of consuming flame to describe the effects of Proust's involuntary memory: "it abstracts the useful, the opportune, the accidental,
because in its flame it has consumed Habit and all its works, and in its
brightness revealed what the mock reality of experience never can and
never will reveal – the real", *Proust*, p. 20.) Mayoux writes of Beckett's
art as "a mirror of truth": "Must we not see that it reflects the depths,
cutting through appearances to what is hidden?"[66] Yet it is again Beckett's
own words which describe the caustic action of his art most impressively,
as he contrasts Proust's works to those of the realists: "Whereas the
Proustian procedure is that of Apollo flaying Marsyas and capturing
without sentiment the essence, the Phrygian waters" (*Proust*, p. 59). Accepting only the essential, Beckett is merciless before intervening veils,
even if they be made of flesh. All illusory surfaces must be rent, though
beneath them lurk a skeleton. Indeed, the essence he often reveals in his
art is our doom, a dreadful sight rather than a diversion. But the harsh
reality which he lays bare makes his art eternally true and satisfies our
desire for reliable statements about our common misery. As Harvey
writes, "devant lui les surfaces conventionnelles de la vie quotidienne se
dissolvent pour nous mettre en contact avec une réalité plus satisfaisante
bien que plus dure".[67] To explore "the essence of the experience of being",[68]
Beckett must "strip away the inessentials",[69] for he aims "to distinguish
between the merely accidental characteristics that make up an individual
and the essence of his self".[70] He searches for the nature of reality "by
eliminating and discarding layer after layer of accidental qualities, by
peeling off skin after skin of the onion".[71] Inevitably, then, use of this
caustic technique produces "solutions toward the insoluble kernel or
void"[72] and leads to the revelation of a *néant* – that which remains at the
core of the onion. Thus making visible the invisible essence of our existence, Beckett's works move us by their fearful starkness, for they frame
the miserable emptiness and utter futility of the human condition.

[65]   Hassan, *The Literature of Silence*, 199.
[66]   Mayoux, "Beckett and Expressionism", 239.
[67]   Harvey, "Initiation du poète", 166.
[68]   Esslin, "Godot and His Children", 137.
[69]   *Ibid.*
[70]   *Ibid.*
[71]   Esslin, "Samuel Beckett", 129.
[72]   Harvey, "Life, Art, and Criticism", 562.

2. HABIT AND SUFFERING

The caustic effect of Beckett's art reduces the human figure to the minimal dimensions of its importance. Engulfed by the infinite universe, bowed and worn beneath his endless misery, the Beckettian protagonist is deprived of every characteristic which would make him seem the master of his situation. Unlike the human figures of classical art which seem to take on the eternal quality of stone (so altogether foreign to the human being), Beckett's men demonstrate to the fullest the transience and fragility of the human condition. Constantly aware of their utter gratuitousness, they themselves are thin transparencies which make clearly visible our plight. Indeed, one can say that they appear "dans leur nudité dernière".[1] It is not surprising, then, that Beckett's work should be compared to that of Giacometti "whose figures cosmic vastness whittles to such a painful smallness".[2] The "spare, barren atmosphere"[3] of this painter's canvases recalls Beckett's own denuded fictional world. Similarly, Giacometti displays in his works adherence to the same kind of principles which give Beckett's art its caustic effect: "Giacometti treats the surface of the canvas and its frame as a field to be emptied rather than filled.... His destruction of the frame results in 'a true void,' a quality of transparency described by Sartre as 'layers of emptiness'."[4] Despising frivolous art that fills up and paints over, hides and stuffs, both artists practice that kind of serious art which pares and chisels, strips and empties. According to Harvey, it is "the eternal conditions of human existence with which art is concerned";[5] and, hence, "all true art lays bare the human condition".[6] Beckett would seem to agree, for in one of his essays on the painters van Velde he writes:

[1] Lamont, "La Farce métaphysique", 99.
[2] Updike, "How How It Is Was", 315.
[3] Bauer, *Sartre and the Artist*, 114.
[4] *Ibid.*
[5] Harvey, "Life, Art, and Criticism", 557.
[6] Harvey, 559.

"au fond la peinture ne les intéresse pas. Ce qui les intéresse, c'est la condition humaine." [7] Irrefutable concurrence can be found in his works.

Careful study of the novels and plays discloses that Beckett "has distilled the work of art in order to focus it on the metaphoric representation of the human condition".[8] As John Erickson says, "in sloughing off the skin of artificiality and convention Beckett has brought the concrete human condition into a much truer perspective than have any of the present day existentialists".[9] Rather than forcing himself to follow the conventions of traditional literary forms, Beckett reduces these conventions to their fundamental elements, producing purified forms that work for him, that are capable of "presenting a vision of life stripped to its bare, degrading essentials".[10] In his works he "shows man's existence to be what it is: Transient, and for much of the time unhappy, ended by a death that makes nonsense of hope."[11] Further, he emphasizes this basic misery by presenting the human condition as "increasingly pathetic"[12] in each successive work. Indeed, chiselling away at his concept of man's destiny, he is left with less and less of what makes life endurable. Finally, in the later works, as Claude Mauriac writes, "il subsiste une donnée existentielle brute qui récuse, et tout à la fois implique, l'idée obsédante et nue de la mort."[13] As early as *Murphy* Beckett formulates concisely the gamut of man's existence in the phrase: "from the spermarium to the crematorium" (p. 78). In *Watt* he traces human destiny at greater length in a threnody (pp. 34-35) and a short poem (p. 247). Sidney Warhaft describes the former as follows: "The content of both stanzas... forms a kind of fragmented summary of, and commentary upon, the human condition moving through the full term of life in a cold meaningless universe."[14] Here Beckett underscores the futility of human activity. "From generation to generation", Warhaft writes, "man slips through life in a kind of music-hall routine"; and he continues, "To the accompaniment of seemingly inane exchanges, humanity dwindles away through division and inanition into tedium and forgottenness."[15] In the Addenda to *Watt*, Beckett specifically designates the revelation of human fate as the task of the artist and seems to imply

[7]   "La Peinture des van Velde", 354.
[8]   Bishop, "Samuel Beckett", 59.
[9]   Erickson, "Objects and Systems", 121.
[10] Glicksberg, "Samuel Beckett's World of Fiction", 35.
[11] Fletcher, *The Novels of Samuel Beckett*, 226-227.
[12] Cohn, *The Comic Gamut*, 117.
[13] Mauriac, "Samuel Beckett", 77.
[14] Warhaft, "Threne and Theme in *Watt*", 262.
[15] Warhaft, "Threne and Theme", 176.

by his interrogatory tone that no one is really capable of effecting it:

who may tell the tale
of the old man?
weigh absence in a scale?
mete want with a span?
the sum assess
of the world's woes?
nothingness
in words enclose? (p. 247)

Since the core of existence can only be expressed in negative terms – age, absence, want, woe, nothingness –, the duty to speak of it in the positive medium of art becomes exceedingly difficult. Still, there is nothing else to tell of according to Malone, who says of his stories: "de vie et de mort, si c'est bien de cela qu'il est question, et je suppose que oui, car il n'a jamais été question d'autre chose, á mon souvenir" (*Malone*, p. 93). The narrator of "Texte VI" seems to agree, saying he will relate "une petite histoire, aux êtres vivants allant et venant sur une terre habitable bourrée de morts, une brève histoire, sous le va-et-vient du jour et de la nuit" (*Textes*, p. 174).

Life is a coming and going, but in spite of its repetitive aspects it is above all a journey with a definite end in store: "[un] long voyage faisable, destination tombe, à faire dans le silence, petit pas irrévocable après petit pas, dans les longs couloirs d'abord, puis en plein air mortel, à travers jours et nuits, de plus en plus vite, non, de plus en plus lentement" (*Textes*, p. 191). Once born, man breathes the mortal air – mortal because living is dying: "tant tout meurt, à peine né" (*Textes*, p. 189). As the trilogy of short stories[16] illustrates, man is expelled from the womb ("L'Expulsé"), waits for death ("Le Calmant"), and dies ("La Fin"). Onimus writes of Beckett's men: "Le mouvement qui entraîne les personnages est celui du temps destructeur: ils sortent de chez eux, de leur coquille natale et les voilà pour toujours condamnés à errer.... Nous sommes tous des expulsés, tous tombés du nid."[17] Caught up in the passage of time, we are born, live, and die; but, though our individual destinies are linear, we participate in the cyclical development of all existence. Beckett has integrated this aspect of life into his most concentrated portrayal of the human condition, the play *Breath*.[18] In this brief production (lasting only about thirty seconds), a series of utterances – birth cry, inspiration, and expiration or death

---

[16] The *Nouvelles* appear with *Textes pour rien* in the single volume *Nouvelles et Textes pour rien*; hereafter, reference to the *Nouvelles* will be included in the text with the appropriate page number in parentheses.

[17] Onimus, *Beckett*, 56-57.

[18] *Breath*, produced by the British Broadcasting Company for television, was presented by the National Broadcasting Company on its program "First Tuesday", April 7, 1970.

rattle – summarizes man's lot. It must be noted, however, that the death rattle is followed by a second birth cry. Though one man dies, another is always available to take his place. The absurd human situation forever perpetuates itself.

Elsewhere in his works Beckett stresses the intimate rapport between man and the earth, showing the former to be nothing but a momentary extension of the latter.[19] Thus, Estragon's insisting that he has lived all his life "au milieu des sables" and in the Merdecluse (*Godot*, pp. 103, 104) reflects not only the terrible poverty (both physical and spiritual) that he has endured but also his close relationship with the barren soil he treads. In the *Textes* there are more references to the desert, indicating that it is all we have before us (p. 189) and that it is our natural habitat ("tu peux déboucher dans la haute dépression de Gobi, tu t'y sentiras chez toi", p. 145). The traveller in *Comment c'est* lives in the mud, becoming almost one with it. His existence seems to depend on it, for he suggests that he has come forth from it and that it will swallow him up at some future moment: "je sors du sommeil et y retourne entre les deux il y a tout à faire à supporter à rater à bacler à mener à bonne fin avant que la boue se rouvre" (p. 28). The mud even serves as a source of inspiration for his visions. Writes Mrs. Cohn: "In *Comment c'est*, it is the narrator who breathes into the mud, and who draws the image from mud which he rolls on his tongue."[20] But, because of his infinite misery, death (the only effective purifier) would be a relief: "plus souiller la boue... le noir... plus troubler le silence... crever... CREVER hurlements JE POURRAIS CREVER hurlements JE VAIS CREVER hurlements bon" (p. 177). So do many other Beckettian characters long for their final reassimilation into the dust. For the narrator of "From an Abandoned Work", the prospect of worms awaiting him is welcome: "Just under the surface I shall be, all together at first, then separate and drift, through all the earth and perhaps in the end through a cliff into the sea, something of me. A ton of worms in an acre, that is a wonderful thought, a ton of worms, I believe it".[21] This state of dissolution he compares with the nonexistence which precedes life, as he speaks of becoming "as when I was not yet" (p. 145). His eager anticipation of annihilation is equalled in intensity by the frantic desire of Mrs. Rooney in *All That Fall* "to be in atoms, in atoms! (*Frenziedly.*) ATOMS!"[22]

---

19 The epigraph to Beckett's *Proust* is Leopardi's "E fango è il mondo".
20 Cohn, *The Comic Gamut*, 200.
21 "From an Abandoned Work", 145; referred to hereafter in the text with the appropriate page number in parentheses.
22 *All That Fall*, 43.

Beckett uncovers, then, those aspects of existence which most men would rather overlook: "le fait d'être là pour mourir" [23] and "man's fundamental solitude".[24] Alone and aware of our mortality, we prefer to flee from the truth of our situation, even though we can never succeed in evading it completely: "Nothing, the negation of all that is, permeates existence, despite the struggle mankind wages to keep it hidden and slumbering in the dark. All existence is shot through with this inescapable experience of dread, which can arise suddenly at any time." [25] But Beckett, refusing to compromise with our cowardice, places before us through his art the emptiness of our condition and the nothingness of our fate. As Hassan explains it, "In revealing man in his absolute nudity, doubt, and solitude, he has bravely revealed what modern man has experienced and wished to conceal from himself.... [his] darkest dread: the void." [26]

Faced with the real horror of his situation, man tries to elude it through "the beguiling narcotic of habit". [27] As Vladimir remarks, "L'air est plein de nos cris.... Mais l'habitude est une grande sourdine" (Godot, p. 157). Through habit we divert our thoughts from our misery, dull our sensibility, and, hence, deaden the pain of existing. (Even the tormented Worm of L'Innommable could expect his pain to be numbed by habit. Wonders the narrator, "The dulling effect of habit, how do they deal with that?")[28] In his essay on Proust, Beckett defines habit at length: "Habit is a compromise effected between the individual and his environment,... the guarantee of a dull inviolability, the lightning-conductor of his existence. Habit is the ballast that chains the dog to his vomit. Breathing is habit. Life is habit. Or rather life is a succession of habits... the pact must be continually renewed.... Habit then is the generic term for the countless treaties concluded between the countless subjects that constitute the individual and their countless correlative objects" (Proust, p. 7). Some pages later he explains its function: "The fundamental duty of Habit... consists in a perpetual adjustment and readjustment of our organic sensibility to the conditions of its worlds" (p. 16). Habit works against man's seeing the uncomfortable truth of his condition. It can even blind him to his own mutability, helping him shift with a minimum of discomfort from youth to maturity to old age. As Pronko explains, "Man is born through suffering into a world in which he continues to suffer, until soon, numbed by

[23]   Onimus. Beckett, 14.
[24]   Hassan, The Literature of Silence, 122.
[25]   Glicksberg, "Forms of Madness in Literature", 43.
[26]   Hassan, The Literature of Silence, 209.
[27]   Todd, "Proust and Redemption in Godot", 175.
[28]   The Unnamable, 367; L'Innommable, 164.

habit, he is overtaken by death."[29] Man possesses a "first nature... corresponding... to a deeper instinct than the mere animal instinct of self-
preservation" (*Proust*, p. 11), but the glimpses of the truth which it affords
are cut short by habit: "Habit has laid its veto on this form of perception,
its action being precisely to hide the essence – the Idea – of the object in
the haze of conception – preconception.... The creature of habit turns
aside from the object that cannot be made to correspond with one or
other of his intellectual prejudices, that resists the propositions of his team
of syntheses, organised by Habit on labour-saving principles" (*Proust*,
pp. 11-12).

Habit, then, is not "a fixed attitude toward an unchanging world", but
"the quality of mind that mechanically adapts the individual's perception
to the changes which may occur momentarily in reality, and thereby
protects him from the shock of change by allowing him to see each occurrence abstractly, generically, and not in its disquieting uniqueness".[30] To
refer problems to habit for solution becomes a habit in itself. Thus enslaved
by habit, one might even spend one's days "wondering what there was for
dinner" ("From", p. 142). (In *Mercier et Camier* the image of the bourgeois ruled by habit is more extensive: "Chacun se hâte vers son petit
royaume, vers sa femme qui attend, vers ses bêtes bien au chaud, vers ses
chiens à l'affût du maître," p. 75.) As Huguette Deyle says, "pour Beckett
l'habitude engourdit la conscience humaine".[31] His characters themselves
admit to practicing evasion. "Et pour ce qui est de laisser de côté l'essentiel, je m'y connais je crois", writes Molloy (*Molloy*, p. 122); and Moran
reveals a similar weakness: "Le noeud de l'affaire Molloy, j'évitais toujours d'y penser" (*Molloy*, p. 152). Ever fearful of being lost in the infini-
tude of reality, "man clings blindly to oversimplifications rather than to
vital forms of perception".[32]

There is more than one mode of evasion, however. Indeed, as Beckett
notes in *Murphy*, "How various are the ways of looking away!" (p. 264).
Ironically, art, which makes visible the inner essential truth, can also be
used to divert man from his nothingness. Because of its stylized nature
even the sparest art has the effect of a mask or veil, creates a distracting
surface beneath which the terrible verity lies hidden. In fact, men expect
art to divert them from their misery, as one of the "Letters of Protest"
appended to an early collection of essays on *Finnegans Wake* illustrates.

---

[29]   Pronko, *Avant-garde: The Experimental Theater in France*, 34.
[30]   Torrance, "Modes of Being and Time in *Godot*", 79.
[31]   Deyle, *Samuel Beckett*, 74
[32]   Brick, "The Madman in His Cell", 43.

G. V. L. Slingsby, author of the letter, explains how he was reduced to approaching the new work: "I tried to put myself in the place of, say, the dentist's waiting room reader, who will bury himself in any bit of printed matter, from Archaeology to steam fitting, to escape the acute apprehension of his impending doom."[33] Yet it may be, as Frederick Hoffman suggests, that "the fact of existence is only palliated by the imagination".[34] Song and story do seem to just make life bearable for many of Beckett's characters. In *More Pricks Than Kicks*, Beckett's first collection of short stories, the Smeraldina, one of the hero's sweethearts, writes to him of the comfort she derives from playing the piano; even though the execution of a Beethoven sonata is not easy for her, "it is the onely [sic] thing that can take [her] away from [her] misery".[35] Similarly, in the radio play *Words and Music*, the aged Croak relies on the songs he demands from his servants Words and Music. As Kenner explains it, Croak requires "a dismal, gratifying song. To rehearse in the mind, in time of need, the gratifications life never offered, or, offering, saw refused: this is Croak's need and Croak's comfort."[36] The author-heroes attempt to lose themselves in their stories. "Ce dont j'ai besoin c'est des histoires, j'ai mis longtemps à le savoir", writes Molloy (*Molloy*, p. 16). The narrator of "Le Calmant" declares: "je vais donc essayer de me raconter encore une histoire, pour essayer de me calmer" (*Nouvelles*, p. 42). As for Malone, he "indulges in the creation of other lives, hoping in this way to ease the torment of his last hours".[37] Thus, fiction, like music, appears as "man's comfort",[38] though it can provide only illusory and fleeting relief from the issueless predicament of existence.

Those who consistently prefer fictional illusion to reality, however, have succumbed to as deadly a habit as habit itself. Numbed and blinded, be it by habit or by the diversion art can give, man has only "the dull inertia which in the end becomes a comfortable, living death".[39] By forfeiting self-consciousness, man virtually ceases to live; he lives but is not alive. The demanding art of essences is not for those who have given up their

---

[33] Slingsby, "Writes A Common Reader", *Our Exagmination Round His Factification for Incamination of Work in Progress*, ed. by Sylvia Beach (Paris: Shakespeare and Co., 1929), 190. There are many indications that Slingsby is Beckett's creation.

[34] Hoffman, *Samuel Beckett: The Language of Self*, 129.

[35] *More Pricks Than Kicks*, 86; referred to hereafter in the text with the appropriate page number in parentheses.

[36] Kenner, "Progress Report, 1962-65", 67.

[37] Hayman, *Samuel Beckett*, 95.

[38] Kenner, *A Critical Study*, 89.

[39] Butler, "Anatomy of Despair", 19.

lucidity. As Beckett writes in an epigraph to a collection of Bram van
Velde's paintings: "A painting of life and death. Natron lovers, abstain."[40]
In danger of embalming ourselves in life, we must be on guard lest we fail
to perceive the truth of our experience. We must be ready to "cast off our
protective cloak of habit and stand vulnerably naked"[41] before every new
phenomenon. Above all, we must refuse the easy, cheap comfort of a
frivolous art that bows to the service of habit. To seek escape from oneself
and one's misery is useless and can only postpone temporarily the necessary confrontation with being. Furthermore, ineffective measures of dealing with the truth of our condition prove deceptive. They are, as Onimus
describes them, "Consolations qui, sous une apparence tonique, sont des
poisons: cela aveugle, cela endort, cela procure un faux bien-être qui
estompe la pure souffrance d'exister."[42]

Serious art, on the contrary, pierces the protective shield of habit,
stimulates perception, opens our eyes to the torment of existence. Indeed,
to be effective, art must be able to penetrate the thickest armor of complacency: "Il faut rompre la carapace d' indifférence que l'adaptation au
monde a formée pour atteindre l'individu authentique."[43] Though art
cannot save man from his plight, it can rescue him "from the clutch of
routine" and enable him "to perceive the... truth behind the veil of con-
cealment".[44] Perception of the truth is painful, however, as numerous
images from the works demonstrate. Molloy, for example, speaks of float-
ing "au fond d'une torpeur miséricordieuse traversée de brefs et abomina-
bles éclairs" (*Molloy*, p. 81). The protagonist of "La Fin" tells of "les
bruits qui coupent, percent, lacèrent, contusionnent" (*Nouvelles*, p. 119).
Yet he prefers the suffering of awareness to the illusory comfort of evasion,
even in the midst of his own nothingness: "Ce que j'aurais voulu, c'étaient
des coups de marteau, pan, pan, pan, frappés dans le désert" (*Nouvelles*,
p. 118). Suffering at least seems real, representing "notre seul repère
valable dans la fluidité de la conscience. Elle arrête le temps."[45] For
Beckett, suffering is that mode of apprehension diametrically opposed to
habit.[46] Possible only when habit has relaxed its hold on our consciousness
(and before it has had time to reorganize its forces), the experience of

---

40   *Bram van Velde*, 72; natron, a hydrated sodium carbonate, is used in embalming.
See Harvey, "Life, Art, and Criticism", 548.
41   Torrance, "Modes of Being and Time", 77.
42   Onimus, *Beckett*, 48.
43   Deyle, *Samuel Beckett*, 74.
44   Glicksberg, "Forms of Madness", 43.
45   Deyle, *Samuel Beckett*, 42.
46   Mayoux, "Samuel Beckett and Universal Parody", 88.

suffering is necessarily brief. Describing these rare moments, Beckett writes: "The periods of transition that separate consecutive adaptations... represent the perilous zones in the life of the individual, dangerous, precarious, painful, mysterious and fertile, when for a moment the boredom of living is replaced by the suffering of being.... The suffering of being: that is the free play of every faculty. Because the pernicious devotion of habit paralyses our attention, drugs those handmaidens of perception whose co-operation is not absolutely essential" (*Proust*, pp. 8-9). The "tense and provisional lucidity" (*Proust*, p. 9) that reigns when habit has been momentarily put to confusion represents our "first nature" [47] which "is laid bare during these periods of abandonment. And its cruelties and enchantments are the cruelties and enchantments of reality" (*Proust*, p. 11). Lucidity brings pain. In fact, the interval between the death of an old habit and the birth of a new one may be fraught with suffering. In the strange hotel room at Balbec, the child Marcel can find no peace: "All his faculties are on the alert, on the defensive, vigilant and taut, and as painfully incapable of relaxation as the tortured body of La Balue in his cage, where he could neither stand upright nor sit down" (*Proust*, p. 12). Yet even if habit is only temporalily suspended, the result of its absence may be shockingly painful. On his hasty return to Paris, motivated by anxiety for his grandmother whose voice had sounded so unfamiliar on the telephone, Marcel (now a young man) finds that "his habit is in abeyance.... The notion of what he should see has not had time to interfere its prism between the eye and its object. His eye functions with the cruel precision of a camera; it photographs the reality of his grandmother", revealing "a stranger whom he has never seen" (*Proust*, p. 15). Thus, when habit ceases to function, suffering "opens a window on the real" (*Proust*, p. 16).

To reveal essences, then, art must use suffering, "the tool which penetrates the shield of habit ruling normal lives and allows the truth to be perceived".[48] It must present a clear image of man's plight, of the suffering of being itself. By stating in simple terms the bare facts of mutability and mortality, art can expose the illusory nature of our blind contentment and compel us to behold the agonizing truth. Beckett's protagonists inspire horror "parce qu'ils mettent en présence d'évidences que la vie par tous les moyens s'efforce de masquer";[49] they succeed in putting habit to flight because "ces monstres témoignent de la condition humaine avec une

---

[47]   As opposed to habit, which Proust has called "a second nature", *Proust*, 11.
[48]   Beebe, *Ivory Towers and Sacred Founts*, 246.
[49]   Onimus, *Beckett*, 138.

force qui arrache tous les masques".[50] An art which unmasks does not aim
to amuse; rather it seeks to produce in the observer a painful recognition
of his own personal truth. (The experience might be likened to that of
Poe's hero upon seeing the House of Usher: an "utter depression of soul",
"the hideous dropping off the veil".)[51] Whatever the shock or pain involved, however, there can be no doubt that Beckett prefers the kind of
art which deals in the revelation of disquieting truths. Such an art is not
popular, for, as Sir Herbert Read points out, people admire those in
public performance who voice commonplace thoughts and instinctive
judgments like their own. Labouring under the illusion that "truth need
not be disturbing", they view complacency as "the ultimate ideal of a
democratic way of life".[52] "Art, on the other hand", writes Sir Herbert,
"is eternally disturbing, permanently revolutionary. It is so because the
artist, to the degree of his greatness, always confronts the unknown, and
what he brings back from that confrontation is a novelty, a new symbol,
a new vision of life, the outer image of inward things."[53] To make visible
the invisible, to strip existence of its illusory surfaces, to unseal the eyes of
men, is not a joyous or pleasant task. Nor will it gain for the artist immediate acclaim. Still, Beckett chooses this *via dolorosa*, for it brings him
ever closer to the ideal representation of his vision in art.

His predilection for an art that lays bare the suffering of being takes on
a new dimension when we understand that reason has no place in this
kind of artistic activity. Like Proust, Beckett espouses an "anti-intellectual
attitude" (*Proust*, p. 65)[54] and affirms "the value of intuition" (*Proust*,
p. 66). He hails Proustian impressionism as the "non-logical statement of
phenomena in the order and exactitude of their perception, before they
have been distorted into intelligibility in order to be forced into a chain
of cause and effect"; and he identifies Elstir as "the type of the impres-
sionist, stating what he sees and not what he knows he ought to see"
(*Proust*, p. 66). Art, then, should not fulfill the expectations of minds
bound up in logic, nor should it anticipate the preconceptions of the
popular majority. The artist must consider every experience as unique,
and his works must reflect that uniqueness in their own. To explain this
idea, Beckett recalls "Schopenhauer's definition of the artistic procedure

---

[50]   Onimus, *Beckett*, 139.
[51]   Edgar Allan Poe, "The Fall of the House of Usher", *The Literature of the United States*, ed. by Walter Blair et al. (Chicago: Scott, Foresman and Company, 1966), 769.
[52]   Read, "The Necessity of Art", 26.
[53]   *Ibid.*
[54]   See also the essays on van Velde.

as 'the contemplation of the world independently of the principle of reason'" (*Proust*, p. 66). The work of art conceived in this way is "a private object, intellectually inaccessible and inexplicable – non-rational".[55] But we must not consider the artist's abjuration of reason as a mere whim indulged in for the sake of novelty. Reason is incapable of ordering or explaining phenomena, and because of its inadequacy the artist has no choice but to search among his other faculties for the means to perceive and interpret the world. Speaking in an interview, Beckett has said: "I think anyone nowadays, who pays the slightest attention to his own experience finds it the experience of a non-knower, a non-can-er.... The other type of artist – the Apollonian – is absolutely foreign to me."[56] Here he not only denies the power of reason to uncover truth but also rejects its use entirely by identifying himself with the Dionysian artist.

There are a number of important analogues between Beckett's artistic preferences and Nietzsche's philosophy of art. For instance, Nietzsche explains that through Dionysian art, we "are to perceive how all that comes into being must be ready for a sorrowful end; we are compelled to look into the terrors of individual existence".[57] In other words, Dionysian art focuses our attention on the misery of the human condition. This perception itself, according to Nietzsche, is experienced as a feeling of oneness with "Primordial Being"[58] and with one's neighbor, "as if the veil of Mâyâ had been torn and were now merely fluttering in tatters before the mysterious Primordial Unity".[59] Thus, Dionysian art rends the veil of illusion that conceals the essence of being. In her study of Beckett and Nietzsche, Edith Kern describes the Dionysian revelation as an experience which resists rational investigation: "Being itself invading the poet and filling him with its mystery, overflowing, untamed, never to be captured or fathomed entirely by man's mind or reason."[60] Possessed by being, the artist creates works "full of a realization of the horrors and suffering of life and death".[61] Yet to achieve such insight, the artist himself must suffer, as Miss Kern shows in her analysis of *Molloy*. Moran's torturous quest for Molloy appears as "a departure from the Apollonian and an arrival

[55]   Harvey, "Life, Art, and Criticism", 552.
[56]   Shenker, "Moody Man of Letters", 3.
[57]   Friedrich Nietzsche, *The Birth of Tragedy or Hellenism and Pessimism, The Complete Works* 1, ed. by Oscar Levy, trans. by William A. Haussmann (New York: The Macmillan Co., 1923), 128.
[58]   *Ibid.*
[59]   Nietzsche, *The Birth of Tragedy*, 27.
[60]   Kern, "Samuel Beckett – Dionysian Poet", 36.
[61]   Kern, "Dionysian Poet", 34.

at the Dionysian element in art".[62] The bourgeois rationalist's world
becomes "the world of the writer-become-Molloy...the world of the macrocosm where individual existence shrinks into meaninglessness and
human relations are reduced – or heightened – to the universal, the subconscious, the mythical".[63] It is Molloy's own quest for his mother, however, that represents the necessary "penetration into the innermost core
of existence".[64] Like Faust, Molloy descends to "the Mothers of Being, to
the innermost heart of things".[65] As a result, his language "becomes the
Dionysian's inarticulate cry of pain and passion. For the Apollonian language of reason, whose purpose it is to name, to arrange, and to create
order, he can muster only contempt."[66] Thus, the artist who has plumbed
the depths knows that Apollonian methods are useless when dealing with
essences. Writes Beckett: "Impossible de raisonner sur l'unique.... Impossible de vouloir autre l'inconnu.... Impossible de mettre de l'ordre
dans l'élémentaire."[67]

What distinguishes Dionysian from Apollonian art, then, is more than
the rejection of reason as an epistemological tool. Kinds of form, too, set
the one apart from the other. In fact, the artist's attitude toward his form
may well determine the very nature of his work. As Nietzsche demonstrates, the plastic art of Apollo "has an altogether different object" from
Dionysian art: "Apollo vanquishes the suffering of the individual by the
radiant glorification of the eternity of the phenomenon; here beauty
triumphs over the suffering inherent in life; pain is in a manner surrepti-
tiously obliterated from the features of nature."[68] Preoccupied with the
outward beauty of forms, the Apollonian artist loses sight of the essential
significance of his subject. His overriding concern for perfectly molded
surfaces obscures the inevitable decay that lies beneath them, and he
forgets the ephemerality and suffering inherent in existence. Thus, in
sculpting a human figure the Apollonian artist distorts the transient
nature of his model by allowing the eternal quality of exquisitely chiselled
stone to dominate the actual fragility of the flesh, "concealing all ugliness
and horror of life and death".[69] Clinging to his predilection for perfect
forms, he subordinates reality to the shallow consolation of appearance

---

[62]   Kern, "Moran-Molloy: The Hero as Author", 191.
[63]   Kern, "Moran-Molloy", 191.
[64]   Kern, "Dionysian Poet", 34.
[65]   Nietzsche, *The Birth of Tragedy*, 121.
[66]   Kern, "Dionysian Poet", 35.
[67]   "La Peinture des van Velde", 352-353.
[68]   Nietzsche, *The Birth of Tragedy*, 128.
[69]   Kern, "Dionysian Poet", 34.

and produces merely a superficial view of the world. Wary of the blinding power of formal concerns, Beckett advocates an art whose form is not pretentious. Comparing Bram van Velde with Braque, he notes how some of the Frenchman's canvases "ressemblent à des méditations plastiques sur les moyens mis en oeuvre".[70] As a result, in Braque's work "[le] définitif est toujours pour demain".[71] Bram van Velde, on the contrary, does not permit himself to be diverted by superficial attention to form: "Ses moyens ont la spécificité d'un speculum, n'existent que par rapport à leur fonction. Il ne s'y intéresse pas suffisament pour en douter. Il ne s'intéresse qu'à ce qu'ils reflètent."[72] His means – materials, methods, techniques – are indeed, means not ends in themselves. They exist in order to help the painter make visible on canvas his particular perception of existence. They are necessary to his work but secondary to his vision. The artist would betray himself were he to allow them to come between him and that vision; and he must realize that, after all, they are only poor instruments which by their very nature throw up a screen between the artist's idea and the mind of the beholder. To remove this screen Beckett works at making his means as transparent as possible, his ideal being exemplified by musical form. According to Nietzsche, the opposing concerns of Apollonian and Dionysian art distinguish the one as plastic art, the other as music. This distinction seems reasonable too from our study of Beckett. Appearance can easily become the principal preoccupation of painters and sculptors, but music is the art form farthest removed from appearance, existing not for the eye but for the ear. Moreover, music lends itself more readily to the direct expression of the Dionysian revelation: "The plastic artist... is sunk in the pure contemplation of pictures. The Dionysian musician is, without any picture, himself just primordial pain and the primordial re-echoing thereof."[73] Above all, music differs from every other art form in that it is not a reproduction of something else. As Nietzsche writes, "Music is distinguished from all the other arts by the fact that it is not a copy of the phenomenon."[74] Thus, in musical form lies the possibility for a truly accurate statement of the artist's vision. Through it, or another form refined to match its transparency, one may be able to speak with voice undistorted by muffling masks.

Beckett's self-consciousness, then, is not a limited Apollonian concern

---

[70] "La Peinture des van Velde", 353.
[71] *Ibid.*
[72] *Ibid.*
[73] Nietzsche, *The Birth of Tragedy*, 46.
[74] Nietzsche, 124.

with the quality of surfaces. Recognizing all surfaces to be illusory, he underscores their artificiality and thus refuses to collaborate in the deception they would produce. Painfully aware that creation is impossible without a medium, and that, hence, all creation must be plagued with a veil, he calls attention to his art as art, not in order to place importance on the artistic means but rather to make plain its flimsiness. Moreover, Beckett is preoccupied with the meaning that lies behind the form, as he has indicated in an interview: "In my work there is consternation behind the form, not in the form."[75] In particular, he is concerned with making the form transparent enough to reveal the meaning behind it. To achieve this end, he refines conventions to their basic elements and reduces traditional forms radically to fit his caustic insights. Each new work is a renewed attempt to do away with all intervening veils, to uncover once and for all the flawless image for his vision. Yet the last veil can only be removed in silence, which is the total absence of form, the absence of creation. Every effort in this direction, then, is doomed to failure, for one cannot express in the positive medium of art the negative qualities of absolute silence and absence. Still, Beckett continues to chisel away at the conventions, producing a series of parallel evolutions involving every aspect of his work.

In general, the Beckettian evolution is distinguished by a marked reduction in surface elements and by a corresponding augmentation of meaning beneath the surface. Inspired by his intense self-consciousness, this movement in the works traces his attempts to strip form of its conventional devices in order to "discover... a way of telling the only unique truth"[76] of his vision. But his rigorous asceticism may seem unsettling to some, for "his surface does not correspond to his profundity".[77] As Mlle Deyle explains, "Le mot simple s'alourdit du poids d'un concept métaphysique. Devenu 'précipité,' il implique sous des dehors inoffensifs, toute une philosophie qui s'y trouve secrètement décantée. C'est ce qui fait à la fois l'apparente simplicité superficielle et la difficile richesse profonde de l'oeuvre beckettienne."[78] Ruby Cohn, too, has remarked the degree of concentration in his style: "Beckett's prose is a skilfully composed verbal texture, gravid with suggestion beneath a comically threadbare surface. A rich poverty."[79] Later in the same work she appreciates the fine tool which

[75] Shenker, "Moody Man of Letters", 1.
[76] Mayoux, "The Theatre of Samuel Beckett", 155.
[77] Mayoux, "Beckett and Expressionism", 239.
[78] Deyle, *Samuel Beckett*, 81.
[79] Cohn, *The Comic Gamut*, 5.

Beckett makes of his art: "The reduced remainder of Beckett's broad comic gamut serves to etch man's desperate state all the more incisively."[80] Similarly, Maurice Nadeau observes of Beckett's narrator-heroes that "leur histoire deviendra toujours plus gratuite... plus dépouillée et... plus significative dans le manque de signification".[81] Claude Mauriac, also, notes the paradoxical impression of richness in poverty that Beckett's works give him; it is an extraordinary impression "je n'ose dire d'enrichissement, puisqu'il s'agit de la conscience d'une pauvreté absolue.... Pauvreté qui est notre seule richesse."[82] Molloy himself concurs in these judgments: "Je veux dire qu'à la réflexion, à la longue plutôt, mes excès de parole s'avéraient pauvretés et inversement" (*Molloy*, p. 50). So, just as Beckett perceives the essence of our condition beneath the cluttered surface of everyday existence, we must sharpen our sight to perceive his concentrated meaning behind the barren superficies of his works, for as his surface wanes his meaning waxes.

Beckett's art, then, concentrates meaning through contraction. Growing ever thinner, his form reveals more and more of the viscera and skeleton of his work. Thus, Hassan can speak of "the contractive metaphor of his art"[83] and can refer to Beckett as "a virtuoso of contraction".[84] The secret of this technique seems to lie in the formal structure of the works, for symmetry "enhances the emptiness Beckett creates in each work".[85] This kind of form, as transparent as it is clearly articulated, throws into relief the void it frames. Ultimately, however, "Beckett's contractive form... seeks to disengage itself from the world of phenomena",[86] to become as music. Indeed, according to Walter Pater, "All art constantly aspires towards the condition of music."[87] Music represents the ideal because in it the idea and its expression are one.[88] It unites what the plastic arts separate – form and content. In his critical essays Beckett often refers to the traditional division between form an content and argues for their unity. Writing of *Finnegans Wake*, he says: "Here form *is* content, content *is* form"; "[Joyce's] writing is not *about* something; *it is that something itself*."[89] To illustrate his point, he explains: "when the sense is sleep, the

80 Cohn, 179.
81 Nadeau, "Samuel Beckett ou le droit au silence", 1274.
82 Mauriac, "Samuel Beckett", 83.
83 Hassan, *The Literature of Silence*, 136.
84 Hassan, *The Literature of Silence*, 137.
85 *Ibid.*
86 *Ibid.*
87 Fletcher, *Samuel Beckett's Art*, 75, note 1.
88 Chambers, "Vers une interprétation de 'Fin de Partie'", 90.
89 "Dante . . . Bruno . Vico . . Joyce", 14.

words go to sleep.... When the sense is dancing, the words dance." [90]
Even Slingsby observes how Joyce makes "words serve as music... letting
their sound convey a meaning quite apart from the actual specific meaning
of each word." [91] In his study of Proust, too, Beckett remarks the coincidence of these traditionally diverse elements: "Indeed he [Proust] makes
no attempt to dissociate form from content. The one is a concretion of the
other, the revelation of a world" (*Proust*, p. 67).

One does not choose form for itself but for the idea it makes visible.
Hence, for Beckett, as for Proust, "style is more a question of vision than
of technique" (*Proust*, p. 67). Proust himself adds in this regard: "Il [le
style] est la révélation, qui serait impossible par des moyens directs et con-
scients." [92] Vision dictates form, is indeed perceived as one with form.
Harvey writes: "Beckett understands style as a correlative of vision, not
as its consequence or effect. Both arise spontaneously from the same
occasion." [93] In his work, "the form is indigenous to the material"; [94]
"the manner of saying and the matter said completely and organically
coincide". [95] Rightly, then, his writing can be compared to music, [96] for
in it he creates an effect like that of the ideal musical experience, which is
"'non-extensive, entirely original, irreducible to any other order of impression... sine materia'" (*Proust*, pp. 71-72); he approaches "the ideal
and immaterial statement of the essence of a unique beauty, a unique
world" (*Proust*, p. 72). Still, even in the realm of musical form he finds
room for improvement, surfaces for reduction. Moments of silence, like
sustained rests or pauses in a musical score, punctuate all his works. As
early as his essay on Denis Devlin, he displays fascination for the elo-
quence of silence and absence, which he describes as "the extraordinary
evocation of the unsaid by the said". [97] In the same way, he notes in a later
essay: "pertes et profits se valent dans l'économie de l'art, où le tu est la
lumière du dit, et toute présence absence." [98] But it is because music exists
in time that it yields the purest expression of the human experience.
Bounded by silence, like the nonexistence that precedes and follows life,
music reflects perfectly the contrast between being and nothingness. Thus,

[90] *Ibid.*
[91] Slingsby, "Writes A Common Reader", 190.
[92] Proust, *Le Temps retrouvé, Œuvres complètes*, 7, pt. 2 (Paris: Nouvelle Revue
Française, 1932), 47.
[93] Harvey, "Life, Art, and Criticism", 561.
[94] Gerard, "Molloy becomes Unnamable", 315.
[95] Esslin, "Samuel Beckett's Poems", 60.
[96] Cohn, *The Comic Gamut*, 5.
[97] "Denis Devlin", 293.
[98] "La Peinture des van Velde", 351.

Susan Seneff observes of the threnody in *Watt*: "The music begins and ends in the silence of a quarter rest; its music comes from naught, from silence, and goes to naught, to silence." [99] She concludes: "this threnody seems to summarize Watt's life."[100] By closing his essay on Proust with the word "defunctus" (*Proust*, p. 72), Beckett not only illustrates how music reveals its gratuitousness and that of all existence through the silence that encompasses it, but he also achieves the same kind of coincidence in his own form and content. It is as though he had concluded with the words *the end*. Thus, in his very first book one can see his creative efforts aimed toward an ever closer rapport between vision and image.

A careful study of all his works furnishes abundant evidence of a full-scale evolution, for both "his prose and plays have become ever more spare".[101] As Mlle Deyle expresses it, "L'oeuvre d'art devient la note pure, 'l'os de l'écho.'"[102] Beckett will settle for nothing less than a form purified and reduced to its last transparency. Writes Kenner: "Beckett invariably backs the mode he is practicing into its last corner."[103] In fact, the work, be it novel or play, must be doubly transparent, doubly coincident. It must represent precisely the artist's vision while at the same time maintaining its own lucid self-consciousness. For this reason, Beckett's fiction and drama, stripped of one device after another (actually made self-consuming), become more and more self-reflecting as they mirror more distinctly his essential vision of existence. Minimizing the centrifugal force of art to divert and entertain, he intensifies its centripetal capacity to draw man into the depths at the core of reality. Thus, the general evolution in his works takes the shape of a dynamic spiral moving downward toward the perfect coincidence of form and content, an ideal that can be attained only in immobility and silence.

[99]   Senneff, "Song and Music in *Watt*", 131.
[100] *Ibid.*
[101] Bishop, "Samuel Beckett", 26.
[102] Deyle, *Samuel Beckett*, 82.
[103] Kenner, *A Critical Study*, 105.

3. THE EVOLUTION OF SELF-CONSCIOUS FORM IN THE PLAYS AND NOVELS OF SAMUEL BECKETT

An examination of specific evolutions in Beckett's works shows in greater detail how the perpetual self-conscious reduction of conventions etches in deeper and deeper relief his vision of man's plight and his essential understanding of art. His plays, for instance, "tend towards a more and more barren simplicity",[1] as he dispenses with one conventional device after another. Reducing scenery and properties to the minimum, he actually empties the stage of almost everything and implies that soon there will be nothing left but the bare boards. By doing so, he emphasizes not only the growing misery of his characters but also the fact that the play is a play. Abandoning illusion, he makes no compromises with the traditional expectations of theatergoers. Furthermore, his rigorous straightforwardness in the matter of the play itself carries over into its content, reinforcing his spare metaphors. In the later plays, Beckett sweeps the stage clean of everything but the one element essential to theater – "un personnage et qui parle".[2] As Mrs. Cohn puts it, his "drama is concentrated down to man acting".[3] Here is the truth of drama and of life, "*theatrum mundi* in our time", for "man is an actor in the cosmic farce".[4] The dramatic form in itself becomes increasingly important, as Beckett proceeds from one exploration of it to another. Jean-Jacques Mayoux writes: "Beckett's theater turns in upon itself, seeks to coincide with itself in a pure theatrical reality".[5] Rather than trying to substitute an illusion for reality, Beckett presents in his plays a dramatic reality, a theatrical experience true to itself in its own right: "Beckett's theater is an extraordinary and paradoxical *Dasein*, a presence, not an imitation of the real but the real itself."[6]

---

[1] Fletcher, "Action and Play", 249.
[2] Nadeau, "Le chemin de la parole au silence", 66.
[3] Cohn, "Acting for Beckett", 237.
[4] Fletcher, *Samuel Beckett's Art*, 74.
[5] Mayoux, "The Theatre of Samuel Beckett", 142.
[6] Mayoux, 153.

Even in his earliest play *Eleutheria* (written about 1947 and still un-published),[7] the characters speak of the play in which they participate, and there is "a pirandellesque allusion to the author, named Beckett, pronounced Bequet".[8] *En attendant Godot* (written in 1949 but not prod-uced until 1953) contains many more clear indications that the play is a play (e.g., "Charmante soirée", "Garde ma place", p. 56). Here "the play is a game that is conscious of itself as a game".[9] Writes Judith Radke: "The players are fully cognizant of the fact that they are involved in a game, not in significant, purposeful activity."[10] Further, they underscore "the gratuitous 'art' of their play ('play' which is both game and thea-ter)".[11] But at the same time that Beckett strips the theater to its bones he reaches the summit of the dramatic genre: "la tragédie, 'acte pur,'... mise à nu de la condition humaine",[12] "the stripping bare of our fates in a phenomenological revelation of lean, driving force".[13] Thus, in spite of its purged, barren surface, *Godot* is a play of universal import.[14] Apparent nonsense conceals the distressing truth of our condition; for example, Lucky's tirade on man (pp. 71-75) contains the statement: "l'homme... est en train de maigrir et... de rapetisser" (p. 73). Arid landscapes drama-tize the endless boredom and futility of existence. The formal symmetry of the play frames the dreadful nothingness at the center of being, the consciousness that man has no *raison d'être*. Paring the theatrical form to its core, Beckett bores deep down into reality. In this way, he "achieves poetry through barrenness"[15] and presents us with a "distillation of dramatic essence".[16] In *Godot*, then, Beckett demonstrates how form can be coincident with itself and with content; already he draws near to the ideal of pure artistic statement. As Harold Hobson writes, in his review of the play after its opening night in London, "It showed that Archer's dictum that a good play imitates the audible and visible surfaces of life is not necessarily true. It revealed that the drama approximates, or can approx-imate, to the condition of music, touching chords deeper than can be

---

[7] Unless otherwise noted, all dates of writing and publication are taken from Raymond Federman and John Fletcher, *Samuel Beckett: His Works and His Critics*.
[8] Cohn, "Play and Player", 43.
[9] Hassan, *The Literature of Silence*, 182.
[10] Radke, "The Theater of Samuel Beckett", 60.
[11] *Ibid.*
[12] Domenach, *Le Retour du Tragique*, 13.
[13] Wilson, "The Social Psychology of Emptiness", 70.
[14] Johnston, "Waiting with Beckett", 26.
[15] Grossvogel, *The Self-Conscious Stage*, 330.
[16] Rexroth, "The Importance of Waiting", 82.

reached by reason, and saying things beyond the grasp of logic."[17]

But, apparently unsatisfied with *Godot* as the ultimate in concentrated drama, Beckett renewed his efforts at contraction to create *Fin de partie* (1957).[18] Here the focus upon the play as play is relentless. From beginning to end the verb *jouer* predominates, and the players frequently use other self-conscious terms such as *comédie* (p. 29) and *soliloque*(p. 102). Still, with all its emphasis on itself as drama, *Fin de partie* speaks eloquently, too, of existence. As Ruby Cohn says, "no other Beckett play offers so elaborate a version of the metaphor of *theatrum mundi*".[19] In short, "toute cette pièce n'est qu'une longue image d'elle-même, se commentant en tant que pièce et commentant ainsi la comédie qu'est la vie".[20] So again there is a "juxtaposition of a formal surface with serious, often terrifying depths".[21] Easthope writes: "The surface of *Endgame* insists upon itself as a meaningless technical exercise of the medium in its own right and refuses to acknowledge anything beyond its own expertise."[22] Yet Beckett makes us painfully aware of "the expressive significance of what is suggested beneath it",[23] of the meaning concealed by this apparent absence of meaning – the *cul-de-sac* of life, the inevitable final curtain. More than ever symmetry makes the work self-coincident; for example, Hamm's removal and replacement of the handkerchief at the beginning and end of the play (pp. 16, 112) seem to parallel the raising and lowering of the curtain. In fact, the replacement of the handkerchief serves as the signal for the lowering of the curtain. In the text the direction "Il approche le mouchoir de son visage" is immediately followed by the word *RIDEAU* (p. 112). Among Hamm's last words is the resolution "ne parlons plus" (p. 112).

Beckett pushes on, however, to reduce his dramatic structure even further. *Acte sans paroles I* (1957) and *Krapp's Last Tape* (1968) present us with a single protagonist each; and though *Happy Days* (1961) has a cast of two, in it "there is... no longer a trace left of traditional theatre concerned with character, action and episodes that have a beginning, a middle, and an end".[24] Still, while Beckett's caustic art eats away at the formal barrier between the stage and the spectator, his lucid focus on

17   Hobson, "The First Night of *Waiting for Godot*", 25.
18   Referred to hereafter in the text with the appropriate page number in parentheses.
19   Cohn, "Play and Player", 46.
20   Chambers, "Vers une interprétation de 'Fin de Partie'", 94.
21   Easthope, "Hamm, Clov, and Dramatic Method", 432.
22   *Ibid.*
23   Easthope, 429.
24   Kern, "Beckett's Knight of Infinite Resignation", 50.

human existence grows more and more intense. As Fletcher notes, "light is the most active element"[25] in his latest pieces. Its incessant burning brightness makes Winnie's life (in *Happy Days*) scarcely endurable, and in *Play* (1964) it pinpoints each immobile player, forcing him to speak. Indeed, with this work Beckett seems to have come as close as possible to his ideal, for here he achieves "astonishing unity of form and content".[26] Dukore says: "The theatrical form of *Play* is a brilliant reflection of its content".[27] Moreover, no title could be less pretentious, no technique could reveal more precisely the essential nature of the theater: the eyes of the curious audience behind the probing spotlight compel the actors to play their parts, to speak their lines.[28] Yet Beckett goes still further in his exhaustive reduction of the drama. In the short pantomines *Acte sans paroles I* and *Acte sans paroles II* (1963) and in the 'dramaticule' *Come and Go* (1967), he gives to gesture the most important expressive functions, thus showing mime to be the basic language of the stage. As Mayoux says, "Mime is a complementary and immediate dramatic language, which reveals the man of the theater."[29] Similarly in Beckett's scenario, predictably entitled *Film* (1967), all is silent action followed by the relentless eye of the camera. It is, as Raymond Federman explains, "a dialogueless experiment whose main theme is the picture itself,... vision within vision", "the simple reaffirmation of the essence of cinema... visual expression of life and movement through photographic manipulation", designed "to develop in the... spectator an extra sense of perception".[30] (A parallel experiment can be seen in the radio plays where the playwright must rely on voices and sound effects alone.)

But it is in his most recent stage production *Breath*[31] that Beckett creates his *tour de force* of concentrated drama. Within a period of time roughly equivalent to that of a few breaths, he telescopes an entire life. As integral parts of the 'performance', the raising and lowering of the curtain establish the temporal boundaries of the drama. When the curtain rises, we see that a large rubbish heap occupies the stage and that there is no cast. Yet every one of the thirty seconds during which the play lasts is filled with tension. One virtually holds one's breath from the moment the curtain

---

[25]   Fletcher, "Action and Play", 249.
[26]   Dukore, "Beckett's Play, *Play*", 22.
[27]   *Ibid.*
[28]   Kenner, "Progress Report", 63.
[29]   Mayoux, "The Theatre of Samuel Beckett", 154.
[30]   Federman, "*Film*", 47, 48, and 50.
[31]   Produced by the British Broadcasting Company for television, presented by the National Broadcasting Company on its program "First Tuesday", April 7, 1970.

rises until it mercifully falls once more, for what Beckett dramatizes so incisively in these brief moments is the ceaseless perpetuation of mankind's futile existence. Four poignant utterances span the seconds, taking man from the silence of nonexistence to the shock of birth, through maturity, and finally to a slow and agonized death; but at this moment (which might seem to signal a conclusion) a second natal cry reveals that the process is a cycle from which there is no escape. Here, then, is the distilled essence of the human condition captured in the essence of theater itself. For what is theater but the experience framed by the rise and fall of the curtain? The lifting off of the veil and its replacement are highly significant for us as for Hamm. When the curtain rises, our eyes are opened to what lies behind it; in fact, we are compelled to look at the scene before us. It is as though the stage were the inner eye of the playwright, through which we experience the intensity of his piercing insight fixed on existence. When the curtain falls, the mind of the author disappears from view, and we are free to re-claim our habitual blindness to reality. Surely there is no dramatic state-ment more fully aware of itself or more perfectly transparent to its content than this. Thus, it seems to justify the judgment of Hassan that the "pure and terrible art of Samuel Beckett finds its consummation in his plays".[32] Indeed, this brief dramatic work crowns the evolution which we have traced through the plays, an evolution which takes the form of a down-ward spiral. Writing of this dynamic development, Geneviève Serreau eloquently describes the penetrating action of Beckett's art: "Il ne fait pas de doute qu'elles [les pièces] tendent à un dépouillement, à une contrac-tion sur l'essentiel. L'art devient foreuse, et de plus en plus aiguisée, pour percer de plus en plus loin les couches stratifiées du réel et atteindre l'unique vérité dont il se soucie: vérité de soi-même et de la condition humaine."[33]

The same general analysis applies, too, to the development of Beckett's fiction. But his novels and short stories span a larger portion of his career than the plays and thus give a more nearly complete impression of the evolution in his style. Linked by similar situations and by the reappearance of characters from one work to the next, the books "form a closed circle, a unity, almost one extended novel".[34] Protagonists not only recall their predecessors but actually seem to recognize their own stories as part of a continuing tale, variously alluded to as "le vieux thrène stupide" (*Textes*, p. 182) or "la même histoire" (*Comment*, p. 132), and which it seems they

[32]   Hassan, *The Literature of Silence*, 174.
[33]   Serreau, "Samuel Beckett", 116.
[34]   Fletcher, *The Novels*, 117.

have been repeating to themselves incessantly: "toujours marmonnant, les mêmes propos, les mêmes histoires, les mêmes questions et réponses" (*Textes*, p. 133); "toujours la même imagination à bout cherchant un trou" (*Comment*, p. 159). For them it has all been nothing but unbearable monotony: "tout est vieux, tout se vaut, c'est décidé" (*Textes*, p. 144); "l'écoute d'un seul de nos murmures et sa rédaction sont l'écoute et la rédaction de tous" (*Comment*, p. 167); "dans cette fange où tout est pareil" (*Comment*, p. 137). Yet when one observes the whole of Beckett's fiction "as a continuous flow of words, as a homogeneous creation",[35] the enormous difference in form between his earliest and latest writings bears undeniably the mark of his caustic process. Looking more closely, one can see how gradually he removes layer after layer of conventional detail, how little by little his fiction progresses toward "un dépouillement de plus en plus complet où tout se décompose, personnages, intrigue et expression".[36] Pared down in one work, certain fictional elements may be reduced "to a still barer minimum"[37] in the next. Like his drama, Beckett's fiction does not pretend to be anything more than it is; and, in fact, turning inward, it probes itself to uncover its own essence. But to become coincident with itself, to reveal its true nature, fiction must come to terms with the fact that it depends on the existence of a narrator or author for its own existence. (For what is fiction if not a man telling a story, or more precisely, a story a mind tells itself?) Fiction cannot become transparent, cannot reveal "the mechanism of its own creation",[38] until the creator's existence becomes one with it. As the stories concentrate more intently on the mind that is at that very moment inventing them, they begin to approach Beckett's ideal of flawless self-reflection. Insisting more and more on "its own difficult progress",[39] the fiction lays bare bit by bit a self-conscious narrator ever more alert to the esthetic imperfections in his work.[40] Finally, "we find ourselves within the limits of the mind",[41] where the creative process holds sway before our very eyes. The evolution in the fiction, then, resembles a spiral whose center is the image of the artist creating. As Mrs. Cohn writes, "Through the years, Beckett's fiction has pared away narrative garb to zero in on man narrating."[42] Indeed,

[35] Federman, *Journey to Chaos*, 16.
[36] Fletcher, "Sur un roman inédit", 152.
[37] Federman, *Journey to Chaos*, 16.
[38] Federman, 5.
[39] *Ibid.*
[40] A more detailed study of the evolution of the narrator-hero follows in Chapter 4.
[41] Fletcher, *The Novels*, 117-118.
[42] Cohn, "Acting for Beckett", 237.

Beckett's fiction moves "from narrative through interior monologue to exacerbated meditation in the dark",[43] as each work makes more clearly visible the process of its own creation.[44]

In his earliest creative works – a collection of short stories *More Pricks Than Kicks* (1934) and the novel *Murphy* (1938) –, Beckett observes many of the orthodox conventions. Characters are relatively numerous and are "differentiated with some care, however bizarre their behaviour";[45] recognizable events take place; and the formal structure, which includes standard punctuation and paragraphing, resembles that of traditional works of fiction. Yet on closer inspection Beckett's obvious violation of many generally accepted principles makes his scrupulous observance of others ludicrous. The early fiction is, in fact, a parody of conventional fiction. As John Fletcher puts it, "*Murphy*... is so carefully and intricately constructed as by its very complexity to constitute a defiant parody of the traditional novel."[46] Of the same work, Claude Mauriac writes: "Tout Beckett était déjà là,... sous une forme plus accessible que celle qu'il devait choisir ensuite, renonçant depuis à toute compromission avec le superficiel et les conventions."[47] Already the narrator makes his presence known, intervening often to ridicule a pompous character or to comment on his own choice of words. *Watt* (written during the war but not published until 1953) deviates even more from traditional fiction than *Murphy*. Although the omniscient storyteller remains, the whole fabric of the novel differs greatly from the earlier works. According to Esslin, "*Watt*... marks the transition from conventional narrative to the mythological present of [the] French novels."[48] Though aloof during the first part of the novel, the narrator alludes to his role in the second part and tells his own side of the story in the third part, revealing his relationship to Watt and his function as transcriber of Watt's story (pp. 164-169). Here he refers to his inadequacy – his difficulty in understanding Watt and his inability to faithfully retell Watt's adventures. But even before his overt appearance on the scene, certain events in the tale itself reinforce the impression that this is not at all an ordinary piece of fiction. In particular, the visit to Mr. Knott's establishment of the piano-tuners the Galls, father and son, disturbs Watt

43 Kenner, *Flaubert, Joyce and Beckett*, 105.
44 What follows is a brief summary of the evolution in the fiction. Detailed analyses of the development of particular fictional elements will constitute the remainder of this chapter (after the summary) and all of the next.
45 Davin, "Mr. Beckett's Everymen", 37.
46 Fletcher, "Beckett and the Fictional Tradition", 151.
47 Mauriac, "Samuel Beckett", 77.
48 Esslin, "Samuel Beckett", 134.

afterward by its utter gratuitousness. For him, "it developed a purely plastic content, and gradually lost, in the nice processes of its light, its sound, its impacts and its rhythm, all meaning, even the most literal"; it "became a mere example of light commenting bodies, and stillness motion, and silence sound, and comment comment" (pp. 72-73). With each renewed effort to understand the event, to conjure it up as a solid occurrence, Watt only encounters once again its undeniable hollowness. The results of his repeated discovery are not good: "This fragility of the outer meaning had a bad effect on Watt, for it caused him to seek for another, for some meaning of what had passed, in the image of how it had passed" (p. 73). Worse, similar incidents follow, "incidents that is to say of great formal brilliance and indeterminable purport" (p. 74). In describing Watt's problem, however, Beckett actually prepares the way for the future development of his fiction. The insight Watt attains in the Knott house enables him to perceive the nothingness of existence. It eliminates the possibility of his attaching importance to superficial matters, as he has done in the past. Kinds of experiences that Watt once understood with no trouble at all now prove too meaningless to survive the onslaught of his concentrated thought. The effect of his caustic perception parallels that of Beckett's art, for from *Watt* on Beckett shows the fragility of all surfaces and directs our attention to the meager skeleton or gaping void beneath them.[49] Comparing this sort of vision with its opposite, he writes: "Some see the flesh before the bones, and some see the bones before the flesh, and some never see the bones at all, and some never see the flesh at all, never never see the flesh at all' (p. 73). The uneventful surface of *Watt* itself reflects Watt's image of the Gall incident and poses for the reader Watt's kind of problem. Thus, this novel's "surface lack of finish is a subtly controlled formal device"[50] that makes it an important stage in the evolution toward perfect coincidence in the fiction.

Mercier et Camier (written about 1946 but only recently published),[51] Beckett's first French novel, is the last of his works to be related by an omniscient narrator.[52] The story contains situations similar to those in *Watt*, and Watt himself reappears. Even Murphy's name is mentioned, so

---

[49] In *Premier amour*, 46, he suggests that language itself is a hollow form utterly without foundation: "J'avais si peu l'habitude de parler qu'il m'arrivait de temps en temps de laisser échapper, par la bouche, des phrases inpeccables au point de vue grammatical mais entièrement dénuées... de fondement."

[50] Cohn, "*Watt* in the Light of *The Castle*", 155.

[51] Date of writing given as 1946 on page 212. See also Federman and Fletcher, *His Works and His Critics*, 108.

[52] Fletcher, "Sur un roman inédit", 148.

that the novel appears to be the third in a series of interrelated works. Yet with its pair of heroes (in contrast to the earlier single protagonists) and with much stichomythia, this piece of fiction bears a striking resemblance to the play *En attendant Godot*, written some years later. *Mercier et Camier*, then, seems to form a branch in Beckett's writing from the fiction to the dramatic works. Perhaps more important to the development of his theater than to that of his novels, this work, according to Beckett's own judgment (as Fletcher cites him), "est un 'faux départ' qui ne mérite pas de figurer parmi ses oeuvres complètes".[53]

The *Nouvelles* ("L'Expulsé", "Le Calmant", and "La Fin") and *Premier amour* (all written in 1946),[54] on the contrary, are of major importance to the evolution of the fiction. The first three stories published together seem to prefigure exactly the later trilogy of novels.[55] Moreover, as noted before, they reflect the familiar Beckettian image of life – birth, the evasion of suffering in the wait for death, and death itself. Told by lucid first-person narrators, the stories are coincident with the existence of the mind at their center and thus represent the first stage in the principal development of the fiction. Beckett applies this same self-conscious method and develops it even further in the trilogy of novels (written between 1947 and 1950), which Esslin calls "the centre-piece of Beckett's oeuvre".[56] Here Molloy and Moran, the storytellers in the first of the novels *Molloy*, propose to recount faithfully certain of their adventures, the latter because he must write a report, the former for no apparent reason at all. Writing from memory, they are not always certain of what really happened and their immediate feelings at the moment of composition come to have more importance than the past events they have set out to record. Malone, author-hero of the second novel *Malone meurt*, announces from the outset that he plans to tell himself stories in order to take his mind off his dying, to pass the time until he dies. It soon becomes evident, however, that the fictions he creates are based on memories of his past. Interspersed among parts of the tales are his reflections on his present condition; and, as the novel continues, these meditations become more and more involved. In addition, he frequently criticizes his own creative efforts, undercutting at every turn the power of illusion. Still, although he realizes that he may well inhabit another's head (i.e., that he may be himself a fiction), Malone maintains his own identity, remaining separate from his creatures. Such

---

[53] Fletcher, 139.
[54] Though written during the same period as the other three stories, *Premier amour* was not published until 1970.
[55] Cohn, *The Comic Gamut*, 114.
[56] Esslin, "Samuel Beckett", 135.

is not the case in the concluding novel of the trilogy, *L'Innommable*. Here the boundary between the first-person narrator and his fictions becomes much less clearly defined. Recognizing that he himself has no more real existence than his own inventions, the Unnamable assumes mask after mask, gliding from one of his creatures to another, and even attempts to solve his dilemma of identity by speaking of himself in the third person: "Je ne dirai plus moi, je ne le dirai plus jamais, c'est trop bête. Je mettrai à la place, chaque fois que je l'entendrai, la troisième personne, si j'y pense.... Ça ne changera rien. Il n'y a que moi, moi qui ne suis pas, là où je suis" (p. 139) The frantic condition of the narrator in his search for identity affects the very style of the novel, bringing form and content close together: "The sentences run to pages in length, are composed of breathless, mutually interactive phrases, and render difficult all isolation of language from event."[57] Realizing that he cannot exist except in language, the protagonist spins out an existence for himself through the novel while at the same time revealing the essence of fiction to be nothing more than words a man mumbles to himself. In this book, "with its successive collapses of pretense, its peelings away, monologue within monologue, of falsification",[58] Beckett probes the workings of the creating mind and in so doing draws near to the essence of creation itself.

In the *Textes pour rien* (begun in 1950), he renews his efforts to tear away the last intervening layers and to achieve the purity of musical expression. Underscoring the futility of the creative act, the title of this collection sets the tone for a thoroughly unpretentious and deeply self-conscious work. Here the diverse authors of the thirteen *Textes* come close to unwavering lucidity, making their works mirror-images of their own creative struggle as they penetrate the very nature of art. For example, commenting upon his own "stripped fiction",[59] the narrator of "Texte XIII" writes of art as one could of life, laying bare its utter gratuitousness and fragility: "c'est vraiment le minimum, non, c'est du roman, encore du roman, seule la voix est, bruissant et laissant des traces. Des traces, elle veut laisser des traces, oui, comme en laisse l'air parmi les feuilles, parmi l'herbe, parmi le sable, c'est avec ça qu'elle veut faire une vie, mais c'est bientôt fini, il n'y aura pas de vie, il n'y aura pas eu de vie, il y aura le silence, l'air qui tremble un instant encore avant de se figer pour toujours, une petite poussière qui tombe un petit moment" (*Textes*, p. 216). Beckett's last complete novel *Comment c'est* (1961) gives a similar but even more intense impres-

[57]   Cohn, *The Comic Gamut*, 121.
[58]   Gerard, "Molloy becomes Unnamable", 317.
[59]   Cohn, *The Comic Gamut*, 170.

sion of the futility in creation. Telling of his existence in the darkness of primeval slime, the protagonist attempts to reveal his own consciousness of creating as he creates, to recount how it is to watch oneself relating one's experience. Since, however, he has but a single mind, he cannot express even to himself his experience of duality, the vision of himself looking at himself in the mirror of self-consciousness. He cannot state while he creates his consciousness of being conscious of himself creating. The perfect transparency he seeks is unattainable. Even here, where Beckett goes "further than ever before" in "stripping away plot and character",[60] the last mask remains intact. Self-consciousness remains unexorcised. Still, *Comment c'est* represents the culmination of Beckett's efforts to lay bare the essence of the novel, to create a perfectly coincident fiction. Through innovation in form (Beckett dispenses with punctuation and orthodox paragraphing), he achieves a new "bareness of language" which reflects clearly the "spareness of situation".[61] Further, employing "writing as a metaphor for itself",[62] he traces in the course of the novel's narration the "agony of its creative movement".[63] Thus, Beckett's caustic method leaves nothing but the bare bones of the novel form, unmasking and mocking the pretension of fictional realism by revealing the source of all literary creation to be a restless mind babbling to itself.[64]

To produce such a revelation, Beckett goes far beyond the mere parody of traditional conventions. In his novels he gradually assimilates basic fictional elements in order to make them work for him. Taking the familiar use of landscape description as an example, one can trace the way he first ridicules a device and then transforms it into a tool suited to his own end. In "Fingal", the first story of *More Pricks Than Kicks*, the hero's reaction to landscapes distinguishes him and his story from conventional heroes and tales: "Landscapes were of interest to Belacqua only in so far as they furnished him with a pretext for a long face" (p. 13). Some pages later, describing a fictitious film in the words of the Smeraldina, Beckett pokes fun at the traditional use of landscapes in cinema: "it was realey [*sic*] something quite different from all other Films, nothing to do with Love (as everybody understands the word) no silly girls making sweet

---

[60]   Cohn, 182.
[61]   *Ibid.*
[62]   Kenner, *A Critical Study*, 189.
[63]   Federman, *Journey to Chaos*, 7.
[64]   Among his latest pieces of short fiction (collected under the title *Têtes-mortes*) are two fragments of unfinished novels, "Bing" and "Imagination morte imaginez", which present the essence of fiction in brief intensely concentrated texts like those in *Textes pour rien.*

faces, black lakes and grand Landschaften" (p. 85). The Smeraldina's use of her native German to name the cliché in question adds still more to the caustic tone underlying her remarks and emphasizes the pretension and artificiality of such techniques. Finally, at the conclusion of the last story in this collection, Beckett unmasks the ironic deception that the conventional use of landscapes promotes. Here at the site of Belacqua's grave the groundsman meditates on the surrounding landscape in an attempt to classify it according to the proper tradition: "he was at a loss to determine off-hand whether the scene was of the kind that is termed romantic or whether it should not with more justice be deemed classical. Both elements were present, that was indisputable. Perhaps classico-romantic would be the fairest estimate. A classico-romantic scene" (p. 107). Ignoring the worms busy beneath his feet, this man, like so many others, turns his back on the stark truth of his inevitable doom to take refuge in the superficial contemplation of indifferent scenery. Parodying traditional description, Beckett underscores the illusoriness of the scene: "the company of headstones sighing and gleaming like bones, the moon on the job, the sea tossing in her dreams and panting, and the hills observing their Attic vigil in the background" (p. 107). Even tombstones play a role in conventional landscapes where they become part of the diverting surface and lose their real significance. But Beckett, fully aware that they both resemble and represent bones, overthrows the convention by pointing out its fallacy. In the conclusion to *Watt* he composes a similarly playful description of what, for an orthodox writer, could be a conventional landscape: "the sky falling to the hills, and the hills falling to the plain, made as pretty a picture, in the early morning light, as a man could hope to meet with, in a day's march" (p. 246). Yet Beckett shows, three pages later in the Addenda, that he can do more than mock conventions. In his rendering of Watt's "soul-landscape" he prepares the way for the "mindscapes"[65] of his French novels:

The sky was of a dark colour....
The waste also, needless to say, was of a dark colour.... Watt also was very naturally of the same dark colour....
   The source of the feeble light diffused over this scene is unknown.
   Further peculiarities of this soul-landscape were:
   The temperature was warm.
   Beneath Watt the waste rose and fell.
   All was silent.
   Above Watt the sky fell and rose.
   Watt was rooted to the spot. (p. 249)

[65] Torrance, "Modes of Being and Time in *Godot*", 95.

The object of his own inner vision, Watt resembles his successors who occupy first closed rooms and then the tightly sealed, mirror-filled realms of their minds. Conventional landscapes are not to be found in these later works, for the world of the narrator-hero shrinks to the confines of his own skull. Beckett's landscapes, then, become "a world from which the world has all but vanished, leaving only the mind that conceived it, caught up in its own close-meshed snares".[66] Thus Beckett refines this fictional convention to its essence, making it transparent and one with itself.

In the same way, he assimilates the common literary device of making erudite allusions to artists and works of art. From the start he uses his erudition imaginatively, molding it to illustrate his vision; and, always mindful of what he is about, he mocks his own use of this technique. Soon, however, he begins refining it. Direct allusions to artists and works become indirect or uncertain; then allusions yield to imaginary creations (e.g., paintings, sculptures, books). Finally, his references to art involve only forms, colors, and words – the basic elements of art. Here the purified convention reveals not only its own feebleness but also the meager reality of the artistic product. Paintings are no more than shapes and colors, books no more than words. By reducing erudite allusion to direct discussion of the fundamental elements of art, Beckett reinforces the effect produced by the gradual disappearance of other traditional narrative techniques, making every aspect of his work intensely self-conscious. With its basic elements laid bare, art can no longer conceal its fragility and gratuitousness.

A detailed examination of the allusions to art in Beckett's fiction demonstrates how he refines conventions and how their transformation affects the evolution in his works. At first, he makes use of allusions in the conventional way and seems to revel in exhibiting his erudition. Yet even as early as *More Pricks Than Kicks*, he integrates the frequent references to artists and works with the basic material of his story, so that the allusions serve to illustrate situations and characters without ordinarily forming long digressions. But an exception occurs when, describing the heroine of "Love and Lethe", Ruby Tough, he compares her to "the Magdalene in the Perugino Pieta in the National Gallery of Dublin" (p. 47). This allusion seems awkwardly specific; and, prolonged by remarks critical of the manner in which the painting is displayed, it gets a bit out of hand. In a later story of the same collection, he becomes quite playful with the con-

---

[66]   Torrance, "Modes of Being and Time", 95.

vention, composing a *tour de force* on a small scale with allusions to Rodin, Dürer, and Maupassant all in the same sentence (p. 78). More unorthodox than ever at the end of the volume, he uses his knowledge of the styles of individual artists to describe the Smeraldina, who has a "pale Pisanello of a birdface" and "Botticelli thighs" (p. 99). Finally, he reinforces his parody of the landscape convention by describing the view from the cemetery as though it had been painted by an early Renaissance Florentine known for his study of perspective: "the mountains [were a] swarthy Uccello behind the headstones" (p. 102). Direct allusions to artists and works abound in *Murphy* too, but they seem less stilted that those in the earlier work and are more tightly woven into the fabric of the novel. Here the hero describes his landlady Miss Carridge as having "a Doric pelvis" (p. 64); a dachsund reminds him of Parmigianino's Mannerist vision of the world (p. 101); and his mental image of a barroom pun makes him think of Tintoretto's *Origin of the Milky Way* (p. 140). Adding *correspondance* to allusion, Beckett describes the color of the walls in Murphy and Celia's room: "The lemon of the walls whined like Vermeer's" (p. 228). An example almost as detailed as the Perugino one above – "Claude's Narcissus in Trafalgar Square" (p. 228) – does not get out of control here; rather, Beckett uses it skillfully to set up a close-knit series of mirror-images which stress the illusory nature of surfaces: "even Miss Counihan [a woman of easy virtue who has been pursuing Murphy]... was inclined to regret her reflection in the linoleum. Similarly before Claude's Narcissus in Trafalgar Square, high class whores with faces lately lifted have breathed a malediction on the glass" (p. 228). As they observe ideal beauty gazing at its reflection in the pool, the prostitutes realize what poor imitations they are. Even the artificial scene before them (which, after all, is nothing but paints applied to canvas and placed behind glass) throws into relief the shoddiness of the beautician's work and makes them see in its own reflective covering that the cosmetic treatment fails to mask their dissolution. Thus, the kind of allusion that was an obvious erudite digression in the earlier story becomes an intricate part of the novel here and serves to heighten its self-consciousness by demonstrating the importance of getting beneath deceptive surfaces.

Some pages later, in a *tour de force* much more impressive than the earlier one, Beckett refers to three sculptors in a single passage (pp. 238-239) and goes on to create an imaginary artist – a "Pergamene Barlach" – representing Murphy's plastic interpretation of the human figures (sleepers and insomniacs in the asylum where he works) before him. This variation of the conventional device is especially significant, since the author's choice of

sculptor reflects his own vision of man's lot. For Barlach, as for Beckett,
man "is a humble creature at the mercy of forces beyond his control; he is
never the master of his fate."[67] A further illustration of this idea is the
image of Murphy (minutes before his accidental death) lying naked in a
"tuft of soaking tuffets" and seeing in his mind "the clenched fists and
rigid upturned face of the Child in a Giovanni Bellini Circumcision,
waiting to feel the knife" (p. 251). (Still another example is this description
of the sleeping inmates: "Those that slept did so in the frozen attitudes of
Herculaneum, as though sleep had pounced upon them like an act of God",
p. 239.) Employing learned allusions in this way, Beckett purges them of
their usual pretension and makes them instrumental in expressing his
inner vision. Yet from the very first reference in *Murphy* he is lucid and
self-mocking in his use of this familiar technique. Describing the linoleum
in Murphy and Celia's room as "a dim geometry of blue, grey and brown
that delighted Murphy because it called Braque to his mind", he goes on
to make fun of his hero's taste for such intellectual games: "Murphy was
one of the elect, who require everything to remind them of something else"
(p. 63). After this, allusions are wherever possible attributed to the mind
of the hero, not to that of the author. But one important exception appears
in the scene where Neary, in his attempt to be perfectly truthful while
speaking with Wylie and Miss Counihan, takes on "a great look of Luke's
portrait of Matthew with the angel perched like a parrot on his shoulder"
(p. 215). Though no such portrait is known to exist, the image could have
been suggested by various medieval paintings and illuminations in which
an Evangelist is pictured at work with the Holy Spirit in the form of a dove
at his ear, revealing to him the Holy Word.[68] Such an image is of great
importance not only for a discussion of the portrait of the artist (as we
shall see later) but also as a unique transformation of the convention.
An indirect, half imaginary reference, it actually presents a mirror-image
of the novel as it is being written, as it is created by a man covering blank
pages with words. Furthermore, since the reference made involves a *portrait* of a man writing, the reflection is more intricate still. A man writing
a novel speaks of an artist (himself a writer too) who has painted a por-

[67]   H. W. Janson, *History of Art* (Englewood Cliffs, N.J.: Prentice-Hall and New York:
Harry N. Abrams, 1962; rpt. 1964), 511.
[68]   See, for example, Janson, *History of Art*, colorplate 20, 236, a Romanesque illumination of St. John the Evangelist from the *Gospel Book of Abbot Wedricus*. Other possible
sources for this image: Poussin's *Le Paysage avec Saint-Mathieu et l'Ange* in Anthony
Blunt, *Nicolas Poussin*, 2 (Bollingen Series 35.7) (New York: Bollingen, 1967), plate
150; Carel Fabritius' *St. Matthew Writing His Gospel, The New Yorker*, 1 August 1970,
65.

trait of a man writing. In both the novel and the portrait, art is the subject of art; the creative act composes the center of the work. As a result, the work of art becomes transparent, reveals its essential nature. Exploring the convention of allusions to its limits, Beckett cultivates those aspects of it which make possible penetrating insights into art itself.

With *Watt*, even indirect allusions grow scarce – a development that reflects the increasingly caustic action of Beckett's method and marks a turning point in the evolution of the novels. The two allusions that do appear are entirely incorporated into the text and serve to enhance it from the inside out rather than to simply ornament it. We should note, too, that in both examples the hero is compared to Christ – first as one whose sacrifice has been made: the "postcrucified position" (p. 140), then as one in the midst of his suffering: "His face was bloody, his hands also, and thorns were in his scalp" (p. 159). Like the allusion in *Murphy* to a portrait of St. Matthew, the first reference here could have been suggested by any of a number of suitable paintings (perhaps even by the Perugino Pieta of *More Pricks*). In the second instance, however, the narrator Sam is more specific, comparing his friend Watt to "the Christ believed by Bosch, then hanging in Trafalgar Square" (p. 159). Certainty being rare in this novel, it is not surprising that one finds here an allusion to a painting that cannot be positively identified. Furthermore, the very mention of Bosch helps reinforce the grotesque image of Watt's infernal suffering and indicates a rapport between Beckett's vision and that of the painter. (Noting this relationship, Edith Kern writes that in early German criticism of *Godot* the "paintings of Hieronymus Bosch were invoked for comparison".)[69] That Beckett and Bosch share common insights into the human situation seems even more evident when Sam, having described Watt in terms of the Bosch allusion, suddenly fears that it is not Watt he sees but his own image reflected in a mirror. Then, although he comforts himself saying, "For if anyone, at that time, could be truly said not to resemble the Christ supposed by Bosch, then hanging in Trafalgar Square, I flatter myself it was I" (p. 159), the comparison which this momentary impression established between all men and the tormented Christ remains intact; and similar comparisons in other works (including the reference to the Bellini Circumcision in *Murphy*) support the basic image. In *Molloy* an indirect allusion to Rodin furnishes another example of this kind. Here Moran imagines

---

[69] Kern, "Drama Stripped for Inaction", 41. A similar comparison is made in Danielle Bajomée's article "Lumière, ténèbres et chaos dans *L'Innommable*", 139, note 1: "Le roman étudié ici s'inscrit, lui aussi, dans cet univers à la Jérôme Bosch où règnent la solitude, l'angoissante certitude du néant et la cruauté sous toutes ses formes."

himself deserted by his son (whom he has considered linking to himself by a rope) and left to continue his journey on foot "tout seul suivi d'une longue corde traînant dans la poussière, comme un bourgeois de Calais" (p. 199). But Beckett subtly undercuts this indirect reference to a touching historical event and its well-known monument by supplying Moran with the imagination to see what would inevitably transform his tragic pose into slapstick comedy: "Jusqu'au moment où la corde s'accrochant à un objet fixe ou lourd, briserait mon élan" (pp. 199-200). In a second indirect allusion, he again calls into question the convention of landscapes and shows how nature can be an accomplice in promoting this superficial kind of vision. From his vantage point "au sommet d'un monticule" Moran discovers how the scene before him seems to have been arranged by a landscape painter: "Et je fais cette remarque curieuse, que la terre à cet endroit, et même les nuages du ciel, étaient disposés de façon à amener doucement les yeux vers le camp, comme dans un tableau de maître" (p. 237).

The last direct allusions appear in *Malone meurt* and illustrate two of Beckett's most predominant obsessions – the portrait of the artist as the subject of art and the deceptive nature of surfaces. In the first case, Malone, describing his fictional creature Macmann (who is seated on a bench by a river), compares his rigid pose to that "du colosse de Memnon, fils bien-aimé de l'Aurore" (p. 98). This comparison not only illustrates the worn condition of Macmann's clothes (imagine the weather-beaten condition of the ancient statue) and his absolute immobility (fixed as stone),[70] but also suggests through the myth that it represents an image of the artist similar to the one we remarked in *Murphy*. Here it is a goddess-mother's power, rather than that of the Holy Spirit, that inspires creation, but (as we shall see later) this image is as important as the earlier one to an understanding of Beckett's conception of the artist. In the second instance, Malone demonstrates his distrust of surfaces by relating his thoughts about the window beside him: "cette fenêtre dont je me dis quelquefois que c'est du trompe-l'oeil, comme le plafond de Tiepolo à Würzburg" (p. 114). The enormous capacity of painted surfaces to deceive is underscored by the example of Tiepolo, master of illusionistic painting, and especially by reference to the Würzburg frescoes in which the artist's "powers are [seen] at their height".[71] Able to obliterate spatial boundaries

---

[70] For other comparisons of men to stone figures see *Murphy*, 142, 168, and 232; in *Watt*, 49, Arsene's desire "to be turned into a stone pillar or a cromlech" recalls Stonehenge, as does the reference in *Malone*, 214, to "des vestiges druidiques dans l'île".
[71] Janson, *History of Art*, 420.

by painting over them, he could create "illusionistic openings of every sort",[72] demonstrating the deceptive effect of that art which seeks to veil rather than to reveal. But Malone, himself an artist, does not stop at the surface in his art. Perfectly lucid about his creative activity, he observes upon writing the name Würzburg, "quel touriste j'ai dû être, même le tréma m'est resté, mais ce n'est pas un vrai tréma" (p. 114). A sophisticated orthographer, he even notes the difference between the diaeresis and the umlaut. With these and other like comments he continually points to the fundamental nature of his art – the act of writing – and to its essential component – words. Thus, what may appear to be nothing more than an erudite allusion serves in effect as a basis for essential revelations about art and the artist. As the evolution continues, such basic insights become overwhelming preoccupations.

As direct allusions to works of art vanish from the novels, references to imaginary works take their place. In *Murphy* imaginary books abound – philosophical (Neary's tractate *The Doctrine of the Limit*, p. 50), theological (*Bishop Bouvier's Supplementum ad Tractatum de Matrimonio*, p. 72), and literary (*The Pathetic Fallacy from Avercamp to Kampendonck*, by Miss Counihan's Hindu suitor, p. 196). Each work by its very title is a parody of its genre and indicates the futility of man's efforts to know and to create. Moreover, the absurdity of literature in all its forms suggests the inadequacy and fragility of all art. Similar fictitious titles appearing in *Watt* stress even more the meaninglessness of most writing. Mr. Spiro's periodical *Crux* and his contribution to it (*A Spiritual Syringe for the Costive in Devotion*) (pp. 27-28), Louit's dissertation *The Mathematical Intuitions of the Visicelts* (p. 171), Martin Ignatius MacKenzie's *The Chartered Accountant's Saturday Night* (p. 28), and Cangiamila's *Sacred Embriology* (p. 248) reflect all the petty pretentiousness of common attitudes toward writing. Made to serve the ends of dogma and vanity, literature has no chance to be significant in its own right. But, in addition to these works, *Watt* contains several other kinds of imaginary art. There are musical inventions of every kind, including an arrangement of the croakings of three frogs (pp. 137-138). Most notable among the songs are the threnody (pp. 34-35), heard by Watt lying in the ditch on the way to Mr. Knott's, and the descant (p. 253) he hears on his way to the station after his departure from Knott's. In both, human destiny is laid bare simply and straightforwardly. For example, in the descant the soprano sings: "With all our heart breathe head awhile darkly apart the air exile of ended

72   *Ibid.*

smile of ending care darkly awhile the exile air" (p. 253). The musical form of these works reinforces the meaning of the words, the whole returning to silence at the end as man must return to the nothingness of non-being. In the French translation *exile air* becomes *l'éther asphyxiant*,[73] suggesting that to live, to "breathe awhile the exile air", is in reality to die. The end of life, like the end of a piece of music, is implicit in its beginning. Another image of the human condition is contained in a fictional picture which Watt finds in the room of his fellow servant Erskine and which he studies carefully for some time. Composed only of a circle "broken at its lowest point" (p. 128) and a dot (both of which appear to be moving in space and time), this picture represents for Watt the sorrowful human predicament: "and at the thought that it was perhaps this, a circle and a centre not its centre in search of a centre and its circle respectively, in boundless space, in endless time, then Watt's eyes filled with tears that he could not stem" (p. 129). Expelled from the womb, man wanders through life seeking a substitute for his lost paradise. Since he cannot return to the prenatal state, he is condemned to stumble on until at last death summons him to the tomb, his "new home" (p. 130). Watt himself is a nomad with "no fixed address" (p. 22); even his stay at Knott's cannot be permanent, as Arsene explained to him when he arrived. Like the picture itself, expulsion is "part and parcel of Mr Knott's establishment" (p. 130), so Watt, doomed to be expelled from the house even as he gazes at the picture, readily identifies himself with the ever roaming dot. He even experiments with the picture to see how the breach in the circle would look in other positions. But to please him the gap must be below, for, reasons Watt, "It is by the nadir that we come,... and it is by the nadir that we go" (p. 130). Later, however, when Watt occupies Erskine's room, the painting yields "nothing further" (p. 208). In fact, its significance diminishes with the passage of time. Dulled by habit and by the numbing influence of Mr Knott, Watt becomes indifferent even to what was once for him a poignant illustration of his miserable existence. This indifference to life finds its own image in another fictional picture, "a large coloured print of the horse Joss", which Watt notices in the waiting room of the railroad station after his expulsion from Knott's: "This horse, its four hooves firmly planted on the ground, its head sunk, seemed to consider, without appetite, the grass.... The light was that of approaching night, or impending storm, or both. The grass was sparse, sere, and overrun with what Watt took to be a species of cockle. The horse seemed hardly able to stand, let alone run"

---

[73] *Watt* (Paris, 1968), 267.

(p. 236). Completely disenchanted with his situation, which, in fact, could not be much worse, the weary old animal, like the man beholding him, seems only to be waiting for the night to come, for the storm to blow him away. Watt, waiting for a train to carry him off, resembles the horse in his utter loss of interest in existence. Worn in mind and body, he awaits the end with complete detachment. The print is a mirror in which Watt's own image is reflected.

In *Malone meurt*, one finds two more imaginary works in which the human condition is central. The first, a photograph of an ass at the seashore, illustrates the idea that existence is a joke which a nonexistent creator plays on his creatures.[74] The ass, a creature of the photographer, finds its lot a sad one. Like the horse Joss, its head is lowered: "On a essayé naturellement de lui faire lever la tête, pour que ses beaux yeux s'impriment sur la pellicule, mais il la tient baissée. On voit aux oreilles qu'il n'est pas content. On lui a mis un canotier sur la tête. Les maigres jambes dures et parallèles, les petits sabots à fleur de sable" (p. 146). But this pathetic figure only serves to amuse the operator behind the camera: "Les contours sont flous, c'est le rire du photographe qui a fait trembler l'appareil" (p. 146). The inhumanity of the creator here is reinforced by Malone's observations concerning the background in the photo: "L'océan a l'air si peu naturel qu'on se dirait au studio. Mais ne devrais-je pas dire plutôt le contraire" (p. 146). Nature, in fact completely impassive to human distress, seems 'natural' to man only through human eyes. When the point of view changes from human to divine, the real indifference of nature to suffering is revealed. Man, then, like the ass, is alone in a hostile environment and at the mercy of a creator who does not even exist (who remains always outside of the picture). That Malone calls attention to the photographer is significant in itself. By so doing, he destroys any illusion the photo might produce and lays bare the creative act – in this instance, the arrangement of the subject and the effect of the operator's sentiments on the picture-taking process. Moreover, he portrays an artist who is in truth absent; he makes visible the invisible, encloses nothingness in words. The second example, another photo, or more precisely a daguerreotype, represents the ephemerality of life and the process of decay that is a very real part of it. The picture is of Moll (Macmann's late companion at the asylum) as a young girl: "Elle se tenait debout à côté d'une chaise et elle serrait dans ses mains ses longues nattes. Il subsistait, derrière elle, des traces d'une sorte de treillage où grimpaient des fleurs, des roses sans

[74] In *Fin de partie*, 76, Hamm curses God with the words: "Le salaud! Il n'existe pas!"

doute, elles aiment grimper.... Ce qu'il préférait de cette image, c'était la chaise, dont le siège semblait être en paille. Moll serrait ses lèvres avec application, afin de cacher ses grandes dents saillantes. Les roses aussi devaient être jolies, elles devaient embaumer l'air" (pp. 200-201). Capturing both the girl and the season at the moment of bloom, this photo obscures the decay already in progress. Just as Moll's lips hide her buckteeth, so the picture conceals the inevitability of her death. Only the straw-bottomed chair, Macmann's favorite object in the picture, reflects the way things really are. The grass grows high and then is cut down. Like the roses, which were dying even as she stood in front of them, Moll herself has withered and gone. Her end belies the impression of eternal youth represented by the photograph. As soon as it was made, it became an anachronism. Unable to bear the deception of it, "Macmann déchira cette photo finalement et jeta les morceaux en l'air, un jour de grand vent. Ils se dispersèrent alors, quoique soumis tous aux mêmes conditions, on aurait dit avec empressement" (p. 201). Mirroring its subject's true fate, the picture seems to welcome annihilation like a long overdue relief. Macmann's own artistic efforts echo the idea that death is a release, the grave a "lifelong promised land".[75] In his two poems written for Moll he uses understatement to emphasize the misery of existence and then speaks of the local cemetery as might a fiancé of the altar:

Poupée Pompette et vieux bébé
C'est l'amour qui nous unit
Au terme d'une longue vie
Qui ne fut pas toujours gaie
C'est vrai
Pas toujours gaie.   (p. 167)

C'est l'amour qui nous conduit
La main dans la main vers Glasnevin
C'est le meilleur du chemin
A mon avis au tien aussi
Mais oui
A notre avis.   (p. 168)

Though not great poetry, these verses, in contrast to the daguerreotype, reveal the true nature of the human situation. Furthermore, as the creature of the writer Malone, the poet Macmann represents a portrait of the artist, a reflection of Malone himself.

Two important portraits of this kind appear in imaginary works in

75   *Malone Dies*, 262.

Watt. The first is a bust of Buxtehude in the music-room at Knott's: "The head, and neck, in plaster, very white, of Buxtehude, was on the mantel-piece" (p. 71). A commonplace sort of ornament, this plaster bust is an example of self-conscious art. The sculptor making a bust of a musician recalls the painter at work on a portrait of a writer. The artist who chooses a fellow creator as his subject produces in effect a self-portrait; and, in so doing, he discloses the nature of his own work. His art becomes transparent, mirroring the process of its creation. The most revealing example of this kind in *Watt* is the imaginary painting included in the Addenda. Referred to as the "Second picture in Erskine's room", it represents a "gentleman seated at piano... naked save for stave-paper resting on lap" (p. 250). Shown in the throes of creation, as though seized by a painful catharsis, this pathetic composer produces for all his effort and distress a mere C-major chord. Closely observant of the details in the painting, the narrator strips away every possibility of illusion by remarking how the artist, a certain Mr. O'Connery, "had lavished all the resources of Jesuit tactility" (p. 250) on his work. Some sentences later he again mentions the painter (noting his "love of significant detail", p. 251) and thus reinforces the barrier to deceptive impressions. A portrait of the artist, this picture of a composer about to be delivered of his musical creation presents the creative act in all the anguish of its impossibility and necessity; at the same time it is transparent, with the hand of its maker pictured (by the narrator) at work on its many grotesque details. One of the most self-conscious of the imaginary works, this painting serves, too, as an important example in the study of the artist's dilemma.

As the process of assimilation continues, imaginary works give way to the essential elements of art – form, color, and word. It is as though the Beckettian persona gradually empties his mind, first, of all superficial knowledge and then even of imagination, reducing his resources for creation to the artistic means themselves. Murphy, for example, in his mental exploration strikes down to the fundamental elements of perception: "landscapes, hands, eyes, lines and colours evoking nothing" (*Murphy*, p. 252). For Molloy, the journey to his mother's room is nothing but the "pénultième d'une forme pâlissante entre formes pâlissantes" (*Molloy*, p. 22). In other words, his memories of the past have been reduced to fading forms. As the body weakens, so do the mind and all its faculties. Imaginative detail is lost, leaving only vague shapes in its stead. As Camier remarks, "Je garde l'impression... de formes vagues et cotonneuses" (*Mercier et Camier*, p. 28). But, paradoxically, such vision represents the only true perception of reality. Sapo, Malone's first creature, achieves a kind of essential insight through his mathematical cogitations: "Et les chiffres qui alors manoeuvraient dans sa tête la peuplaient de couleurs et de formes" (*Malone*, p. 22). More often, however, uncluttered perception comes only with the infirmities of age, when, purged of illusion, one can see the folly of perpetual attempts to evade one's own nothingness. Thus, Malone, bedfast and solitary, realizes that his diversions are only forms with which he seeks to mask the formlessness of his essential nature and imminent dissolution: "Les formes sont variées où l'immuable se soulage d'être sans forme" (*Malone*, p. 42). In art, the very mediums are veils covering the kernel of meaning. Still, beyond these basic elements the artist cannot go without yielding to silence and the blank page. In his later fiction, Beckett approaches this kind of essential expression – silence and absence – through his frequent references to form, color, and word.

Allusions to the shape of the handle of a can-opener (*Comment*, p. 41), to the forms of hands,[76] and to the geometrical shape of a cubicle (*Têtes*, p. 61) are examples of the obsession with simple forms that appears everywhere in the later works. But, recurring most often, the "basic figure of Beckett's work"[77] is the circle. In *More Pricks Than Kicks* it is used in the traditional manner to illustrate eternity. Describing to Belacqua the eternal revolutions of heaven, a woman in a pub whirls her arm to dramatize her words: "Heaven goes round... and round and round and round and round" (p. 23). In *Watt*, however, the circle is broken (see above the discussion of the first imaginary picture in Erskine's room, p. 64). Here Beckett adds a new dimension to the familiar figure. Human existence, though the result of a cyclical process of generation, must have a beginning and an end. The broken circle adequately represents the inevitable doom of every man, while at the same time calling to mind by its imperfection (by its failure to be a full circle) the perfect and eternal kind of existence to which man vainly aspires. Moreover, its circularity, though incomplete, suggests the continuing cycle of reproduction in which man participates. In this way, the broken circle presents both the irresistible and perpetual current of life in which all men are caught up and the common end of each. An infinity of broken circles (individual human beings) compose together the full circle of endless human existence. A German round[78] sung by Vladimir in the second act of *Godot* (pp. 96-97) and summarized by the Unnamable (*L'Innommable*, pp. 187-188) demonstrates this principle clear-

---

[76] In "Assez", *Têtes-mortes*, 36; hereafter, reference to the pieces in *Têtes-mortes* will appear in the text with the appropriate page number in parentheses.

[77] Hoffman, *Samuel Beckett*, 133.

[78] Fletcher, "Roger Blin at Work", 26.

ly with its continuous tale of the death and burial of one dog after another. As Beckett writes of the circular movement in *Finnegans Wake*, "In a word, here is all humanity circling with fatal monotony about the Providential fulcrum";[79] and, in the same essay he observes: "There is a continual purgatorial process at work, in the sense that the vicious circle of humanity is being achieved."[80]

The circle takes on a different kind of significance in later works, where the protagonist inhabits an ever shrinking circular space (perhaps vast, perhaps only "douze pieds de diamètre" in *L'Innommable*, p. 15, it is reduced to a diameter of "80 centimètres" in "Imagination morte imaginez", *Têtes*, p. 51), often described as a rotunda ("une minuscule rotonde", *L'Innommable*, p. 62; "La rotonde", *Têtes*, p. 51). This enclosed space frequently has no entrance or exit ("Pas d'entrée", *Têtes*, p. 51; "sans fenêtres", *L'Innommable*, p. 62) and, hence, resembles the interior of the mind. Indeed, as early as *Murphy*, the three-dimensional circular figure represents the mind: "Murphy's mind pictured itself as a large hollow sphere, hermetically closed to the universe without" (p. 107). For one immured in his head, there could be no more fitting image, as Ruby Cohn remarks: "the circle is the perfect symbol of a self-contained cosmos. When that cosmos is the self, the circle becomes the symbol of solipsism, and indeed Murphy is explicitly designated as a 'seedy solipsist', who pictures his mind as a sphere."[81] (Similarly, according to Jacqueline Hoefer, a "circle seems to be the right symbol for Watt's world, for it so forcefully asserts a limit – solipsistic, self-contained, and inescapable".)[82] Confined to bed in a sparsely furnished room, Malone believes at times that he inhabits a skull: "et il me semble souvent en effet que je suis dans une tête" (*Malone*, p. 87). Significantly, the Unnamable invents just such a small closed world for himself: "faire un endroit, un petit monde,... il sera rond... au plafond bas, aux murs épais" (*L'Innommable*, p. 242). Yet for the artist, the circle or sphere is static. It cannot bore down into the heart of consciousness; it can only represent the mind closed in upon itself. The descending, cone-shaped spiral, on the other hand, illustrates the probing action of art, and actually resembles a circle actively in search of its center (compare the description of the first imaginary painting in

---

[79]   "Dante . . . Bruno . Vico . . Joyce", 9.
[80]   "Dante . . . Bruno . Vico . . Joyce", 22. Cf. the extensive passage from Arsene's discourse in *Watt*, 46-47, beginning: "And the poor old lousy old earth, my earth and my father's and my mother's and my father's father's and my mother's mother's and my father's mother's and my mother's father's and...."
[81]   Cohn, *The Comic Gamut*, 46.
[82]   Hoefer, "*Watt*", 70.

Watt above, p. 64). The Unnamable, in the guise of his creature Mahood, describes how he manoeuvres himself on crutches in just such a spiral: "Je m'étais probablement empêtré dans une sorte de spirale renversée, je veux dire dont les boucles, au lieu de prendre de plus en plus d'ampleur, devaient aller en rétrécissant, jusqu'à ne plus pouvoir se poursuivre" (*L'Innommable*, pp. 59-60). Ironically, this kind of motion leads to immobility, for the circle can never reach its center; the mind can never contemplate its hollow core. Even the artist can perceive consciousness only through the veil of self-consciousness. Thus, though the characteristic shape of its development is the cone-shaped spiral, the evolution of the novels cannot end in a vacuum. Some form or color or word must always remain to frame the void at the center. Perhaps that is one reason why spirals, noticeable only in the trilogy, disappear from the most recent works in which the diminished circle dominates. Even in *L'Innommable* the three-dimensional spiral yields to a plane figure: "J'avais cru comprendre que je passais ma vie à faire le tour du monde, en colimaçon. Erreur, c'est dans l'île que je ne cesse de tourner. Je ne connais rien d'autre, seulement l'île. Elle non plus je ne la connais pas, n'ayant jamais eu la force de la regarder. Quand j'arrive au rivage, je m'en retourne, vers l'intérieur" (pp. 80-81). Confined to the island of his mind, the Unnamable is alternately drawn toward its center and repulsed from it without ever being able to contemplate any part of his mental landscape – circumference or center. The dynamic movement of the spiral becomes the vain and monotonous in and out motion of an ever expanding and contracting circle.[83]

Grey and white are the dominant colors in the later works. The first represents mental obscurity, the second, silence and emptiness. In *Malone meurt*, light and color vanish, leaving an odd twilight: "il n'y a vraiment pas de couleur ici, sauf dans la mesure où cette sorte d'incandescence grisâtre en est une" (p. 85). The author-hero even believes that he himself gives off a grey light: "Moi-même je suis gris, j'ai même l'impression quelquefois de jeter du gris, au même titre que mes draps par exemple" (p. 86). A few pages later, after suggesting that he inhabits a skull, Malone remarks how "toutes ces grandes superficies, ou devrais-je dire infraficies... ont sensiblement blémi" (p. 90). He notes how parts of the body undergo such transformations, reinforcing the earlier suggestion of his cerebral location. Still, he asks: "Est-ce à dire qu'il fait plus clair chez moi maintenant

---

[83]   Cf. Georges Poulet's essay on Rousseau in *The Metamorphoses of the Circle*, trans. by Carley Dawson and Elliott Coleman in colloboration with the author (Baltimore, Md.: The Johns Hopkins Press, 1966), 70-90.

que je sais ce qui se passe? Eh bien, je dois dire que non, c'est le même gris qu'auparavant, qui par moments étincelle littéralement, puis se trouble et faiblit, s'épaissit si l'on préfère, au point de tout cacher à mes regards sauf la fenêtre" (p. 91). The grey, then, is a permanent veiling of the mind which demonstrates the limits of reason. For the Unnamable, the air itself forms grey veils: "D'un gris tout juste transparent dans mon voisinage immédiat, en dehors de ce cercle charmé il s'étale en fines nappes impénétrables, d'un ton à peine plus foncé" (*L'Innommable*, p. 26). Though thin, the veils cannot be pierced by perception. Possessed by doubt and uncertainty, the mind is a dim realm which thwarts all efforts of consciousness to know it. In the words of Onimus, it is "cette grisaille... où la conscience s'épuise en tâtonnements et en vaines hypothèses".[84]

The color white predominates in the most recent works. Representing the blank page, the purification longed for by earlier heroes (see above, pp. 26-27), it becomes the annihilating nothingness into which the works themselves dissolve. Onimus writes: "Le blanc n'est-il pas la couleur de l'Absence, du Rien qui est aussi celle de l'Absolu, une couleur si intense qu'elle a dévoré toutes les couleurs? Le blanc est inhumain, insoutenable, antiseptique: rien ne suggère mieux la transparence totale du regard intérieur, une nudité écrasante, une brûlure solaire, l'absence de toute ombre protectrice, de toute trace de souillure vivante."[85] White, then, represents too the relentless lucidity of the self-conscious artist and his art. In "From an Abandoned Work", the narrator reveals his predilection for white animals when he sees a white horse (pp. 140-141). He dreams of animals, too, and says of them: "I couldn't describe them, lovely creatures they were, white mostly" (p. 142). Admitting his general sensitivity to the color white, he declares: "White I must say has always affected me strongly, all white things, sheets, walls and so on, even flowers, then just the thought of white, without more" (p. 141). White envelopes everything in the last two stories of *Têtes-mortes*. In the first, "Imagination morte imaginez", the narrator begins by accepting the fact that his imagination is dead. As a result, typical background elements of fiction are immediately discarded from his mind: "Iles, eaux, azur, verdure, fixez, pff, muscade, une éternité, taisez" (p. 51). All is expelled, "Jusqu'à toute blanche dans la blancheur la rotonde" (p. 51). That the rotunda represents the interior of the narrator's mind is suggested by the following observation: "Sortez, une rotonde sans ornement, toute blanche dans la blancheur, rentrez, frappez, du plein partout, ça sonne comme dans l'imagination l'os sonne" (p. 51). Everything is

---

[84] Onimus, *Beckett*, 52.
[85] Onimus, 51.

white: "Par terre deus corps blancs, chacun dans son demi-cercle. Blancs aussi la voûte et le mur rond" (p. 51). Even the woman's hair is white, though "d'une blancheur incertaine" (p. 55). The whiteness is associated with emptiness and silence: "Vide, silence, chaleur, blancheur" (p. 52). Twice during the course of this short piece the narrator describes the rotunda from outside, emphasizing how it almost merges with the whiteness around it: "Ressortez, reculez, elle disparaît, survolez, elle disparaît, toute blanche dans la blancheur" (p. 52); "Extérieurement tout reste inchangé et le petit édifice d'un repérage toujours aussi aléatoire, sa blancheur se fondant dans l'environnante" (p. 55). Finally, the entire image is lost: "plus question de retrouver ce point blanc perdu dans la blancheur" (p. 57). The vision of a stripped mind, this bleached and barren scene vanishes as suddenly as it appeared. Having come out of the whiteness, it returns to it, just as men are born of nothing and are called back to it in the end. Here Beckett shows fiction to be as gratuitous as life by underscoring the whiteness of the very pages upon which it takes form.

In "Bing", he demonstrates much the same thing but with even more repetition. The major development here is the narrator's revelation that everything is becoming white after having been some other color. For example, he says of the body: "Donné rose à peine corps nu blanc fixe un mètre blanc sur blanc invisible" (*Têtes*, p. 62). Onimus suggests how such a process takes place by reference to Beckett's short piece "Dans le cylindre": "C'est dans une lumière de fournaise que s'agitent les prisonniers du *Cylindre*, saignés à blanc par une clarté verticale qui abolit leurs ombres."[86] Enveloped in whiteness, almost everything is invisible: "Mains blanches invisibles pendues ouvertes creux face" (*Têtes*, p. 62). Only the eyes (the one touch of color in "Imagination morte", p. 56) and the mysterious traces on the walls break the monotony: "Seuls les yeux seuls inachevés donnés bleus trous bleu pâle presque blanc seule couleur fixe face" (p. 63); "Traces seules inachevées données noires gris pâle presque blanc sur blanc" (pp. 61-62). But they too must succumb to the whitening power which unifies all, eradicating everything in its path: "tout blanc achevé... murs blancs rayonnants sans traces yeux couleur dernière hop blancs achevés" (p. 66). Vanishing from sight these last distinguishable elements complete their destiny, merge with the nonexistent from which for a moment they had surged into being – the eyes, windows of consciousness, and the signs, expressions of that consciousness. Still, as long as the piece continues there must be some organ of perception focused on the

---

[86]   *Ibid.* "Dans le cylindre" is a fragment of the now completed *Le dépeupleur* (Paris: Éditions de Minuit, 1970).

scene; hence, a single eye remains, one that the narrator apparently has never seen before ("ça de mémoire presque jamais", p. 65): "oeil embu noir et blanc miclos longs cils suppliant" (p. 66). It, too, disappears, however, when the end of the piece is proclaimed by the final word *achevé* (p. 66; *over* in the English translation).[87] Here in the concluding story of *Têtes-mortes*, the self-consciousness of Beckett's art seems to reach its summit. By insisting on the whiteness that surrounds his fiction, he goes further than ever in underscoring the creative act, the attempt to fill blank pages with words. In *Comment c'est*, the narrator calls attention to the empty spaces between each group of lines: "les blancs sont les trous", he admits self-consciously, and then goes on, "sinon ça coule plus ou moins plus ou moins grands les trous on parle des trous impossible d'indiquer pas la peine" (p. 104). The gaps are the silences between his utterances, the white spaces on the page that frame the words. The word *blanc*, meaning both the color white and the blank spaces in a text, reinforces the multi-valent significance of white in the fiction. It is the purity of silence and nothingness to which all Beckett's author-heroes aspire, and it is the menacing blank page upon which they must write.[88] But *white* is also a word – "there is that word white again" ("From", p. 145) – and by remarking it to be so, the narrator of "From an Abandoned Work" indicates that for the writer there can be no more persistent obsession than words.

In the last stage of the process of assimilation, the words – themselves the basic elements of literature – come to the fore, replacing the superficial allusive detail of conventional fiction. This essential refinement of the convention makes the works transparent to their own true nature and dramatizes the creative act by revealing the rapport between the creator-heroes and their medium. As early as *Molloy*, the narrator meditates upon what he has just written: "Quelle bonté dans ces petits mots, quelle férocité" (p. 127). Later the hero of "From an Abandoned Work" admits his weakness for certain words: "over, I love the word, words have been my only loves, not many" (p. 147).[89] Explaining this passage, Jean-Jacques Mayoux writes: "Words and phrases remain apparitions full of meaning...

---

[87] "Bing", 168.

[88] Comparing Beckett's passion for purity and awareness of creative inadequacy to those of Mallarmé, Rose Lamont writes in "La Farce métaphysique", 107: "Ecrire pour créer du silence, écrire pour dire qu'on ne peut écrire, évoquer l'absence d'une rose dans une chambre vide, telle était la tâche que se proposait Mallarmé, poète de la stérilité idéale, alchimiste du verbe, exilé comme son Cygne dans la contrée glacée de l'impossible pureté. Tout est de trop également dans l'univers de Beckett, tout se voudrait absence."

[89] Cf. the verbal predilection of the hero in *Premier amour*, 44: "J'ai beaucoup aimé, enfin assez aimé, pendant assez longtemps, les mots vase de nuit".

They are the nuclei, the raw materials of a nebulous structure that forever rises up and partially disintegrates, in the midst of which a voice heroically persists."[90] In *L'Innommable*, the nameless protagonist repeatedly refers to the nature of his art: "Tout se ramène à une affaire de paroles" (p. 98); "Ce qui se passe, ce sont des mots" (p. 119); "les mots qui tombent, on ne sait pas où, on ne sait pas d'où, gouttes de silence à travers le silence" (p. 195); "ce sont des mots, je n'ai que ça" (p. 259). Implicitly comparing himself to a painter, he illustrates how fundamental words are to fiction by comparing a collection of twenty basic ones to a similar assortment of paints: "la palette y serait, je les mélangerais, je les varierais, la gamme y serait" (p. 248). Further, he demonstrates how he must depend on words in order to make progress through his story: "moi qui suis en route, de paroles plein les voiles" (p. 134). Similarly, the narrator of "Texte IX" acknowledges, "je suis encore en route, par oui et par non" (*Textes*, p. 203). More revealing still is the hero's realization that as a persona he himself is made of words, that they compose his own existence: "je suis en mots, je suis fait de mots"; "je les suis tous" (*L'Innommable*, p. 204). At times he cannot actually believe that he is coexistent with his story: "errer... de mot en mot... être ce lent tourbillon sans bornes et chacune de ses poussières, c'est impossible" (*L'Innommable*, p. 235). More often he accepts the rapport as inescapable: "de mot en mot, ça tournoie d'ahan, on est là-dedans quelque part" (*L'Innommable*, p. 236); "Des mots, des mots, la mienne [sa vie] ne fut jamais que ça que pêle-mêle le babel [sic] des silences et des mots" (*Textes*, p. 172). In fact, in "Texte VIII" the narrator compares his words with tears, making the former as essential a sign of existence as the latter are in other works:[91] "je les confonds, mots et larmes, mes mots sont mes larmes, mes yeux ma bouche" (*Textes*, p. 181). A few pages later this same narrator describes his own death and rebirth as a phenomenon of words: "Moi, ici, s'ils [les mots] pouvaient s'ouvrir, ces petits mots, m'engloutir et se refermer, c'est peut-être ce qui s'est produit. Qu'ils s'ouvrent donc de nouveau et me laissent sortir, dans le tumulte de lumière qui m'a scellé les yeux, et d'hommes, pour que j'essaie d'en être de nouveau" (*Textes*, p. 184). Words take the place of primeval slime here, for this is after all a work of fiction in which everything is made of words. Thus, in the same way, the hero of "Texte XI" yearns for his own annihilation to be achieved through a final purifying negation:

---

[90]   Mayoux, "Samuel Beckett and Universal Parody", 90.
[91]   For example, see *Fin de partie*, 84. When Hamm asks Clov to look into Nagg's ashcan to see if he is dead, Clov obeys and reports: "Il pleure." Hamm's reply is: "Donc il vit."

"il faut trouver... un nouveau non, qui ne se laisse dire qu'une fois, qui ouvre sa trappe et me lampe, ombre et babil, dans une absence moins vaine que d'existence" (*Textes*, p. 209). In *Comment c'est* the dependency on words is more marked than ever: "les mots ne viennent pas aucun mot même muet j'en ai besoin d'un mot" (p. 22). The words even seem to control the speaker: "les syllabes remuent mes lèvres" (p. 22). He, too, exists by virtue of them, but it is his own voice uttering the words that gives him a presence: "un mot de moi et je resuis" (p. 32); "je me suis nommé... et je suis un instant" (p. 132). Behind every word, then, there must be a mind to choose and a voice or a hand to express. Words have an enormous capacity for establishing one's existence, for, according to the narrator of *Comment c'est*, "un seul suffit" (p. 32). Still, if he wants to exist, he must continue to say words incessantly: "vieux mots par-ci par-là les ajouter les uns aux autres faire des phrases" (p. 129). Through statements like this one the self-conscious author-hero displays the direct rapport between himself and his work. He and the work are coincident, his existence in words being the stuff of the fiction itself. Indeed, narrator and narrative appear as one and inseparable. Thus, through his chiselling away at the convention of allusions, Beckett transforms an outworn traditional device into a fine new tool for his caustic art.

A final example from among the conventional techniques assimilated in the fiction is the conclusion. As early as *Murphy*, Beckett makes the concluding phrase of the novel reflect its function. After Mr. Kelly loses his kite, Celia wheels him home while the park rangers call, "All out" (p. 282). Through the use of significant detail, the self-conscious author acknowledges that his story is coming to an end. Here the conclusion plays an essential role in the formal structure and helps make the novel transparent. In the French works, his efforts to reveal the illusory nature of fiction lead to more subtle symmetry. Molloy traces a circle in his story as he describes how he travelled to his mother's room, which he occupies at the time of composition. Moran, who begins by setting the scene for his own report, concludes by denying that his first words were true and, hence, calls into question the veracity of all that followed them. Recounting at the end of his tale how he began to write it, he says: "Alors je rentrai dans la maison et j'écrivis, Il est minuit. La pluie fouette les vitres. Il n'était pas minuit. Il ne pleuvait pas" (*Molloy*, p. 272). In *Malone meurt*, the conclusion of the novel coincides precisely with the ebbing existence of the author-hero. The words in the text are even arranged so as to reflect his diminishing powers. Heralding the end is the phrase "Glouglous de vidange" (p. 216), and the final words standing alone on the page are "plus rien" (p. 217).

Sculptured to match the slow emptying of the creative mind, this conclusion is a *tour de force* in self-conscious writing. Some examples in the *Textes pour rien* are simply more refined variations of earlier ones (for example, "Voilà, c'est fait, ça finit là, je finis là", p. 142), but others go further, revealing that the narrator-hero is actually an endless Chinese puzzle of one consciousness within another: "on commence à être bien fatigué, bien fatigué de sa peine, bien fatigué de sa plume, *elle tombe, c'est noté*" (*Textes*, p. 166, my emphasis). As long as someone is there to write "elle tombe", the narrator is not limited to his first persona. In effect, the real storyteller can never be identified; slipping into one disguise after another, he evades all pursuit and has no existence but that of his creations. To surprise the creating consciousness at its source, unwavering lucidy is maintained throughout *Comment c'est*, persisting to the very end as the narrator closes: "comment c'était... après Pim comment c'est" (p. 177). But it is in "Bing", his last piece of short fiction, that Beckett comes closest to rending the veil of the persona and to creating the effect of pure consciousness recording perception. Using a telegraphic style, he eliminates almost all traces of conventional novelistic technique and produces his most concentrated fictional work. Self-consciousness survives, however, and seems to be completely integrated into the fabric of the piece, for the concluding word is *achevé* (*Têtes*, p. 66; *over* in the English translation).[92] The end of the work, implicit in its beginning, is reflected in the elements of the initial scene. Almost every object named is white and, hence, "achevé"; the two exceptions (the traces and the eyes) are in the process of becoming "achevé" also. Once their transformation is complete, all will be an indistinguishable whiteness. Only the impression of an absence of image, like that of the silence at the end of a tale or musical performance, will remain. This piece, then, not only anticipates its inevitable conclusion but also calls attention to the kind of nothingness (the whiteness, emptiness, and silence of the blank page) that will succeed its end. An unprecedented example of coincident writing, "Bing" represents a culmination of Beckett's efforts to create perfectly lucid works of art. Mayoux summarizes his achievement in the fiction as follows: "He does not go in for the tricks of fiction, with its logical and temporal successions. He renders the impossible silence, the impossible concentration at the firm and motionless heart of being, by a continual movement, reconsidering and making us reconsider whatever he provisionally sets down, arresting time, destroying illusion... remaining obstinately in the present."[93]

---

[92] "Bing", 168.
[93] Mayoux, "Samuel Beckett and Universal Parody", 87.

4. THE EVOLUTION OF THE PROTAGONIST
IN SAMUEL BECKETT'S FICTION

The assimilation of conventions to the Beckettian vision reveals more than the essence of fiction. As a part of the caustic process, it lays bare the human condition – one of Beckett's principal concerns (as noted earlier). Indeed, the attempt to make visible the true misery and helplessness of mankind plays an important role in the evolution of the novels. As Germaine Brée suggests, "Beckett, avec *Comment c'est*, semble avoir vidé son monde imaginaire de tout ce qui n'était pas nécessaire à une vision fondamentale de la condition humaine."[1] Showing man to be "voué à la désintégration physique, en route vers la mort",[2] Beckett underscores the inevitability of death. "Le drame auquel Beckett nous fait assister", writes Mme Lamont, "est celui de la dégénérescence inéluctable du corps et de l'esprit, du vieillissement, humiliant prologue à la mort qui, elle, surgit à la naissance de l'homme."[3] To reach the core of the situation, in the case of man as in that of the novel, all superfluous detail must be eliminated and the area of exploration reduced "à ses données les plus élémentaires".[4] To get "down to the bedrock of existence",[5] Beckett divests his heroes of all but the bare minimum of human capacities. Yet, just as a minimum of conventional surface detail reflects an enhancement of meaning in the novels, so the increasing physical destitution of the heroes indicates their growing significance and produces an ever clearer image of the inescapable misery of existence. As Ruby Cohn puts it, "Gradually stripped of possessions and clothes, they grow larger in meaning as their silhouettes shrink."[6] The caustic mutilation is designed to pierce the veils of flesh, to reach the heart of being. Writes Hélène Cixous: "on voit le corps... être graduellement supprimé. On perd les membres, le tronc; reste la tête; la tête aussi disparaîtra"; and she adds: "L'élimination du corps, de la matière, se fait en faveur d'un

---

[1] Brée, "L'Etrange monde des 'grands articulés'", 96.
[2] *Ibid.*
[3] Lamont, "La Farce métaphysique", 100.
[4] Abirached, "La Voix tragique de Samuel Beckett", 85.
[5] Moore, "Some Night Thoughts", 535.
[6] Cohn, *The Comic Gamut*, 295.

Moi."[7] The body vanishes in order to disclose the consciousness, that consciousness which remains even after the flesh dwindles to almost nothing. Thus, the evolution of the heroes in the fiction reflects "Beckett's incessant endeavour to strip his characters of accidental qualities and to penetrate to the core of their being – the consciousness of being."[8] Still, the absurdity of the human conditon is evident when one considers that "the continued existence of our consciousness depends absolutely on the continued existence of our bodies";[9] as the narrator of "Texte I" says, "Je devrais m'en détourner, du corps et de la tête, les laisser s'arranger, les laisser cesser, je ne peux pas, il faudrait que moi je cesse" (*Textes*, p. 128). To exist, consciousness requires a minimum of mind and body, even though "the body, as Beckett repeats unceasingly, is a frail machine subject to depreciation and built-in obsolescence".[10] Paradoxically, the nothing of consciousness, that hole in the center of being, the core of being itself, must be encased in mortal flesh. As a result, thus illuminated from within, the utter ephemerality of the body becomes undeniably visible.

In *Murphy*, Beckett exposes man's infinite fragility and impotence while indicating at the same time how one must bring the body under control in order to explore the mind. Our first view of Murphy shows him "naked in his rockingchair of undressed teak" (p. 1) where he seeks to "appease" his body (bound to the chair by seven scarves) so that he may "come alive in his mind" (p. 2). Some pages later, however, an untimely accident interrupts his spiritual exercise and mocks his efforts to escape the prison of flesh. Discovered by Celia,

Murphy was as last heard of, with this difference however, that the rocking-chair was now on top. Thus inverted his only direct contact with the floor was that made by his face, which was ground against it. His attitude roughly speaking was that of a very inexperienced diver about to enter the water, except that his arms were not extended to break the concussion, but fastened behind him. Only the most local movements were possible, a licking of the lips, a turning of the other cheek to the dust, and so on. Blood gushed from his nose. (p. 28)

Emphasizing the humor and pathos of his plight are the sounds which bring Celia to his side ("An appalling sound issued from Murphy's room, a flurry of such despairing quality that she dropped the bag, followed after a short silence by a suspiration more lamentable than any groan", p. 28) and the revelations which accompany her rescue efforts. As she

[7]   Cixous, "Le maître du texte pour rien", 13.
[8]   Esslin, "Looking for Beckett", 923.
[9]   Fletcher, *Samuel Beckett's Art*, 140, note 1.
[10] *Ibid.*

pries the chair off him, he falls to the floor in a posture which suggests the torment of existence: "Part by part he subsided, as the bonds that held him fell away, until he lay fully prostrate in the crucified position, heaving" (p. 28). More touching and comic still is the final detail laid bare by the unbinding: "A huge pink naevus on the pinnacle of the right buttock" (p. 29). This physical feature, which stamps its bearer now, as it did when he first came into the world, recalls the helpless babe he was and foreshadows the inert cadaver he must become. Ironically, though most fittingly, the charred remainder of this mark is the distinguishing sign by which Celia identifies Murphy's corpse after his final, fatal accident in the chair (p. 266). In this way, his birthmark literally becomes a deathmark, as the coroner points out (p. 267). Moreover, this episode reveals that in fact every birthmark is inherently a mark of death, since for every human beginning (birth) there must be an end (death).

In *Mercier et Camier*, nakedness, the exposure of human limitations and weakness, undergoes variation to show that even when hidden its nature cannot be changed. Here Watt appears in the greatcoat, a floor-length garment that is the typical costume of Beckett's French heroes: "Il portait, malgré la chaleur, un immense chapeau melon enfoncé jusqu'aux oreilles et un lourd manteau boutonné de tous ses nombreux boutons et dont les pans balayaient le sol. Il était peut-être nu en-dessous."[11] Later, in a similar description of Macmann, Malone suggests that one is always as naked and vulnerable as a worm, no matter how all-enveloping his clothes may be: "Macmann serait nu comme ver sous... cette houppelande, qu'il n'en paraîtrait rien à la surface" (*Malone*, pp. 101-102). The garment itself is referred to as a "cache-misère" (*Malone*, p. 98), indicating clearly the feebleness of what lies concealed beneath it. As for himself, Malone readily admits his nakedness: "Je suis nu dans le lit, à même les couvertures, dont j'augmente et diminue le nombre selon les saisons" (*Malone*, p. 18). Able to take advantage of at least some protection against the changing temperature, he is more fortunate than the Unnamable who must depend only on his jar and the attentions of his patroness to shield him from the snow (*L'Innommable*, pp. 83-84). Crawling through warm slime, the protagonist of *Comment c'est* needs no clothes; still, his naked body lies open to tortures, like those he inflicts on Pim in Part II. Completely exposed to the extremes of heat and cold, the two bodies in "Imagination morte imaginez" seem to present aged fetuses whose womb-like

---

11   From an excerpt of *Mercier et Camier* taken from a copy of the original typescript and published by Fletcher with his article "Sur un roman inédit", 154. This passage does not appear in the edition of the novel published in 1970 by Editions de Minuit.

dwelling does not function for their benefit (*Têtes*, pp. 51-57). As impotent as the unborn, they lie immobile, exhibiting an infinitely pathetic vulnerability. It is in "Bing", however, that the mutability of the human condition assumes its most essential character. Here the narrator, who insists on the blinding whiteness of everything, emphasizes at the same time how things were before this time. Of the body at the center, which is first described as "corps nu blanc" (*Têtes*, p. 61), he twice remarks, "Donné rose à peine" (pp. 62, 64), indicating that it has grown more and more pale until now it is so white as to be invisible against its white surroundings: "blanc sur blanc invisible" (p. 62). Having emerged from nothingness, it must return to the anonymity of nonbeing.

Reinforcing the image of corporal limitation exposed in nakedness, the gradual deterioration of the body helps chart the evolution of the Beckettian hero. Even Belacqua bears the stamp of a faltering constitution. He "always looked ill and dejected" (*More Pricks*, p. 4) and had a "weak bladder and tendency to ptosis of viscera" (p. 27). The importance of such disintegration becomes clear with *Murphy* where Mr. Kelly, Celia's grandfather, appears as the archetype for the decaying hero of later works. Graced with "a fine bulb of skull, unobscured by hair" (p. 11), Mr. Kelly is undergoing a physical metamorphosis which does not affect his head: "Yet a little while and his brain-body ratio would have sunk to that of a small bird" (p. 11). But the changes in his body occupy his mind as he attempts to ward off death by giving mental attention to the debilitated parts: "He found it hard to think, his body seemed spread over a vast area, parts would wander away and get lost if he did not keep a sharp look-out, he felt them fidgeting to be off" (p. 115). Paradoxically, his diminishing body seems to be growing larger; like Malone, who always expected that he would fade away "en me ratatinant, jusqu'à finir par pouvoir être enterré dans un écrin à bijou presque" (*Malone*, p. 113), Mr. Kelly could say "voilà que je me dilate" (*Malone*, p. 113). But the pathos of his situation remains in his acute awareness of his own lingering dissolution. The unnaturally large size of his head and the inversely proportionate and ever decreasing size of his body underscore the role played by each. As the body declines, the mind takes note of each impoverishment, as if its feverish activity could stem the inevitable outflow of vitality. But rather than arresting the disintegration to which it bears witness, ever alert consciousness of self deepens the pangs of slow decay. The final effect, the ultimate in human absurdity and pitifulness, can be seen in the last chapter of *Murphy* when Celia takes Mr. Kelly to the park: "He wore his kiting costume, a glistening slicker many sizes too large for him and a yachting-cap many sizes too small, though the smallest and largest of their kind obtainable" (p. 276). Later in the same scene when he makes a futile effort to retrieve his lost kite, he appears as "a ghastly, lamentable figure" (pp. 281-282): "The slicker trailed along the ground, the skull gushed from under the cap like a dome from under its lantern, the ravaged face was a cramp of bones, throttled sounds jostled in his throat" (p. 282). Even though his body is little more than a skeleton ("figure de danse macabre" in the French translation),[12] the mind dominates it, forcing it to do what lies beyond its powers. The image of an enormous head recurs in the same novel to describe the mysterious Mr. Endon, Murphy's favorite patient at the Magdalen Mental Mercyseat. As one who retreats often into the life of the mind, according to Murphy, Mr. Endon is another example of mental hyperactivity combined with a diminutive physique: "The skull, large for any body, immense for this" (p. 186).

All through the trilogy, too, the image reappears, though with some variations. In *Malone meurt*, for instance, Macmann's greatcoat, which provides such ample covering for his nakedness, cannot conceal his head; the coat has the effect "d'être sur et par-dessus le tout, à l'exception évidement de la tête, qui s'élève, altière et impassible, hors de son étreinte" (p. 99). The mind, then, remains impervious to what befalls the body, though it is continuously aware of the latter's steady decline. In *L'Innommable*, the hero envisions his head as a ball mounted on a stick: "le cou droit et sans torsion et là-dessus la tête, bien assise, comme sur son bâtonnet la boule du bilboquet" (p. 35). Later he sees himself in his jar as a sort of bust with his head "montée en épingle et artistiquement éclairée dès la tombée de la nuit" (pp. 116-117). Reduced radically in body but with a large head still intact, Beckett's heroes resemble the stripped figures of Giacometti. (A specific description of Mr. Kelly's head illustrates the similarity in detail of the two artists: "the hairless domes and bosses of his skull... [the] ravaged face [scored] with shadow", *Murphy*, p. 115.) For both artists, consciousness of self dominates the human figure and makes what little remains of the physical self seem even less. As Geraldine Cmrada says of Malone, "Only his consciousness or thought is hyperactive."[13] In fact, the weight of the mind seems too much for the body to bear. Onimus, confirming the comparison between writer and sculptor, expresses most vividly the common features of their work: "la recherche ascétique et presque enragée de l'essentiel: l'être humain, filiforme ou larvaire, réduit à un regard, mais quel regard! Un corps dévoré de mai-

---

[12]   *Murphy* (Paris, 1965), 201.
[13]   Cmrada, "*Malone Dies*: A Round of Consciousness", 202.

greur, mais un esprit brûlant"; "c'est à force de manques que cet être apparaît si vivant".[14] Aware of his perpetually worsening debilitation, the Beckettian hero realizes ever more forcefully with each new loss the constant, piercing gaze of his mind. "Il y avait des jours", says Molloy, "où mes jambes étaient ce que j'avais de mieux, abstraction faite du cerveau capable de former un tel jugement" (*Molloy*, p. 126). Eventually, nothing remains but the consciousness fixed on itself, mirroring its own incessant self-perception.

To capture the essence of being, Beckett concentrates on that period in man's life when the body's disintegration makes itself felt most strongly – old age. In the Addenda to *Watt*, he specifies this period first in his verse list of concerns: "who may tell the tale of the old man?" (p. 247). Mr. Kelly is at least ninety (*Murphy*, p. 115), and his successors are so old as to be without any specified age. The narrator of "Le Calmant", for example, refers to his body as "ce vieux corps" (*Nouvelles*, p. 46), and cannot even think of his age later in the story (p. 66). As for the Unnamable, he says of himself: "j'ai toujours été vieux, toujours vieillissant" (*L'Innommable*, p. 229). Aging, then is recognized as an inescapable aspect of life. Living is growing old and dying, and the entire process can seem to occupy very little time. As the narrator of "Texte XI" puts it, "c'est vite fait, un vieux morveux"; and he goes on to describe his diminished self: "vieux comme le monde, foutu comme le monde, amputé de partout, debout sur mes fidèles moignons" (*Textes*, p. 206; here we recall Nagg and Nell in *Fin de partie*, pp. 24, 31). In *Comment c'est*, the direct rapport between birth and death, living and dying, becomes clear when the hero expresses "l'impression d'être né plutôt octogenaire à l'âge où l'on meurt dans le noir la boue" (p. 87). Man is born dying but the fact is usually admitted only after many years. By focussing on men who are undeniably in the proces of wasting away, waiting for the end, Beckett presents an image of the human condition uncluttered by superfluous detail. Fletcher says of this period: "man is best seen then, when his passions are largely dead"; and he goes on to explain that Beckett "prefers to look at man in that state... for then he can examine [man's] essential nature unhindered by any distracting features".[15] The disintegrating hero himself (Molloy, Malone, the Unnamable) finds a refuge in old age, a retreat from the external world with its distractions. Furthermore, his image of himself is less distorted then than at an earlier period, for age strips man of his vanity as it gnaws at his capacities. With a diminished body, one has fewer outward concerns.

---

[14] Onimus, *Beckett*, 122.
[15] Fletcher, *Samuel Beckett's Art*, 143.

As the corporeal side of existence offers less and less to occupy the mind, consciousness itself assumes central importance. In the aged hero, then, one begins to approach the fundamental elements of being, hidden beneath superficial characteristics in younger men.

The dwindling hero seems to welcome his dissolution, regarding it as a liberation from illusory involvement in the world and as the necessary means by which he can return to the freedom of nonexistence. In the *Nouvelles*, the fit of the heroes' clothes indicates how their bodies have shrunk. The narrator of "Le Clamant" notices his coat raking the ground and attributes this change to his having grown smaller (p. 49). In "La Fin", the hero obtains second-hand garments which are apparently a bit small for him at first, since their former owner was "un peu moins grand que moi, un peu moins gras" (p. 78). But he notes that these clothes fit him better in the end, clearly revealing that his body undergoes reduction after the receipt of the costume. Pointing out how he becomes more and more detached from the external world as his body shrinks, this same narrator remarks near the end of his story: "Quant à mes besoins, ils s'étaient en quelque sorte réduits à mes dimensions et, sous l'angle de la qualité, tellement raffinés que tout secours était exclu, à ce point de vue-là" (p. 118). Molloy frankly admits the pleasure of disintegration: "tout ce qu'on peut espérer c'est d'être un peu moins, à la fin, celui qu'on était au commencement, et par la suite" (*Molloy*, p. 47). Continuous dissolution is all one can count on in this life and the only thing worth hoping for. Thus, Malone declares with assurance: "Ma voix s'est éteinte, le reste suivra" (*Malone*, p. 183). Complete physical disability does not appear, however, until *L'Innommable*, where the physical side of the hero's evolution seems to reach its limit. Discussing the application of Beckett's caustic art to the human condition, Mayoux writes: "This experiment in diminution and mutilation culminates in Mahood in *The Unnamable*, a trunk with eyes streaming with tears, stuck in a jar."[16] Another critic suggests that this same image is one of a man being slowly sucked back into the earth: "The jar that has swallowed the torso up to the head is the archetypal image of the Great Mother taking life back into herself."[17] Applicable, too, to Winnie's situation in *Happy Days*, this analysis emphasizes the importance of the head's being the last to succumb and so witnessing the body's disintegration to the very end, "l'âme étant notoirement à l'abri des ablations et délabrements" (*L'Innommable*, p. 88). From the start of his tale, the Unnamable admits his utter helplessness: "Mais

[16]   Mayoux, "Samuel Beckett and Universal Parody", 85.
[17]   Wellershoff, "Failure of an Attempt at De-Mythologization", 102.

l'époque des bâtons est révolue, ici je ne peux compter strictement que sur mon corps, mon corps incapable du moindre mouvement et dont les yeux eux-mêmes ne peuvent plus se fermer" (p. 27). This apparent total paralysis answers to the letter Moran's dream of perfect immobility: "Etre vraiment enfin dans l'impossibilité de bouger, ça doit être quelque chose!... Et qui sait une paralysie de la rétine!... Et juste assez de cerveau resté intacte pour pouvoir jubiler!" (*Molloy*, p. 217). The narrator himself refers to his condition as a "délabrement physiologique" (*L'Innommable*, p. 61) and to his remaining capacities as "mes moyens déclinants" (p. 67). He, too, speaks of diminishing in size: "Je diminuais. Je diminue" (p. 89) and goes on to imagine shrinking so much as to no longer be able to lift his head above the rim of the jar. Yet, though he is "almost pure mind... or... pure cognitive process",[18] the Unnamable is not the last incarnation of Beckett's diminished man.

In the *Textes pour rien*, one narrator suggests a kind of worm-like body for himself: "quelques anneaux peut-être, contractiles, avec ça on va loin" (p. 151). Another speaks of his body as "ce monceau de chair, couenne, os et soies qui attend le départ" (p. 178); still another recalls his bodily existence as something in the past: "les tissus que j'étais" (p. 170). This same narrator describes himself as dust, suggesting that the ultimate dissolution has occurred: "Et bien me voilà, petite poussière dans un petit nid, qu'un souffle soulève, qu'un autre rabat, venus du dehors perdu" (p. 170). Yet absolute liberation seems impossible to the hero of "Texte VIII", who recognizes his fictional nature and dreams of existing as a man so that he might die: "l'espoir de me voir une histoire, d'être venu de quelque part et de pouvoir y retourner... celui de me voir vif, et non seulement dans une tête imaginaire, un galet promis au sable... comme si cela pouvait aider, de devenir moindre, toujours moindre, sans jamais disparaître" (p. 183). In real life one can only return to dust; absolute annihilation is unattainable. Indeed, final dissolution is always inconceivable, for consciousness cannot admit its own nonbeing. Even when envisioning oneself as dust, the eye of imaginary future perception must be focused on the sight, inevitably reassuring one of an illusory immortality. In *Comment c'est* the hero realizes fully the nature of his physical disintegration and states clearly the desire to be reduced to nothing. Here, "crawling naked like a worm in the mud",[19] man is revealed in all his helplessness and misery. Aware of his declining state, the narrator early compares his present condition with that of his youth, and finds the latter to be for the

---

18　Cohn, *The Comic Gamut*, 121.
19　Federman, *Journey to Chaos*, 205.

better, the former for the worse. Underscoring corporeal mutability he describes himself at present as a "suite ininterrompue d'altérations définitives" and even admits to having practiced self-deception in the past: "je me disais ça ne va pas plus mal je me trompai" (p. 12). He goes on to note mental and emotional paralysis: "détérioration du sens de l'humour moins de pleurs aussi... ça manque aussi" (p. 22). Surrounded by impenetrable darkness, he endures perpetual sightlessness and must depend on his other senses, especially that of touch ("poils tout blancs au toucher", p. 67; "la main qui plonge tâtonnante", p. 98). Already diminutive, he imagines himself to be even smaller in the future when he will have nothing but air and mud for nourishment: "je me vois tout petit tel à peu près que déjà mais encore plus petit tout petit plus d'objets plus de vivres et je vis l'air me nourrit la boue je vis toujours" (p. 21). Later he envisions himself carried away by the current of time: "petit tas à l'arrière [d'un bateau] moi tous ceux que je vois moi tous les âges le courant m'emporte le reflux attendu" (p. 105). Human existence seems to him as momentary and as ineffectual as a single breath: "ma vie comme un rien l'homme debout qu'un souffle" (p. 99). Finally, he describes his reduced condition in terms which recall Moran's dream of total immobility and Molloy's hope of being always less than before: "plus de tête en tout cas presque plus de coeur juste assez pour qu'on en soit content un peu content d'être si peu là de baisser un peu enfin étant au plus bas" (p. 126); "moins on est là plus on est gai" (p. 127). Here is the culmination of "la regression vers un être-là minime",[20] here the "shadow of a personality that Beckett wants to erase before he falls back into nothingness".[21] The question "to be or not to be" finds a straightforward answer: "it is better not to be."[22] But, as Wylie Sypher notes, even though all Beckett's heroes "exist with a minimal presence", the great difficulty is "to diminish even this minimal presence".[23] Thus, when the reduction of the body can go no further, the corrosive action of Beckett's art attacks the mind.

Balanced atop a tottering frame, the mind undergoes a disintegration of its own. Most often memory is the first faculty to falter. Molloy can scarcely remember his name (*Molloy*, pp. 31-32); Winnie, heroine of the play *Happy Days*, has forgotten "that unforgettable line"[24] she used to know. In fact, she does not even recall what the word "hog" means (p. 19). Yet

20 Morissette, "Les Idées de Robbe-Grillet sur Beckett", 63.
21 Sypher, *Loss of the Self in Modern Literature and Art*, 148.
22 *Ibid.*
23 *Ibid.*
24 *Happy Days*, 50; hereafter referred to in the text with the appropriate page number in parentheses.

such loss of memory can be considered a boon. Complete, though only temporary, annihilation of memory is achieved by Celia when, practicing Murphy's favorite exercise, she goes back through her past: "Then it was finished, the days and places and things and people were untwisted and scattered, she was lying down she had no history" (*Murphy*, p. 149). With the past erased from her thoughts she is free to explore the deeper regions of her mind. In "Texte VIII" the narrator attains permanent release from his past: "mon passé m'a mis dehors, ses grilles se sont ouvertes, ou c'est moi qui me suis évadé, peut-être en creusant" (*Textes*, p. 182). He cannot even remember how he gained his freedom. The imagination fades too, as the hero of *Comment c'est* admits: "je baisse baisse c'est trop dire plus de tête imagination à bout plus de souffle" (p. 125); "l'imagination qui décline étant au plus bas" (p. 126; cf. the very title of the piece "Imagination morte imaginez"). Commenting upon this mental debility, he confides: "c'est ça le plus triste" (p. 126). Deprived of memory, one cannot escape into the past to evade one's present condition; deprived of imagination, one cannot seek refuge in the future or in the fictional lives of one's creations (perhaps the most diverting kind of evasion). With the disappearance of memory and imagination, little remains in the mind except consciousness, consciousness of self in the present moment. A painful lucidity dominates the mental scene and casts its piercing light into every barren corner, leaving no loss unnoticed. As Claude Mauriac defines it in the case of the Unnamable, the remaining mental faculty consists in "cette douloureuse et vive conscience de sa condition".[25] Describing the heroes in their evolution, Nadeau writes that they are "de plus en plus privés de pouvoirs physiques, de plus en plus soustraits à l'agitation du monde, réfugiés en leur esprit et... réduits à une conscience pure";[26] as a result, "Demeurent la seule réalité des sensations cénesthésiques, la seule souffrance."[27] Similarly, noting the direction of the evolution, Hassan finds that "Beckett leaves only one thing intact: the capacity of human consciousness to reflect upon itself."[28] The hero is left with his minimal state of being and with the mirror of self-consciousness to constantly remind him of his stark situation.

His inner world shrinks, then, to encompass little more than what Beckett calls "the only world that has reality and significance, the world of our own latent consciousness" (*Proust*, p. 3). In his book on the loss of

---

[25] Mauriac, "Samuel Beckett", 92.
[26] Nadeau, "Le chemin de la parole au silence", 64.
[27] Nadeau, 65.
[28] Hassan, *The Literature of Silence*, 30.

the self in modern literature and art, Wylie Sypher cites this statement from *Proust* as the theme of Beckett's fiction and goes on to describe the mental remainder in the later writings: "the consciousness of the central figure is vestigial, a vague residue of man's anxieties".[29] Defining the novels as "studies in the extreme attrition of personality, an advanced stage of entropy in the self",[30] Sypher finds that for Beckett "man is no longer the sole hero, but only the center for what he sees";[31] and he continues: "our sense of identity has withdrawn deeply into what is only a point of attention from which we watch. It must be *our* attention. It must be our awareness, however dim, or our malaise."[32] This awareness is our consciousness of perceiving, our sense of identity, the last veil covering the ultimate core of being – pure perception. Even when all else has been eliminated, this consciousness of perception endures. As Sypher puts it, "we cannot, in spite of everything, annihilate selfhood"[33] and he speaks of the remaining element as "the persistent residue of selfhood", "a nondeductible selfhood", "irreducible selfhood".[34] Consciousness of being is experienced, then, only through awareness of perception; as Beckett notes in *Proust*, there is no "direct and purely experimental contract possible between subject and object, because they are automatically separated by the subject's consciousness of perception, and the object loses its purity and becomes a mere intellectual pretext or motive" (p. 56). Hence, the subject's own consciousness of being is necessarily removed from him by his awareness of perceiving that consciousness. Pure consciousness remains unattainable. Still, the Beckettian hero in evolution aims at winning near the goal, at being one with himself, at dwelling, as Arsene says, "in his midst at last, after so many tedious years spent clinging to the perimeter" (*Watt*, p. 41). But the process involved in this attempt to realize self-coincidence is long and arduous, as Ludovic Janvier points out: "Quant à l'entreprise, en allant de la péripétie au noyau, en se découvrant toujours une enveloppe à dépouiller, elle se donne comme une opération gigogne de l'être."[35]

Images from the novels confirm this analysis and illustrate how layer after layer of extraneous material is stripped from the mind. In *Murphy*, for instance, the hero's mind ridding itself of inessentials is compared to a

---

[29] Sypher, *Loss of the Self*, 147.
[30] *Ibid.*
[31] Sypher, 153.
[32] Sypher, 154-155.
[33] Sypher, 156.
[34] Sypher, 157, 158, and 163.
[35] Janvier, *Pour Samuel Beckett*, 285.

spool unwinding: "Scraps of bodies, of landscapes, hands, eyes, lines and colours evoking nothing, rose and climbed out of sight before him, as though reeled upward off a spool level with his throat" (p. 252). For Mallone, delivery from superfluous mental stuff resembles an emptying of the mind: "dans ma tête je suppose tout glissait et se vidait comme à travers des vannes, à ma grande joie, jusqu'à ce que finalement il ne restât plus rien, ni de Malone ni de l'autre" (*Malone*, p. 92). Speaking of a paradisiacal future, the narrator of "From an Abandoned Work" alludes to a similar sort of ideal mental void:

Then it will not be as now, day after day, out, on, round, back, in, like leaves turning, or torn out and thrown crumpled away, but a long unbroken time without before or after, light or dark, from or towards or at, the old half knowledge of when and where gone, and of what, but kinds of things still, all at once, all going, until nothing, there was never anything, never can be, life and death all nothing, that kind of thing, only a voice dreaming and droning on all around, that is something, the voice that once was in your mouth.   (p. 148)

Dispossessed of every faculty except that of speech, the hero-narrators often propose to purge their minds through speaking: "Parler, il n'y a que ça, parler, s'en vider, ici comme toujours, que ça" (*Textes*, pp. 139-140). Burdened with acute self-consciousness, they seek through verbal exhaustion of the mind the purity of final dissolution: "chaque jour un peu plus pur, un peu plus mort" (*Textes*, p. 184). Still others, finding that they are already completely hollow, can only suppose "qu'il y eût une fois quelque chose, dans une tête, dans un coeur, entre des mains, avant que tout se soit ouvert, vidé, refermé, figé" (*Textes*, p. 197). Determined to do away with every element that is not essential to their being, they "refuse to acquiesce in any kind of dupery, decline all consolation, strip themselves of all illusion".[36] Thus, avows one protagonist, "me dépenser tout est là".[37] The pleasure experienced in this way is described by Onimus as "Bonheur de dépouillement où l'on goûte enfin l'âcre satisfaction de n'être que ce que l'on est – à l'abri des hommes, de leur théâtre d'illusions comme de leurs chambres de torture."[38] The stripped hero, then, becomes "un pur existant", revealing the fundamental human condition and his own individual plight: "Plus on le dépossède, plus il s'approche de la transparence",[39] and even though pure transparence be forever out of

[36]   Mayoux, "Samuel Beckett and Universal Parody", 85.
[37]   "L'Image", 35; this is an excerpt from an early, unpublished version of the novel *Comment c'est*.
[38]   Onimus, *Beckett*, 55.
[39]   *Ibid.*

reach, no fictional creatures come so close as Beckett's to an unlimited exposure of "l'existence dans ses profondeurs".[40] Testifying to the ultimate ephemerality of body and mind, their shrinking world sets in bold relief man's nothingness and his inevitable doom.

Reduction to fundamental consciousness leads to more than a revelation of the human condition. Increasing self-consciousness in the Beckettian hero produces increasing transparency in the novels. Relieved of exterior and corporeal concerns, the protagonist probes within himself. Deprived of the mental faculties which could serve to divert him from his present situation, he is compelled to center his attention upon his own immediate activity; and, for the majority of Beckett's heroes, this means constant preoccupation with the creative act. Aware of himself as writer, the narrator-hero comments on his immediate creative efforts and criticizes weaknesses and gaps in his work. Recognizing himself as author of the stories he tells, he calls attention to his self-scrutiny, to the workings of the creative mind. Finally, he acknowledges that his own existence is fictional, that he has no life outside of the fiction in which he plays the central role. At this point in the evolution of the artist-hero, the creator's life becomes coincident with the created work, and the novel itself achieves almost flawless transparency. As noted earlier, fiction is nothing but a story a mind tells itself; hence, the novel cannot reveal its essential nature until it reflects precisely the existence and activity of its creator's mind. In the French fiction the first-person narrator is the hero-author of the story which he narrates. He initiates and perpetuates his own existence by creating characters, by commenting upon them and upon his artistic endeavor, and by meditating upon his immediate situation in general. The novel, serving him as notebook and journal, echoes his every thought and, thus, mirrors his self-consciousness. Its boundaries determined by his shrinking sphere of mental faculties, his fiction reflects the ever contracting circle of his consciousness (within which, in the end, is sealed awareness of the creative act alone),[41] while representing the only existence of which he is capable – a fictional existence spun out of language. Growing more and more nearly coincident with the life of the mind which created them, the novels become stories of their own creation, accounts of the creative act that produced them. The present moment of creation comes to dominate the scene, as the hero's ability to invent declines. Stripped of physical and

---

[40] Onimus, 71.
[41] For example, Malone describes his shrunken consciousness as "ma conscience périmée", *Malone meurt*, 26.

mental energy, he is an artist "whose art... is exercised continually on less and less",[42] and who is at last reduced to writing only of his own efforts to write. David Hayman notes of the hero's evolution in the novels: "as the series progresses towards *The Unnamable* the narrator's world tightens and shrinks. It is almost as if Beckett were examining layer by layer the mind of the artist and the sources of his inspiration."[43] Ultimately the author-heroes are divested of every inspirational source other than their immediate self-consciousness, their awareness of creating in the present moment; they "spin their world out of their own being",[44] for they have nothing else. In the novels, "the hero watches himself writing, remembering, groping for words, seeking to pin down the ineffable".[45] Comparing him to the Joycean artist "'invisible, refined out of existence, indifferent, paring his fingernails'", Ruby Cohn finds that Beckett's artist-hero, "spitting spluttering and swearing, is biting his nails down to the bones of a perhaps inexistent body".[46] Painfully aware of himself creating, this artist can speak of nothing else. Thus, by intruding "into his novel to comment on himself as writer, and on his book, not simply as a series of events... but as a created literary product",[47] he makes his work as nearly transparent as possible and qualifies himself formally for the designation "self-conscious narrator". The simultaneous and interdependent development of the novel and the artist-hero toward the ultimate in transparency and self-consciousness leaves its traces throughout the fiction.

In *Murphy*, the otherwise conventional omniscient narrator shuns Flaubertian impassivity in order to comment upon his style and characters. Coining a euphemism to refer to Murphy and Celia's relationship, he explains his doing so and at the same time calls attention to the fabricated and ultimately commercial nature of the entire work: "This phrase is chosen with care, lest the filthy censors should lack an occasion to commit their filthy synecdoche" (p. 76). A similar remark follows a description of two minor characters kissing: "The above passage is carefully calculated to deprave the cultivated reader" (p. 118). Again the narrator humorously underscores his own creative act and in this way lays bare the essential illusoriness of all fiction. In effect, he recognizes that he is

---

[42] Scott, *Samuel Beckett*, 68.
[43] Hayman, "Quest for Meaninglessness", 92.
[44] *Ibid.*
[45] Fletcher, *Samuel Beckett's Art*. 92.
[46] Cohn, "Still Novel", 53.
[47] Booth, "The Self-Conscious Narrator", 165. Calling attention to this article, Fletcher writes in "Beckett and the Fictional Tradition", 154: "Beckett's French heroes are usually self-conscious narrators according to Wayne C. Booth's definition."

putting together the present novel and that it is destined to be read by other men, who, if they are truly cultivated, will no doubt chuckle at this candid acknowledgment. All through the novel he makes asides concerning his characters, criticizing them for pretentiousness and bad taste (Miss Counihan, p. 119; Miss Carridge, p. 155) but especially for lack of courage to face the truth of their human condition. Exclaims the narrator as they all stand before Murphy's charred corpse: "How various are the ways of looking away!" (p. 264). Murphy alone escapes harsh criticism: "All the puppets in this book whinge [*sic*] sooner of later, except Murphy, who is not a puppet" (p. 122). Still, here again the critical aside calls attention to the nature of its context – it is a part of a book which the narrator is admittedly inventing. In concluding chapter six, an involved explanation of Murphy's mind, the narrator heaves a figurative sigh of relief that discloses his personal feelings while writing: "This painful duty having been discharged, no further bulletins will be issued" (p. 113). The business of composing a novel can involve difficulty and suffering for the writer, who in this case does not let his pain go unstated. The creative act itself becomes, if only momentarily here, substance for the created work. Near the end of the novel the narrator goes further still in uncovering the essential nature of his piece by actually referring to it as a story. Speaking of Murphy's attempt to arrest the unwinding of his mental spool by getting a familiar image in mind, the narrator seems to mock his own creative effort: "He tried with the men, women, children and animals that belong to even worse stories than this" (p. 251). Thus, the storyteller constantly attacks his fiction's capacity to create illusion by reminding the reader that the novel is a novel, and not reality.

Attention to the mechanics of writing is more detailed in *Watt*, and the narrator reveals his own story, a frame to Watt's, in the third part of the book. Commenting upon the lyrics to the threnody in Part I, he calls attention to individual words and thus underscores the basic element of both the poem and his own writing: "Bun is such a sad word, is it not? And man is not much better, is it?" (p. 35). Later he shows impatience with one of the conventional tools of his trade: "How hideous is the semi-colon" (p. 158). Early in the second part he discloses the source for his story by mentioning "the period of Watt's revelation", and at the same time takes on a fictional personality by adding "to me" (p. 79). Having already suggested the nature of his rapport with Watt by referring obliquely to himself as "his mouthpiece" (p. 69), the narrator goes on to elaborate upon the way in which a particular part of Watt's story (the Gall episode) was recorded, all the while insisting upon the difficulty of the project, his own inadequacy to see it through, and, hence, its inevitable inaccuracies and gaps. Watt's recollections were not clear enough or were too clear, his bodily condition was not the same as at the time of the incident, his communications were obscure, and the conditions under which he made them were far from ideal. Moreover, the narrator finds himself wanting in his role, as he notes "the scant aptitude to receive of him to whom they [Watt's communications] were proposed", and "the scant aptitude to give of him to whom they were committed" (p. 75). Generalizing from this detailed example to the entire task of writing Watt's story, he continues: "And some idea will perhaps be obtained [from the above example] of the difficulties experienced in formulating, not only such matters as those here in question, but the entire body of Watt's experience, from the moment of his entering Mr Knott's establishment to the moment of his leaving it" (p. 75). In the frame story, the narrator even names himself Sam (p. 153),[48] and describes at length his life in company with Watt at an asylum to which the latter must have retired after his adventure at Knott's. Here the difficulty involved in recording Watt's tale becomes clear, for Sam gives examples of Watt's peculiarly, though systematically, distorted speech (pp. 164-168). Varying his verbal pattern from one recital to the next, Watt poses a constant problem for Sam, who repeatedly admits that there are inevitable omissions in his records. Undermining the credibility of his version of Watt's experience, Sam gives no assurance of certainty in his own tale. After all, he himself is an inmate of the asylum, and at one moment in the frame story he cannot even distinguish himself from Watt (p. 159). Having alerted us to his incapacities and to the problems he encountered in writing Watt's story, Sam not only draws attention to his responsibility in the matter but also casts doubt on the possibility that any part of what he says could be true. The piece is a fiction, as minor asides persistently remind us; the whole, a result of a man's creative effort.

Allusions to the artificial quality of the narrative and to the problems of creating recur in *Mercier et Camier*, the last of Beckett's novels told by a narrator removed from the action.[49] Here the narrator comments upon the actions of the two heroes ("Ils continuent à l'appeler le parapluie, que c'est drôle", p. 126) and practices frequent self-criticism ("Que cela pue l'artifice", p. 10). Like Sam, he casts doubt on the accuracy of his

---

[48]   By giving the narrator his own name, Beckett may be reminding us that there is yet another creator behind the one who acknowledges the story as his handiwork. Under layers of telling remains one man's thought.
[49]   Fletcher, "Sur un roman inédit", 148.

tale ("Certaines choses, nous ne les saurons jamais avec certitude", p. 12) and goes still further near the end, insisting that he is uncertain about all that follows: "on ne sait plus rien avec certitude, dorénavant" (p. 181). Indeed, this outspoken storyteller even confides to us his strongest feelings about writing: "Enfin on sait à quoi on s'engage lorsqu'on fait de la littérature, à des déceptions qui feraient insérer au peintre ses pinceaux dans le cul. On ne peut compter sur rien ni personne, c'est simple."[50] Echoed frequently in later works, milder complaints are on the order of the following: "Que tout cela est lamentable" (p. 127). Such persistent dissatisfaction with the work in progress emphasizes not only the present moment in which the piece is being created but also the extremely painful labor involved in its creation. While undermining illusion, the self-conscious writer draws attention away from his characters and focuses it on his own struggle to create.

In the short stories, first-person narrators dominate the fictional scene and prepare the way for the later author-heroes. Like their predecessors, they practice self-doubt and self-criticism, and so constantly unveil the narrative mechanism and call into question the work itself. As Mrs. Cohn explains it, "In each of the four stories, an 'I' conscientiously recounts what he recalls, but all four are aware of the unpredictability of their memories. As the narrator Sam casts doubt on Watt's story, so these 'I's' doubt their own stories."[51] For example, one narrator-hero avows: "Tout cela ce sont des mensonges, je le sens" (*Nouvelles*, p. 85); another says: "Je me demande si tout cela n'est pas de l'invention, si en réalité les choses ne se passèrent pas tout autrement, selon un schéma qu'il m'a fallu oublier" (*Premier amour*, p. 22); still another asks himself: "Est-ce vraiment de moi, cette bassesse?" (*Nouvelles*, p. 52). Acknowledging that they alone are responsible for the tales, these storytellers comment upon their creative efforts with unprecedented candor. Writes one: "Cela tient debout, cocher, hôtel, c'est vraisemblable" (p. 35); and: "Je situe cette conversation sur le trottoir, devant la maison d'où je venais de sortir" (p. 35). Another exclaims: "Les choses qu'on se rappelle! Et qu'on rapporte!" (*Premier amour*, pp. 42-43). They underscore too the problems encountered in writing and the apparent purposelessness of their labors. "Je ne savais par où commencer ni par où finir, disons les choses comme elles sont", states one (*Nouvelles*, p. 11); and near the end of his story he observes: "Pas de raison pour que cela finisse ou continue. Alors que cela

---

[50] *Ibid.*: cited from a copy of the original typescript, this passage does not appear in the edition of the novel published in 1970 by Editions de Minuit.
[51] Cohn, *The Comic Gamut*, 102.

finisse" (p. 37). The hero of "Le Calmant", who announces his creative intention from the start: "Je vais donc me raconter une histoire, je vais donc essayer de me raconter encore une histoire, pour essayer de me calmer" (pp. 41-42), frequently interrupts his narrative to express his "uncertainties about the creative process".[52] Advising himself as to how to conclude, he says: "il faut cesser doucement, sans traîner mais doucement (p. 69). Soon after, he queries: "comment dire la suite?"; then reassures himself: "Mais c'est la fin" (pp. 70-71). Having almost reached the end, he settles for less than precise diction, confessing, after the selection of a conventional term, "trop fatigué pour chercher le mot juste" (p. 74). Most noteworthy of the details here, then, is the importance of the present creative moment in the story. In fact, there are two stories here: the first, one that the hero proposes to tell himself, and the second, one which frames the first and is interwoven with it. This second story, reflecting the creative act as it is carried out, must be conveyed in the present tense. Thus, the author-hero writes: "ce que je raconte ce soir se passe ce soir, à cette heure qui passe" (p. 43). Yet he openly accepts the conventional practice of relating fictions in the past tense: "Je mènerai néanmoins mon histoire au passé, comme s'il s'agissait d'un mythe ou d'une fable ancienne" (pp. 43-44), and later he observes himself using the future tense: "me voilà acculé à des futurs" (p. 47). More than the tale, the manner of telling preoccupies him. Reflections upon the creative act become more important than the thing created and eventually compose the greatest part of the creation. In "La Fin", the hero suggests the ultimate coincidence of fiction with the creator's existence by comparing his story to his life: "Je songeai faiblement et sans regret au récit que j'avais failli faire, récit à l'image de ma vie, je veux dire sans le courage de finir ni la force de continuer" (p. 122). On the point of dying, this narrator can think only of himself and his creation. His world reduced to the size of a coffin, his consciousness confined to self-consciousness, his concerns are limited and basic. For him, as for the heroes who will succeed him, to create is to live creating; to live, to mirror the creative effort in the created work.

The present moment of creative activity becomes more and more important in the trilogy, as self-consciousness and transparency increase from one work to the next. Writing of the three novels, Richard Macksey states:

---

[52] Friedman, "Molloy's 'Sacred' Stones", 8; Friedman compares these self-conscious remarks to those of Laurence Sterne's hero Tristram Shandy. Making a general comparison between Beckett's novels and Sterne's *Shandy*, Fletcher writes in *Samuel Beckett's Art*, 91-92: "in both cases, what goes into the book is what passes through the hero's mind at the very moment of composition".

"Beckett's trilogy can be seen as... the utter immurement in self-consciousness";[53] "the self at the center is immured like Daedalus in the work of
art".[54] Observing how the act of creation takes on major importance, he
finds that the trilogy dramatizes the extremity of the subject turned in
upon itself, the lamp in the mirror", and that Beckett here "collapses
the self in a maze of mirror images and verbal echoes".[55] Molloy, creator-
hero of the first book in the series, calls attention to his occupation of
writing from the start ("Il me donne un peu d'argent et enlève les feuilles",
Molloy, p. 7) and continues making comments on his work throughout
the first part of the novel. "Quelle langue", he writes at one point in his
narrative (p. 16), and at another: "Il faudrait récrire tout cela au plus-que-
parfait" (p. 122). Concerned especially with tenses, he has a predilection
for narrating in the present tense: "Je parle au présent, il est si facile de
parler au présent, quand il s'agit du passé. C'est le présent mythologique,
n'y faites pas attention" (p. 37). Naming his narrative tense the mythological present, he points out in effect that it is to be used in creating myths,
in writing fiction, for the creative activity cannot but take place in the
present moment of writing. Reflected in brief critical remarks such as "non,
ça ne va pas" (p. 8), the struggle of creating is expressed precisely in statements Molloy makes about his story. For instance, at the outset he presents
his original "beginning', introducing it with the admission: "Il [le com-
mencement] m'a donné beaucoup de mal" (p. 8). At the same time, however, he contrasts this recorded beginning with the end of his life which he
is actually approaching at the moment of writing: "C'était le commencement, vous comprenez. Tandis que c'est presque la fin, à présent" (p. 8).
His constant awareness of the reality of the present moment makes his
story of the past seem less real and less important. He even states his
intention to return to his present situation from time to time in order to
remind the reader that he is indeed still in existence: "Ainsi de temps en
temps je rappellerai mon existence actuelle dont celle que je conte ne peut
donner qu'une faible idée. Mais de loin en loin seulement, afin qu'on
puisse se dire, le cas échéant, Se peut-il vraiment que ça vive encore? Ou
encore, Mais c'est un journal intime, ça va bientôt s'arrêter" (p. 93). Still,
for all his perspicacity and ability to anticipate his reader's thoughts,
Molloy purports to tell a true story of the journey to his mother's room
(where at the present moment he is writing): "J'invente peut-être un peu,
j'embellis peut-être", he admits, "mais dans l'ensemble c'était ainsi" (p. 9).

---

[53] Macksey, "The Artist in the Labyrinth: Design or *Dasein*", 252.
[54] Macksey, 248.
[55] *Ibid.*

Moran, writer-hero of the second part of *Molloy*, also presents his narrative as nonfiction. In fact, in writing of his search for Molloy, he fulfills one of the obligations of his profession. Doubt creeps into his report, however, undermining its supposed veracity through general uncertainty, through lies confessed ("J'ai menti en disant que j'avais des dindes, etc.", p. 197), and through avowed weakness of memory ("si je ne confondais pas avec un autre endroit", p. 208). Once again the present moment of writing forms the frame and point of orientation for the narrative; and, since the actual condition of the man writing determines, ultimately, the credibility of his report, the entire work may be called into question by a single comment such as the following: "Mais ce soir, ce matin, j'ai bu un peu plus que d'habitude et je peux être d'un autre avis demain" (p. 204). Thoroughly self-conscious yet detached enough to use imagery, Moran describes the physical act of writing as he observes his hand move across the page: "Une main ferme, inexorable navette qui mange ma page avec l'indifférence d'un fléau" (p. 205). Later on in his account he cannot remember the details of a murder he committed. Aware of the consequent gap this makes in his story, he regards the slip as fortuitous since it prevents him, he thinks, from lapsing into conventional fiction: "Je regrette de ne pas pouvoir indiquer plus clairement de quelle manière ce résultat fut obtenu. Ça aurait fait un beau morceau. Mais ce n'est pas arrivé à ce point de mon récit que je vais me lancer dans la littérature" (p. 235). Thus, though he is not a writer by profession, Moran working away at his report becomes a writer and, inevitably, a self-conscious one. He even touches upon a crucial problem of creation, which will not be thoroughly explored until *Comment c'est* – the problem of registering consciousness of creating while creating. For example, he comments after a lengthy part of his narrative: "Me rapportant maintenant *en imagination* à l'instant présent, j'affirme avoir écrit tout ce passage d'une main ferme et même satisfaite, et l'esprit plus tranquille que depuis longtemps" (p. 239, my emphasis). Unable to recall precisely how he felt while writing the preceding pages, he can only imagine how it was. He could not both write the passage and record at the same time his feelings about writing it. Consciousness of creating cannot be expressed simultaneously with the creation. Even were the creative act itself to become the sole substance of the novel, one's consciousness of writing self-consciously could not be exposed in the same moment with the writing.

Like the hero of "Le Calmant", Malone, creator-hero of *Malone meurt*, declares from the start his intention to tell himself stories. Indeed, his plan is to amuse himself with narratives until he has finished dying: "On va pouvoir m'enterrer, on ne me verra plus à la surface. D'ici là je vais me raconter des histoires, si je peux" (p. 9). Moreover, like the narrator of "La Fin", Malone expects his works to mirror his condition: "Ce seront des histoires ni belles ni vilaines, calmes, il n'y aura plus en elles ni laideur ni beauté ni fièvre, elles seront presque sans vie, comme l'artiste" (p. 9). Perfectly straightforward about his literary project, Malone outlines a program for himself: he will relate first his present situation, then three stories, and finally an inventory of his possessions (p. 13). He does not propose to indulge in fiction alone; he realizes that he must speak of himself, too. Further, unlike Moran and Molloy, he frankly admits to being a storyteller, and his lucidity appears everywhere in the novel. As Macksey puts it, "Senses fail him, but not his self-consciousness.. Alone, in the dark of his own self-consciousness, he enters (with the help of his other extension, the stub pencil) on the artist's journey." [56] A "sophisticated and self-conscious creator of his own fictions",[57] he mixes "criticism with creation, as the artist must",[58] punctuating his narrative with remarks such as "Quel ennui" (p. 22) and "Quelle misère" (p. 29). Laying bare the fictional bones of his story, he congratulates himself on his success: "Que tout cela est vraisemblable" (p. 46). A writer who studies his language, Malone is wary of its hollowness, of the existence it has apart from things: "Je connais ces petites phrases qui n'ont l'air de rien et qui, une fois admises, peuvent vous empester toute une langue. *Rien n'est plus réel que rien.* Elles sortent de l'abîme et n'ont de cesse qu'elles n'y entraînent. Mais cette fois je saurai m'en défendre" (p. 32). Aware that he succumbs to imprecision in his writing, Malone remarks at one point with regard to the two pots he uses: "Ils ne sont pas à moi, mais je dis mes vases, comme je dis mon lit, ma fenêtre, comme je dis moi" (p. 148). Language itself is but an imperfect tool, whose conventional use makes inaccuracies inevitable. In fact, it is so unreliable that Malone interrupts meditation on his present state to query: "Mais je me dis tant de choses, qu'y a-t-il de vrai dans ce babil?" (p. 115). Composed basically of nothing but words, his narrative may hold no truth at all. A fabric of language woven by a dying man, it inspires small credibility. The whole appears, then, as a story a fading mind tells itself.

Intensely self-conscious in the act of writing, Malone, like Moran, speaks of his hand moving across the page: "Mon petit doigt, couché sur la feuille, devance mon crayon, l'avertit en tombant des fins de ligne"

---

[56] Macksey, 250.
[57] Cohn, *The Comic Gamut*, 132.
[58] Tindall, *Samuel Beckett*, 28.

(p. 60), and even notes the sound of his efforts: "j'entends le bruit de mon petit doigt qui glisse sur le papier et celui si différent du crayon qui le suit' (pp. 61-62). Similarly, throughout his story, Malone calls attention to the creative act he performs, interrupting the course of his narrative to express his personal, immediate feelings as creator. Janvier writes of this practice: "L'histoire se supprime quand le narrateur ressent la peine d'inventer." [59] Expressions of weakness ("Non, je ne peux pas", p. 171), encouragement ("Encore un petit effort", p. 175), and self-mockery ("C'est ça bavarde", p. 179) alternate with fictional material. At one point Malone even acknowledges that he is interrupting his story: "Je m'interromps pour noter que je me sens dans une forme extraordinaire. C'est peut-être le délire" (p. 157). Such asides not only remind us of the essentially illusory nature of the novel itself but also focus attention on the hero's continuing dissolution. Inevitably the narrative must end with Malone's death, and, indeed, as noted earlier (see above, p. 67), the novel's conclusion mirrors precisely the passing of its narrator-hero. To preserve lucidity until the very end poses a problem, however, especially since self-consciousness cannot be expressed simultaneously with creation. Undaunted, Malone outlines a plan for himself to meet this challenge: "Voici en tout cas le programme, la fin de programme.... Visite, diverses remarques, suite Macmann, rappels de l'agonie, suite Macmann, puis *mélange* Macmann et agonie aussi longtemps que possible" (p. 180, my emphasis). Alternate attention to his story and to his death will not do in the end; somehow he must mix the two. The result is the chiselled final passage where the position of the words on the page and the choice of concluding words convey at the same time the end of Malone's story and his own end (p. 217). Having existed interdependently, the novel and its author-hero subside as one. Thus, *Malone meurt* is a highly coincident novel, revealing the very fiber of its fabric through its self-conscious creator. As Hassan explains it, "In *Malone Dies*, then, Beckett is not using two narratives, each reflecting the other; he is forcing the same narrative to reflect itself in the course of its own progress"; [60] and he continues: "the interludes of self-examination [become] gradually indistinguishable from the episodes of narrative invention; reality and illusion [are] blurred in a state of consciousness that also [subsumes] death and life". [61] According to Kenner, here "the writing of the word now being written becomes its own subject", "the man in bed [writes] about himself in bed writing, and [proposes] to

---

[59]   Janvier, *Pour Samuel Beckett*, 67.
[60]   Hassan, *The Literature of Silence*, 160-161.
[61]   Hassan, 162.

track himself to his own death, so that his last word may be about his last word – better, may *be* his last word".[62] There is even a hint that Malone realizes the fictional nature of his existence. Unable to do without his pencil and notebook, he seems to know "that the pages of his exercise book are his life, and the movements of his ever shortening pencil his wander-ings":[63] "De ma main lointaine je compte les pages qui me restent. Ça ira. C'est ma vie, ce cahier, ce gros cahier d'enfant, j'ai mis du temps à m'y résigner" (p. 191). He lives, avowedly, only in his creation.

Even more close-knit than *Malone meurt*, *L'Innommable* presents the stark and shrunken world of a tightly sealed consciousness. Here "the narrative and its substance grow absolutely identical"[64] as the artist-hero's mind churns away before our eyes. Portions of invented episodes alter-nate so rapidly with reflections on the present moment that the two elements fuse.[65] The importance of creating dominates the hero's con-sciousness from the outset, for he realizes that he must speak even though he has nothing to say: "Je suis obligé de parler" (pp. 8-9); "J'ai à parler, n'ayant rien à dire" (p. 55). Like his predecessors, he is concerned with tenses ("J'aurai besoin aussi, je le note en passant, de participes futurs et conditionnels", p. 27) and does not hesitate to criticize himself ("Ces comparaisons sont déplacées", p. 35). The crucial matter of actually producing the necessary work haunts him more relentlessly than the others, however, since he fully understands that his existence depends upon his work: "J'espère que ce préambule s'achèvera bientôt, au profit de l'exposé qui décidera de moi" (p. 30). His fate, it seems, hangs on the degree of success he can achieve in his narrative. Innumerable interruptions riddle his work, though, underscoring the artificiality of the novel and the pain-ful labor of creation. Early in the narrative he acknowledges his role as creator (and destroyer): "Je vais avoir de la compagnie. Pour commencer. Quelques pantins. Je les supprimerai par la suite" (p. 9). Some pages later he implies that his creative function is godlike: "Il serait sans doute temps que je donne un compagnon à Malone" (p. 18). But he frequently denies his own credibility ("il ne faut pas croire ce que je dis", p. 226) and reveals anxiety about his task through advice to himself ("Mais doucement, doucement, sinon je n'arriverai jamais", p. 36). Desperate in his attempt to keep the narrative moving and to find something more to say, he clings to every idea that passes through his mind. Thus, after musing upon the

[62]   Kenner, *A Critical Study*, 79; Kenner's emphasis.
[63]   Wellershoff, "Failure of an Attempt at De-Mythologization", 99.
[64]   Kenner, *A Critical Study*, 80.
[65]   Hassan, *The Literature of Silence*, 162.

form and posture of his stripped body, he remarks: "De cette preoccupation si légitime en apparence, quelle tranche de discours à tirer" (p. 38).
Yet even such meditations as this are termed *histoires* by the hero (p. 37).
Later, focusing attention on the bare mechanism of his narrative, he casts
off the first-person point of view with abuse: "assez de cette putain de
première personne" (p. 114). Paradoxically, even as he sheds the first-
person mask and the responsibility which it imposes, he reaffirms his
exclusive control of the story. Indeed, he repeatedly identifies himself as
the author of the piece: "C'est moi qui écris, moi que ne puis lever la
main de mon genou" (p. 28); "C'est donc moi qui parle, tout seul, ne
pouvant faire autrement" (p. 41). Going even further to expose the pain
of his task, he draws attention to the self who exists behind the tissue of
words: "C'est moi qui hurle, loin derrière ma dissertation" (p. 55). Even
though the writing and the writer's feelings require separate moments to
be recorded, the writer must speak of nothing but the difficulty of his
creative activity: "Je n'ai pas de voix et je dois parler, c'est tout ce que je
sais, c'est autour de cela qu'il faut parler" (p. 40). The self-consciousness
of the creator, then, becomes the transparent substance of the creation.
As Mlle Deyle describes the process, "L'artiste... photographie sa propre
conscience dans l'oeuvre d'art."[66] Moreover, the Unnamable insists that
one must always scrutinize one's tale while telling it ("ils feraient mieux
de penser à ce qu'ils sont en train de raconter", p. 178) and reprimands
himself for failure to do so ("j'aurais mieux fait de faire attention à ce que
je disais", p. 226). This kind of novelist, according to Kenner, "becomes
absorbed with consciousness" and "lives in the act of writing ... as consciousness in the act of thinking. If he proposes to stop writing of
himself, thinking of himself, himself entertaining such a proposition
becomes in turn a theme for writing or an object of thought."[67] Being
"one conscious that he is conscious",[68] the Unnamable exhausts himself in attempts to express his dual perception, to probe the essence of
consciousness, for "plus l'oeuvre avance, plus la fureur de la conscience
de se découvrir au bout d'elle-même creuse cet espace vers soi et fait ten-
ter le pari de la réduction".[69] As Macksey writes of him, "Beckett's
metaphoric hero reaches a state of absolute poverty and utter self-consciousness";[70] and later he says, "Beckett immures the narrator and reader

[66] Deyle, *Samuel Beckett*, 74.
[67] Kenner, *A Critical Study*, 34-35.
[68] Kenner, 35.
[69] Janvier, *Pour Samuel Beckett*, 285.
[70] Macksey, "The Artist in the Labyrinth", 251.

in the endlessly reflexive consciousness of a storyteller." [71] Finally, he observes how the hero's existence coincides with his story: "The last vestiges of marginal life are sucked from Beckett's l'Innommable so that he may exist purely as a shattered telling." [72] It would seem that more nearly perfect coincidence in the novel would be impossible, that no more intense self-consciousness in the narrator could be expressed. Yet the last words of the Unnamable announce future attempts to penetrate even more deeply into the essential nature of conscious creation: "il faut continuer, je vais continuer" (p. 262).

Taking up his story from this point, the narrator of "Texte I" avows in his very first sentence: "je n'en pus plus, je ne pus continuer", and soon reveals his dilemma: "Je ne pouvais pas rester là et je ne pouvais pas continuer" (Textes, p. 127). Nevertheless, impelled to babble on self-consciously, this hero and his twelve successors speak of themselves creating. For example, like Moran and Malone, the writer of "Texte V" states: "je tiens la plume" (p. 159), and describes how he observes his hand as he writes: "Du coin de l'oeil je surveille la main qui écrit" (p. 161); "je vois la main, elle sort lentement de l'ombre, celle de la tête, puis d'un bond y retourne, ça ne me regarde pas" (p. 163). But, aware that the scene he beholds cannot be real ("C'est une image, dans ma tête qui est sans force, où tout dort, tout est mort", p. 159), the narrator severs any link the reader might try to construct between the tale and its teller's actual existence. All is fiction, and the creator dwelling behind the work assures us that what he relates consists of mental images and nothing more. The essence of his story, then, can be considered only as figments of a mind that cannot know pure perception, that can only express blurred conceptions of its inner vision. Most unsettling of all, the narrator becomes inextricably entwined with his creatures, producing a haunting echo effect in "Texte III": "Qu'importe qui parle, quelqu'un a dit qu'importe qui parle" (p. 143), and at the very beginning of "Texte IV": "Où irais-je, si je pouvais aller, que serais-je, si je pouvais être, que dirais-je, si j'avais une voix, qui parle ainsi, se disant moi?" (p. 153).

The obsession with the present moment of creative activity reappears in the recently collected short fiction. In "From an Abandoned Work", for example, the hero reveals that it is his habit to tell stories of one day after another, as he requests: "But let me start as always with the morning and the getting out" (p. 146). In "Assez" the author-hero devotes the entire first paragraph to a description of how he goes about producing the story

---

[71]   Macksey, 254 (misspelling in the text: refiexive for reflexive).
[72]   Macksey, 255.

and concludes his preface with the acknowledgment: "Voilà pour l'art et la manière" (*Têtes*, p. 33). But, as the evolution continues, the heroes question more and more intensely the reason for their creative efforts. As one narrator asks repeatedly, "But why go on with all this, I don't know, some day I must end, why not now" ("From", p. 143); "But what is the sense of going on with all this, there is none" ("From", p. 147).

A similar remark ("mais question à quoi bon", p. 146) characterizes the tone of the last novel *Comment c'est*. Here every word echoes the laboriousness involved in its expression, as the narrator-hero pants ("quand ça cesse de haleter", p. 9 and passim) through his story. Sealed within the darkness of his mind, he uses a limited vocabulary, often repeating himself. For instance, one general self-criticism recurs frequently, reinforcing the impression of continuous creative effort: "quelque chose là qui ne va pas" (p. 11 and passim). Like his predecessors, he is concerned with language, especially tenses, but rather than explain his notions about verbs he simply mentions them in passing as part of the fabric of his story: "un peu moins du temps être et ne pas être passé présent futur et conditionnel allons allons suite et fin" (p. 46). The unpunctuated telegraphic style used here reflects the haste and urgency with which the creative act is carried out. Calling attention to this method which he uses exclusively, the author-hero describes it in the second part of the novel where he has the opportunity to scratch words on the back of his victim Pim: "d'une traite pas un alinéa pas une virgule pas une seconde laissée à la réflexion avec l'ongle de l'index jusqu'à ce qu'il tombe et le dos fatigué saignant par endroits" (p. 87). The meaning of the words here describes the way they look on the page, making this passage almost perfectly transparent. More impressive, however, is the attempt, prolonged throughout the novel, to reveal the unrecounted fourth part of the story. Hinted at from the start by abrupt repetitions of the same phrase in a different tense (usually a change from present to past such as "comme j'en vois... comme j'en voyais", p. 14, and "je vis encore vivais encore", p. 43), this additional section obviously resembles the fully expounded second part in which the hero extorts utterances from Pim through systematic torture. The narrator, mute during the three parts of his tale that we read, will have a voice in the fourth part when "un autre viendra mieux que Pim... et sur toi soudain une main comme sur Pim la tienne deux cris le sien muet" (p. 28); "tu auras une petite voix elle sera juste audible tu lui parleras à l'oreille ce sera autre chose tout à fait une autre musique tu verras un peu comme Pim une petite musique de vie mais dans ta bouche à toi elle te sera nouvelle" (pp. 28-29). Having compelled Pim to relate the story of his life, the hero foresees a time when someone else will require the same kind of performance from him. Referring again to this Future scene, he describes it in fragments: "arrive... celui qui pour moi pour qui moi ce qui moi pour Pim Pim pour moi", "l'usage de la parole ...un nommé Pim une vie que j'aurais eue avant lui avec lui après lui une vie que j'aurais" (p. 75). Later he calls this fourth segment "la vie avec Bom", whom he envisions "à ma gauche le bras droit autour de moi... l'oreille contre ma bouche" (p. 117), and who he believes will constrain him to recount "ma vie là-haut" (p. 117) and "comment c'était ma vie avant lui" (p. 121). That he will have to perform as he made Pim do is clear later: "les deux couples... composent le même spectacle exactement" (p. 158); and, even though the narrator would like to avoid the encounter with Bom ("si Bom ne venait pas si seulement ça", p. 98), he announces quite definitively that the meeting will take place: "il suffit que cet épisode soit annoncé Bom vient" (p. 159). What, then, is this mysterious fourth part if not the creative activity which is producing the three-part novel in progress? Unable to tell of how he is saying what he says while he says it, the narrator can only suggest that an important part of his story remains untold. In fact, the portion he speaks of encompasses the other three parts, for it is their telling. Near the end of the novel, the hero explains that his story is incomplete and tries to explain why it must be so: "à vouloir présenter en trois parties ou épisodes une affaire qui à bien y regarder en comporte quatre on risque d'être incomplet", "mais nous ne verrons jamais Bom à l'oeuvre haletant dans le noir la boue je resterai en souffrance la voix étant ainsi faite... que de notre vie totale elle ne dit que les trois quarts" (p. 157). Incapable of remarking upon itself speaking as it speaks, the voice cannot express the intense self-consciousness which the hero obviously experiences here. Confined by his faculties and by language, he can speak of his consciousness of present creative activity only as another in a series of temporal events. To express the true simultaneity of his experience is impossible. Thus, what he describes in the future tense ("l'avenir le dira il est en train", p. 85) as his interaction with Bom is actually taking place as he speaks of it and as he tells the story of his life.

Indeed, from the outset it is clear that the novel and his existence coincide: "raconte-moi encore finis de me raconter" (p. 9); "ma vie dernier état mal dite mal entendue mal retrouvée mal murmurée... pertes partout" (p. 9); "c'est le début de ma vie présente rédaction" (p. 11). There is even a suggestion in this last remark that the hero has presented other drafts of his life and that this is just another in the series. (Here again it seems that the novels form one long work whose author undergoes metamor-

phoses and consequent changes in point of view from one book to the
next.) Aware that his life coincides with his murmurings, the narrator calls
attention to the imperfections in it: "je la dis comme elle vient dans l'ordre
mes lèvres remuent je les sens elle sort dans la boue ma vie ce qu'il en reste
mal dite mal entendue mal retrouvée... mal murmurée à la boue au
présent tout ça des choses si anciennes l'ordre naturel le voyage le couple
l'abandon tout ça au présent des bribes" (p. 24). Later he makes repeated
allusions to his life and to his story in the same terms and in almost the
same breath: "ce vieux conte... en moi des bribes" (p. 130), "une autre
histoire... la même histoire" (p. 132), "ces bribes de vie en moi" (p. 137),
"une vieille histoire ma vieille vie" (p. 160), "ma vie entière balbutiement
six fois écorché" (p. 162), "on parle toujours de ma vie" (p. 156), "une
seule vie toute la vie" (p. 162), "des murmures sans nombre tous pareils"
(p. 162), "un antique cafouillis" (p. 162). In the end, one cannot be distinguished from the other, the living is the telling; the only way the hero can
live his life is to relate it: "la voix la raconte seul moyen de la vivre" (p.
156). Since, then, all in the novel is fiction, the narrator himself can have
no real existence and must apply the same term to himself as to his story:
"orgie de faux être" (p. 85). Here the work and the process of its creation
become as nearly one as can be imagined. Transparency and self-consciousness, simultaneously achieved, reveal the essential nature of the novel
and the inevitable difficulties of conscientiously making the self-conscious
creative act. As Michel Gresset says, "il faut conclure avec Maurice
Blanchot que l'oeuvre de Beckett représente 'l'approche pure du mouvement d'où viennent les livres.' Ce mouvement, justement, dont nul écrivain ne rend compte totalement s'il ne restitue le jeu complet des forces en
présence, en remuant le fer dans la plaie, en puisant l'écriture 'aux racines
même de l'être' (Cézanne)."[73] The enormous place Beckett gives to exploration of the creative experience justifies, too, Mrs. Cohn's statement
that "no other modern writer... has integrated the act of creation so consistently and ironically into his own creation".[74] It is only fitting, then,
that the second part of this study be devoted to an analysis of Beckett's
portrait of the artist.

---

[73]   Gresset, "Création et cruauté", 64.
[74]   Cohn, *The Comic Gamut*, 296.

PART TWO:

THE SELF-CONSCIOUS ARTIST

5. THE ARTIST'S DILEMMA

The intense self-consciousness of Beckett's writings reveals itself most clearly in the ever present figure of the artist creating. As demonstrated in Part I, the works become increasingly transparent and more nearly coincident as they contract to reflect only the thoughts of their narrator-heroes. Insisting upon rigorous lucidity in his art, Beckett centers attention on the creative experience, producing a series of portraits of the artist in which each successive subject is still more incapacitated than the last. Finally there remains only a consciousness which can perceive nothing but its own self-perception. Under such conditions of severely limited (though intensely concentrated) awareness, one can think and speak only of one's own self-conscious state (as shown in Chapter 4). The inevitable result for the artist is endless self-reflection – a Chinese puzzle of self-portraits. The obsession with the immediate creative act is both the effect of relentless self-awareness and evidence of it. Yet, the recurring portrait is even more important because it reveals the nature of the creative experience itself. From one work to the next, Beckett chisels away at his description of the artist at work in ever renewed attempts to capture the essence of the creative act. Close examination of these portraits and their contractive development yields abundant detail for a comprehensive interpretation of the artistic process as Beckett presents it.

Extreme mental and physical distress characterizes the creative act throughout all the works. As Ruby Cohn observes, "Beckett's haunted 'I''s are in constant anguish", are images of "the strife-torn writer".[1] Always they "[struggle] helplessly with the process of putting words together".[2] Testifying incessantly to "la peine d'inventer",[3] the Beckettian narrator-hero concentrates ever more intently upon the anguish he undergoes while creating. Indeed, one must agree with Federman when he says:

[1]   Cohn, *The Comic Gamut*, 165.
[2]   Federman, *Film*, 48.
[3]   Janvier, *Pour Samuel Beckett*, 67.

"This agony of artistic expression is the theme Beckett has reiterated throughout his work."[4] From the earliest novels on, the suffering involved in performing the creative act is manifest. Ticklepenny, "a distinguished indigent drunken Irish bard"(*Murphy*, p. 88), appears among the first artist-figures in the novels. To restore his health, this poet, who used to compose at the rate of one "pentameter per pint" (p. 86), arranges to undergo treatment for his dipsomania while working as a male nurse. at the asylum where Murphy eventually replaces him. His rapid recovery, however, suggests to his doctor that there has been "a misdiagnosis" (p. 88) and that "the curative factor at work in this interesting case was to be sought neither in the dipsopathy nor in the bottlewashing, but in the freedom from poetic composition that these confined on his client, whose breakdown had been due less to the pints than to the pentameters" (p. 88). In explaining the extremely adverse effect of creative activity on the creator here, the narrator pokes fun at traditional Irish verse, which he refers to as "the gaelic prosodoturfy" (p. 89), and concludes: "No wonder he felt a new man washing the bottles and emptying the slops of the better-class mentally deranged" (p. 89). *Any* occupation, he insists, is preferable to that of artistic creation which undermines the health of even the least of its practitioners.

For the artist who cannot give up his work, the discomfort and distress are still more acute. An allusion to Balzac in the same novel illustrates the extent of a great author's suffering. Describing the furnishings in Murphy and Celia's Brewery Road room, the narrator mentions that "two massive upright unupholstered armchairs, similar to those killed under him by Balzac, made it just possible for them to take their meals seated" (p. 63). He stresses the extreme hardness of the chairs by noting how Celia and Murphy could scarcely bear to sit in them for the duration of a meal. Yet Balzac wore out numerous chairs of this same formidable kind while producing his monumental *oeuvre*. In his case, the enormous anguish of creation was outweighed by perseverance. The author's determination to persist in his creative endeavor was greater than the torment involved in its pursuit. Possessed by the need to write, the novelist would yield to no other obligation and thus wore out the chairs and himself in his efforts to create. All the difficulty of the creative act is embodied in the image of the straight-backed, cushionless chairs; all the feverish persistence of the artist, in the harsh treatment they receive from him.

The image *par excellence* of the creator's anguish appears in the Adden-

---

[4] Federman, *Film*, 48.

da to *Watt*. Already noted in Chapter 3 (as one of the imaginary works of art which come to replace traditional allusions), it is the second picture in Erskine's room – the portrait of a composer in the grasp of the creative compulsion. Naked and dirty, this creator seems to have already spent a great deal of time at his work. Details of his appearance reveal the enormous effort he must make to compose and the tremendous strain under which he labors. To improve his hearing "he prolongs pavilion of left ear" (p. 250); all his muscles are "standing out like cords in stress of effort" (p. 250), and "beads of sweat... were plentifully distributed over pectoral, subaxillary and hypogastrial surfaces" (p. 250). "His right foot, assisted from above by its fellow, depresses with force the sustaining pedal" (p. 250), while "nasal slaver and buccal froth" (p. 251) discolor his moustache. The total effect is described as follows: "The bust was bowed over the keyboard and the face, turned slightly towards the spectator, wore expression of man about to be delivered, after many days, of particularly hard stool, that is to say the brow was furrowed, the eyes tight closed, the nostrils dilated, the lips parted and the jaw fallen, as pretty a synthesis as one could wish of anguish, concentration, strain, transport and self-abandon" (p. 251). Yet for all his pain this artist produces nothing more than a simple C-major chord. Unlike the reference to Balzac, this image of man creating stresses the agony of the process without hinting in the least that there is any compensation for it. The artistic product is negligible. All that can be said for the gratification of the artist is that he achieves a catharsis, temporary relief from the obligation to create. For the moment he is free, having attained a "dying accord" (p. 251) with which to conclude one particular composition.

This brutally frank image of artistic creation as a kind of painful physical catharsis appears frequently throughout the fiction, though in a somewhat different form. Based on the idea suggested above that one is 'delivered' of one's creation, the comprehensive Beckettian image for the creative act is contained in the phrase "une naissance difficile" (pronounced by Vladimir in *Godot*, p. 156). As Federman observes, "throughout Beckett's fiction... images of physical birth are equated with the act of creating fiction".[5] Even as early as *More Pricks Than Kicks* there is reference to a fictitious piece of literature being "held up in the limae labor [i.e., polishing, revision] stage for the past ten or fifteen years" (p. 79). Later images are more graphic and seem to be prepared by the passage in *Watt* where Tetty Nixon describes her own first labor and delivery. Asked how "it

---

5 Federman, *Journey to Chaos*, 200.

feels to have the string cut" (p. 14), she replies: "For the mother... the feeling is one of relief, of great relief, as when the guests depart" (p. 15). Of subsequent births she remarks: "The feeling was always the same, one of riddance" (p. 15). Expressing this same kind of attitude toward his creature Macmann, Malone writes: "Mais pour Macmann, ouf, le revoilà" (*Malohe*, p. 106). That he gives birth to his persona is further suggested by the fact that his creative tool is a Venus pencil (p. 89). A more extensive use of the childbirth image for artistic creation appears in *L'Innommable* where the narrator-hero says: "je n'en serai pas délivré, je parle de Worm" (p. 106). Worm, the second of the hero's personae, has no existence in the world. Rather he is described as inhabiting a dark, moist place where "il est comme enraciné... c'est comme de la sargasse, non... de la mélasse, non plus, n'importe, il faudrait une convulsion, qui le vomisse au jour" (p. 158). The incomplete persona lodged in the mind of the author resembles a foetus who can be expelled from his interior refuge only through enormous effort. The creatures themselves express some knowledge of their traumatic creation. One's story may begin with a "brutal expulsion from the security of a bourgeois home".[6] But the experience is often described specifically "as a painful birth – the ejection from the womb, or rather the symbolic extraction from the mind of the creator".[7] Recalling that he was driven from his home, the narrator-hero of *Premier amour* imagines how the other inhabitants of the house must have felt upon his departure: "un grand ouf, et puis rappel des mots d'ordre" (p. 16). In the *Textes* the memory of expulsion fades: "et d'où sorti, avec quelle peine, non, j'aurais oublié, tout oublié" (p. 192). But for the creator the longing to be delivered of one's creation never wanes. On the contrary, it becomes the principal anxiety of all the later author-heroes, though they know that the realization of one delivery will only serve to create the need for another. For example, the narrator-hero of "From an Abandoned Work" urges himself to maintain his creative effort with the words: "So on to this second day and get it over and out of the way and on to the next" (p. 145).[8] The artist, then, does not choose to create but rather finds himself forever bound to do so; no sooner does he complete one work than another must be gotten underway. In her study of *Comment c'est*, Ruby Cohn shows how the expression "j'ai fait l'image" (in a fragment of the work

---

[6] Federman, *Journey to Chaos*, 184.
[7] *Ibid.*
[8] In the French translation, the idea of deliverance from the burden of creation is evident: "vite donc cette deuxième journée et en finir et m'en délivrer et à la suivante", *Têtes-mortes*, 23.

published before the completed novel)[9] was changed to "j'ai eu l'image"
in the final version (p. 38).[10] To explain the importance of this observation,
Mrs. Cohn writes: "Changing the verb from *make* to *have* shifts the connotation from creation to parturition, and places the narrator at a further
remove from God, who made man in His own image."[11] The creative act
is involuntary; one does not elect to suffer its pangs, but for the artist there
is no choice. He must create; and though the process is excruciatingly
painful, he will create compulsively. Like the muttering old man in "Assez" who "lâchait ses murmures" without reflection (*Têtes*, p. 37), the
human creator blurts out his creation. Indeed, one can see the whole
series of Beckett's fictional works as the product of such an involuntary
compulsive effort. Germaine Brée has expressed the same idea thus: "de
Murphy à *Comment c'est*, on finit par entrevoir que c'est sans doute le
même aventurier qui poursuit son chemin et qui met au monde, de livre
en livre, l'inimaginable et inévitable livre suivant."[12]

Implicit in the early descriptions of the creative experience, the nature
and source of the artist's suffering become more evident as the novels
coincide more nearly with the existence of their creator-heroes. As the
narrator's self-consciousness increases, more and more details of the
artistic process flow into the work itself. The trilogy of novels provides a
growing wealth of material pertinent to the creative act, for as Ruby
Cohn says, "*Molloy* shows the making of the artist, *Malone Dies* the
artist making, and *The Unnamable* the artist's reflections upon art and the
artist".[13] In particular these three works present an evolving portrait of
the artist in which the creative agony increases in intensity from one narrator-hero to the next. As the anguish grows ever more acute, its source
becomes plain. In the case of each creator, the distress is of one caught up
in a terrible dilemma, of one torn between the obligation to create and the
impossibility of meeting this obligation. Tension mounts from one novel
to the next, for as the creative compulsion intensifies, the capacity of the
creator weakens. The overwhelming need to create is matched in degree
only by the towering inadequacy of the artist. Compelled to make the
creative act, the narrator-hero lacks the means with which to create. Yet
he must create though he cannot. The anguish resulting from this dilemma
characterizes the experience of every Beckettian artist. Always the creative

---

[9] "L'Image", 37.
[10] Cohn, *The Comic Gamut*, 199.
[11] *Ibid.*
[12] Brée, "L'Etrange monde des 'grands articulés'", 94.
[13] Cohn, *The Comic Gamut*, 118.

ordeal involves the unbearable simultaneous presence of obligation and impotence and produces in the artist an ever increasing sense of futility and disappointment.

The creative dilemma appears in ever greater detail from *Molloy* to *Comment c'est* as the tension produced by obligation and impotence paralyses the artist-hero, making him oblivious to everything but his plight. Confined to bed in his mother's room, Molloy admits from the outset that he is unable to perform as he should: "je ne sais plus travailler" (*Molloy*, p. 7); "j'ai oublié l'orthographe aussi, et la moitié des mots" (p. 8). Moreover, he does not even know why he continues to write; he seems to have no motive for his creative activity. Even though an anonymous man comes each week to pay him by the page for his efforts, Molloy declares: "Cependant je ne travaille pas pour l'argent. Pour quoi alors? Je ne sais pas" (p. 7). Yet, in spite of his total lack of desire to create and in spite of his obvious inability to do so, he must compose. More, he must tell of his absurd situation in his work: "Ne pas vouloir dire, ne pas savoir ce qu'on veut dire, ne pas pouvoir ce qu'on croit qu'on veut dire, et toujours dire ou presque, voilà ce qu'il importe de ne pas perdre de vue dans la chaleur de la rédaction" (p. 40). The self-conscious artist has no choice but to mirror his agonizing state in his creation. Obliged to write a report of his quest for Molloy, Moran performs the task grudgingly. Speaking of his mysterious boss Youdi, he mutters: "Il a voulu un rapport. Il l'aura, son rapport" (*Molloy*, p. 185). The creative act he describes as "ce triste travail de clerc" (p. 203; in the English translation: "this paltry scrivening").[14] His pursuit of Molloy appears in itself as a part of Moran's compulsive obligation and, like Molloy, before its demands he maintains "an awareness of his inadequacies and ignorance". [15]Again like Molloy, he can give no clear motive for his actions: "ce que je faisais, je ne le faisais ni pour Molloy, dont je me moquais, ni pour moi, à qui je renonçais, mais dans l'intérêt du travail qui, s'il avait besoin de nous pour s'accomplir, était dans son essence anonyme, et subsisterait, habiterait l'esprit des hommes, quand ses misérables artisans ne seraient plus" (p. 177). Yet Moran suffers extreme physical and mental torment while attempting to carry out his mission and returns home (after failing to find Molloy) with his physical faculties greatly impaired.

Bedridden like Molloy, Malone has even fewer resources for creation than his predecessors. In fact, deprived of all but a very few possessions, he declares: "il ne me reste plus que mon cahier de tout ce que j'ai eu,

14   *Molloy* (New York, 1965), 131.
15   Kern, "Moran-Molloy", 184.

alors j'y tiens, c'est humain. La mine aussi, bien entendu, mais qu'est-ce que c'est, une mine, sans papier?" (*Malone*, p. 183). To make the most of his notebook he resolves to write "sur les deux côtés de la page" (p. 64). It is all he has, and it must see him through his creation. Of the pencil he can only say, "J'espère qu'il fera l'affaire" (p. 65), for it is "très court et taillé des deux bouts" (p. 65). This inadequate writing tool is worn so short that he can no longer tell what color it is. He describes it as "vert encore sans doute" and explains that it is "si court qu'il y a tout juste la place, au milieu, pour mon pouce et les deux doigts suivants, ramassés en étau" (p. 89). In his anxiety not to use it up entirely, he tries to press as lightly as possible on the lead, but again he suffers distress from this imperfect piece of equipment for "la mine est dure et ne laisserait pas de trace si je n'appuyais" (p. 89). He is, then, caught up in a painful dilemma even in the matter of his writing materials. His own continuous physical dissolution aggravates the situation still more. As he withdraws ever further into his mind, his body, which must perform the creative act of writing recedes from sight and his concentration wavers, making composition almost impossible: "Mais mes doigts aussi écrivent sous d'autres latitudes, et l'air qui respire à travers mon cahier et en tourne les pages à mon insu, quand je m'assoupis, de sorte que le sujet s'éloigne du verbe et que le complément vient se poser quelque part dans le vide" (p. 112). Like Moran, he grumbles throughout his work: "Quel ennui" (p. 25); "Quelle misère" (p. 29); and, like Molloy, he reveals that he has had no particular desire to write: "Je ne voulais pas écrire, mais j'ai fini par m'y résigner" (p. 61). Though his avowed purpose in creating is to pass the time until his death (p. 9), to divert himself from his situation through the creation of fictions, his anxiety concerning the size of his notebook and pencil and the admission that he did not want to write but finally resigned himself to it suggest that he is in fact "under a compulsion to write down his thoughts, his fantasies, his memories".[16] One final detail seems to leave no doubt that the force behind his agonized literary efforts is an instinctive need to create: his pencil is a Venus (p. 89). Compelled by a force, as strong and irresistible as man's compulsion to reproduce himself physically, Malone in effect has no choice but to spin out tales peopled by creatures who come more and more to resemble their creator.

Driven to create by a similarly demanding obligation, the narrator of *L'Innommable* seems to be in an even worse plight than Malone, for he can foresee no end to his painful struggle: "je suis obligé de parler. Je ne me

---

[16]   Esslin, "Samuel Beckett", 138.

tairai jamais. Jamais" (pp. 8-9). As Ruby Cohn puts it, "The situation grows increasingly desperate by its very duration."[17] The torment here is heightened still further by utter physical paralysis; the Unnamable has no writing tools and could not wield them even if they were provided: "Mais l'époque des bâtons est révolue, ici je ne peux compter strictement que sur mon corps incapable du moindre mouvement et dont les yeux eux-mêmes ne peuvent plus se fermer" (p. 27). Faced with the obligation to write, he can only query: "Comment, dans ces conditions, fais-je pour écrire, à ne considérer de cette amère folie que l'aspect manuel? Je ne sais pas" (p. 28). Obsessed by his dilemma, this creator-hero describes it repeatedly and thus reveals much about its nature: "je vais avoir à parler de choses dont je ne peux parler" (p. 8); "Si seulement je n'étais pas dans l' obligation de manifester" (p. 17); "Mais il faut que le discours se fasse" (p. 13); "je ne peux parler de rien, et pourtant je parle" (p. 241). Echoing Molloy, he formulates his situation as "ne rien savoir, ne rien pouvoir, et d'avoir à essayer" (p. 236). In another passage he suggests the paralysing effect of combined necessity and impotence: "impossible de m'arrêter, impossible de continuer" (p. 221). In yet another, he explains at length the unbearable tension produced by his dilemma: "Moi... qui ne peux pas parler, ne peux pas penser, et qui dois parler, donc penser" (pp. 28-29); "l'impossibilité où je suis d'y penser [à moi et à l'endroit où je suis], d'en parler, à cause de la nécessité où je suis d'en parler, donc d'y penser peut-être un peu" (p. 29). The obligation itself makes the performance impossible, and the obligation continually renews itself: "l'obligation où je serai, une fois débarrassé, de recommencer, à partir de nulle part, de personne et de rien, pour y aboutir à nouveau, par des voies nouvelles bien sûr, ou par les anciennes, chaque fois méconnaissables" (p. 30). Bereft of every creative resource, the narrator here can speak only of his unspeakable agony, of how he is compelled to speak though he cannot. Summarizing this situation, Fletcher writes: "The artist cannot express and yet he must express: *The Unnamable* is about nothing else."[18] The dilemma arises, then, from the perplexing experience of the writer who "feels the obligation to express as much as he feels the impossibility of it".[19] In the case of the Unnamable, the agony seems to reach the limit of endurance. Describing it and the effect it produces in him, Mayoux writes: "The penitential and agonizing aspect of creation, pitiless exigence on the one hand, face to face with the painful mixture of resistance and im-

17 Cohn, *The Comic Gamut*, 146.
18 Fletcher, *Samuel Beckett's Art*, 22.
19 Furbank, "Beckett's Purgatory", 70.

potence on the other, is one of the things which... makes reading *The Unnamable* one of the most heartrending of experiences." [20]

The narrators of still later works are bound to the same wheel of torment. Immobilized by the opposing forces of obligation and impotence, one declares: "Je ne peux pas rester, je ne peux pas partir" (*Textes*, p. 131).[21] Another fears a possible future dilemma: "Avoir à gémir, sans le pouvoir" (p. 140). The constant suffering of yet another finds expression in incessant tears: "Je pleure aussi, sans discontinuer. C'est un flot ininterrompu, de mots et de larmes. Le tout sans réflexion" (p. 181). In one of the later stories in this group the juxtaposition of imperative and impossibility composes a concise formulation of the writer's plight: "Nommer, non, rien n'est nommable, dire, non, rien n'est dicible, alors quoi, je ne sais pas, il ne fallait pas commencer" (pp. 203-204). Evaluating the importance of this statement, Tom Bishop says: "This starkly anguished sentence is the quintessential statement of Samuel Beckett's universe, organized along the double polarity of the impossibility of saying and the necessity to say.... The paradox of the artist." [22] Still later the narrator-hero of "From an Abandoned Work" resembles his predecessors in not understanding why he must create: "About the narrative itself, the narrator complains that he does not know why he has chosen this day to describe; he does not know why he speaks, but he must speak on." [23] All the same, the extent of the anguish he endures is clear, since it takes the form of an acute sore throat: "All this talking, very low and hoarse, no wonder I had a sore throat" (p. 143); "Throat very bad, to swallow was torment" (p. 148).

Like earlier creator-heroes, the protagonist of *Comment c'est* suffers from paralysis ("on ne peut continuer on continue la même chose... on ne peut continuer on ne peut s'arrêter arrêter", p. 110) and from the fear of having to speak without being able to do so ("le moment où sans le pouvoir j'aurais à dire", p. 131). But his situation surpasses that of all the other narrators in desperateness. In the midst of mud and darkness this creator has not even a voice with which to utter what he must say. His murmurings are mute "mouvements du bas du visage" (p. 9). As Ruby Cohn expresses it, "Having no voice, the narrator knows he speaks only

[20] Mayoux, "Samuel Beckett and Universal Parody", 81.
[21] The theme of tension in immobility can be traced as far back as *Mercier et Camier*, 32, where Camier describes the heroes' common plight: "il n'y a plus moyen d'avancer. Reculer est également hors de question."
[22] Bishop, "Samuel Beckett", 26.
[23] Cohn, *The Comic Gamut*, 180.

when he feels his face move."[24] Still, though voiceless, "the 'I' formulates words as compulsively as he moves towards the East".[25] Here is relentless obligation face to face with "utter and uncalculating incapacity".[26] The torment which results from such a dilemma is illustrated in Part II of the novel. With the arrival of Pim on the scene, the creator's means are momentarily improved. Using torture, he extorts utterances from his fellow being, who, unlike himself, has a voice. The tormentor even resorts to carving words with his fingernail on the back of his victim in order to exact information from him about his former life. More, this particular part of the work reveals the anguish with which the entire novel is composed, for it is a reflection of what transpires in the unrecountable fourth part – the telling of how the three parts are told (as explained in Chapter 4). The pain which the narrator inflicts on Pim is a sample of what the protagonist must endure at the hands of Bom in order to produce the three-part work. Thus, for this hero, the dilemma takes on an aspect of intense brutality, the compulsion being personified by a ruthless tormentor, the impotence by his naked victim.

Perhaps the sparest of formulations for the dilemma, the short piece "Imagination morte imaginez" conveys in its very title the obligation and impossibility of the creative experience. Given a defunct imagination, the artist could not possibly create, and yet the imperative follows: "imaginez". Even when the writer has no more resources, when his consciousness has contracted to its smallest circumference, he feels the overpowering urgency to create. The very first sentence of this piece reads: "Nulle part trace de vie, dites-vous, pah, la belle affaire, imagination pas morte, si, bon, imagination morte imaginez" (*Têtes*, p. 51). Confronted by the insoluble nature of his dilemma, the Beckettian artist accepts the truth of his issueless situation and suffers it with unblunted awareness.

Beckett clearly reveals his preference for such uncompromising lucidity in the critical piece "Three Dialogues". Turning from that modern painting which remains essentially traditional, which does not leave "the plane of the feasible",[27] he calls instead for "the expression that there is nothing to express, nothing with which to express, nothing from which to express, no power to express, no desire to express, together with the obligation to express."[28] In other words, he champions the kind of relentlessly self-

---

[24]   Cohn, 188.
[25]   Cohn, 200.
[26]   Kenner, *Flaubert, Joyce and Beckett*, 76.
[27]   "Three Dialogues", 17.
[28]   *Ibid.*

conscious art practiced by his own narrator -heroes.Their dearth of matter for expression, their ever-diminishing supply of tools, their constantly deteriorating bodies, and their utter lack of desire to create make them perfect examples of the creator who finds himself totally impotent when faced with the exigencies of his vocation. Helplessly suspended between the obligation to create and his utter incapacity to meet that implacable demand, the self-conscious creator in Beckett's fiction can express only his inability to express. Yet he speaks on. Like Bram van Velde, who, according to Beckett, is "the first [artist] to accept a certain situation and to consent to a certain act",[29] the narrator-hero creates in spite of the impossibility of his doing so. For the Dutch painter, "the situation is that of him who is helpless, cannot act, in the event cannot paint, since he is obliged to paint. The act is of him who, helpless, unable to act, acts, in the event paints, since he is obliged to paint."[30] For the author-hero, the situation involves the inability to write and the act of writing in spite of that inability. In both cases, the result is an intensely self-conscious art deeply scarred by the painful conflict which the creator suffered in its production. As Hassan explains it, "Obligation... wrestles with impossibility, and the result is always pyrrhic. The artist, like so many heroes of Beckett, can neither continue nor desist. The work of art itself – painting or play – contracts to express the paradox of its own existence."[31] Given the impossible demands which the obligation to create makes upon the impotent artist, the creative effort, when made, can never be successful; it must always fall short of the ideal demanded by the artistic imperative. This is especially true of "la création littéraire qui est, pour Beckett, obligatoire, bien que vouée à l'échec".[32] In Hassan's words, "Art... is failure and frozen outrage".[33] The wonder is that the artist, consumed by anguish in his work and haunted by the failure which will inevitably result from his tortured efforts, creates at all. "And yet the urge, the inescapable compulsion to express – but what? – remains embedded, as strongly as ever, in the artist's nature."[34]

The force of the compulsion to create cannot be underestimated. Indeed, the obligation to express is one with the artist's existence. Like the pulse, the written or spoken word is a vital sign for the narrator-hero. As Madden

29   "Three Dialogues", 19.
30   *Ibid.*
31   Hassan, *The Literature of Silence*, 136.
32   Fletcher, "Sur un roman inédit", 149.
33   Hassan, 136.
34   Esslin, "Introduction", 2.

of *Mercier et Camier* admits, "Je survivais en parlant, tous les jours un peu plus, tous les jours un peu mieux" (p. 59). Similarly for Molloy, "writing is identical with existence and existence means writing".[35] Driven by a "disposition permanente" to seek out his mother (*Molloy*, p. 134), he responds to the equally constant and vital urge to write of his quest. According to Edith Kern, "his hands almost mechanically move the pen. What keeps him alive is precisely an 'invisible reality' that bids him: write."[36] Referring to his literary efforts as "mon projet de vivre, et faire vivre" (*Malone*, p. 63), Malone provides still further evidence of the intimate rapport between the artist and his writing. Of this dying narrator Janvier says: "vivre, ainsi qu'il le vérifie constamment par le cours de son récit, ce n'est autre chose qu'inventer";[37] and "si vivre c'est inventer, inventer c'est vivre".[38] Malone actually seems to prolong his rapidly declining existence through his creative efforts. Though tempted to cease writing, he will not risk throwing away his pencil, perhaps for fear of dying on the instant: "Je me demande si je vais pouvoir m'arrêter. Si je jetais ma mine. Je ne la récupérerais jamais. Je pourrais en avoir du regret. Ma petite mine. C'est un risque que je ne suis pas disposé à courir en ce moment" (p. 150). It is as though he had contemplated suicide and then withdrawn from the brink. Creation virtually coincides with existence for the hero of *Comment c'est*; his "incessant, compulsive 'murmure à la boue' is tantamount to breath".[39] To exist is to be compelled to create for the Beckettian artist. Thus, the creator-hero appears as one who has always been in the process of composing fiction. When Hamm asks Clov to specify which story he means by the words *ton histoire*, the reply is: "Celle que tu te racontes depuis toujours" (*Fin de partie*, p. 80). As demonstrated in Chapter 4, Beckett's heroes live only in their creations. Their continued existence "is manifested not by a heartbeat but by the word".[40] For these creators, as for Rilke, "Gesang ist Dasein".[41] Conversely, where there is no artistic creation there can be no existence.

The incessant compulsion to create dominates the artist's experience, making the agony of dilemma unavoidable. But how is the creator so compelled? Why is the creative urge so overpowering? To understand the

---

35 Kern, "Moran-Molloy", 183.
36 Kern, "Beckett's Knight of Infinite Resignation", 49.
37 Janvier, *Pour Samuel Beckett*, 68.
38 Janvier, 71; cf. *Malone meurt*, 37: "c'est gravement que j'ai essayé... de vivre, d'inventer".
39 Cohn, *The Comic Gamut*, 186.
40 Bishop, "Samuel Beckett", 27.
41 Cohn, 5.

nature of the irresistible force which drives the artist to create, one must attempt to determine its source. Careful study of the images used to describe its action and effect provides valuable insight into the reasons for its power. As early as *Murphy*, the hero (though not a practicing artist) undergoes the experience of compelled expression. In the climactic scene with Mr. Endon, Murphy "seeing himself stigmatised in those eyes that did not see him... heard words demanding so strongly to be spoken that he spoke them, right into Mr. Endon's face, Murphy who did not speak at all in the ordinary way unless spoken to, and not always even then" (pp. 249-250). Insisting upon Murphy's taciturn nature, the narrator reinforces by contrast the enormous force of the compulsion to speak which momentarily takes possession of the hero. The barrier of his habitual muteness cannot block the urge to express himself in this situation. Hearing words pronounced by an unspecified voice, Murphy violates his customary silence (referred to in his horoscope as one of "his highest attributes", p. 32) to give them the utterance they demand. Watt, too, experiences the compulsion to speak in spite of himself. As Sam says of Watt's discourse concerning the Gall episode, "it may be assumed that Watt would never have thought or spoken of such incidents, if he had not been under the absolute necessity of doing so" (*Watt*, p. 79). Here thought and expression together are affected by the obligation, the absolute necessity of thinking and speaking. Though Watt, like Murphy, would apparently prefer silence to speech, he has no choice. His manner of speaking in an "impetuous murmur" (p. 156) reflects the compulsive nature of his expressive activity: "But Watt spoke as one speaking to dictation, or reciting, parrotlike, a text, by long repetition become familiar" (p. 156). Another description of his almost automatic oral expression appears in the final pages of the novel where, after leaving Knott's house, the hero occupies the waiting room at the railroad station. There he produces from "behind the door, a disquieting sound, that of soliloquy, under dictation" (p. 237). Still later, in the Addenda, the narrator alludes again to Watt's continuous muttering; but here he insists even more upon its incessant nature and goes on to reveal its general content:

Watt will not
abate one jot
but of what

of the coming to
of the being at
of the going from
Knott's habitat   (p. 249)

Sam himself does not escape the compulsive urge to create. Having no desire whatever to record Watt's story, he nonetheless feels the obligation to associate with Watt and to assume the role of his secretary. Describing the compulsion he feels in terms that recall his description of Watt's own similar experience, Sam says: "I found my steps impelled, as though by some external agency, towards the fence; and this impulsion was maintained, until I could go no further... I say an external agency; for of my own volition... I should never have gone near the fence, under any circumstances" (p. 158). Just as Watt would greatly prefer never to think or speak of the inexplicable happenings at Knott's, so Sam would choose not to approach Watt. Neither has the least desire to do what he does, yet both are forced to act in spite of their extreme reluctance.

The 'external agency' mentioned by Sam takes on human form in *Molloy*. In the first part, a strange man makes weekly visits to Molloy's bedside: "Cet homme qui vient chaque semaine.... Il me donne un peu d'argent et enlève les feuilles. Tant de feuilles, tant d'argent" (p. 7). The representative of a mysterious group referred to only as "ils" (p. 7), the demanding caller expresses his dissatisfaction when Molloy fails to produce: "Quand je n'ai rien fait il ne me donne rien, il me gronde" (p. 7). But this anonymous agent soon disappears, to be replaced much later in the tale by what Molloy calls first "un impératif" (p. 132), then "mes impératifs" (p. 132), and finally "cette voix" (p. 133). The voice, like the strange visitor, harries Molloy. Indeed, it seems to convey the creative imperative itself: "Et la voix aurait pu me harceler jusqu'à pied d'oeuvre que je n'y serais peut-être pas arrivé davantage, à cause des autres obstacles qui barraient le chemin" (p. 133). Were it to clamor on forever, he would not be able to do all it demands. Yet this voice serves, too, to reassure him when at the end of his story he finds himself paralysed in a ditch: "je m'entendis dire de ne pas me biler, qu'on courait à mon secours" (p. 140).[42] For Moran, the compulsive force undergoes a similar metamorphosis. At the beginning of his tale he speaks of receiving an order through the messenger Gaber (pp. 142-147) from his boss ("un nommé Youdi", p. 166). The initial order "de m'occuper de Molloy" (p. 142), which coincides with the obligation to write a report of the investigation, permanently affects its recipient. Just as Molloy is gradually reduced to paralysis in his attempts to obey imperatives, so Moran's physical and mental faculties undergo radical changes as he tries to obey the order from Youdi. Comparing his assignment to a poison (p. 149), Moran describes its effects on him: "Le monde changeait

[42]   In the English translation, *Molloy* (New York, 1965), 91: "I heard a voice telling me not to fret, that help was coming".

déjà de couleur et de poids" (p. 149); "Je sentais une grande confusion me gagner" (p. 152); "Je perdais la tête déjà" (p. 153). Even before starting out in quest of Molloy, he feels the anguish of his dilemma: "Je ne comprenais pas ce qui m'arrivait" (p. 158); "Ma vie s'en allait mais j'ignorais par où" (p. 158). Later the duty to make a written report of the journey becomes more important than the adventure itself ("ce récit qu'on m'impose", p. 203), and Youdi fades from view. Like the unnamed messenger in Molloy's tale, he is replaced by a voice which seems more powerful and much more closely related to the narrator-hero. Speaking of it, Moran says: "J'obéis encore aux ordres, si l'on veut, mais ce n'est plus la crainte qui m'inspire. Si, j'ai toujours peur, mais c'est plutôt là un effet de l'habitude. Et la voix que j'écoute, je n'ai pas eu besoin de Gaber pour me la transmettre" (pp. 203-204).

The precise nature of the rapport between the compelled creator-hero and the powerful force which controls his activity appears more clearly in images drawn from the *Textes pour rien*. For example, one narrator reveals utter passivity in the face of his compulsion:: "je ne suis ici qu'une poupée de ventriloque, je ne sens rien, je ne dis rien, il me tient dans ses bras et il fait remuer mes lèvres avec une ficelle" (p. 185). Comparing himself to a helpless, will-less marionette, the creator declares that he is but a mere vehicle for the expression of some vague other, referred to simply as "il", who speaks through him. In a later piece from this same group the hero describes his forced activity in a similar fashion, but here the hands of the manipulator come into direct contact with the head and face of the hapless speaker: "elles [les mains] me tiennent la tête, par derrière, curieux détail, comme chez le coiffeur, et... manoeuvrent mâchoires et langue, pour que j'étrangle, mais mal, et dise, pour mon bien, ce que je dois dire" (p. 198). The image of involuntary speech appears in its most revelatory form as early as *Murphy* where Neary, in his effort to be perfectly truthful with Wylie and Miss Counihan, assumes the possessed attitude of the compelled creator: "Neary began to speak, or, as it rather sounded, be spoken through. For the voice was flat, the eyes closed and the body bowed and rigid.... Altogether he had a great look of Luke's portrait of Matthew with the angel perched like a parrot on his shoulder" (p. 215). Compared to the Evangelist experiencing divine inspiration, Neary demonstrates in his passive though tense posture all the anguish of the artist's dilemma. No force could be more imperious than that of the Holy Spirit, no creative activity more compulsive than that performed at divine command. Designated to carry out the will of God, St. Matthew has no choice in the matter. The angel, who conveys the Word to him for his recording, is his constant companion and taskmaster. Its words claim immediate transcription; the imperative to which it gives voice is irresistible. Being unable not to write what he is told, St. Matthew (as described here) provides the perfect model of the artist who is compelled despite his impotence to speak or write in response to the demands of an all-powerful voice.

Still, the voice is not the only significant image of the compulsive force. In comparing his creature Macmann to the Colossus of Memnon (p. 98), Malone provides further insight into the creative dilemma. Seated on a bench with his back to the river (p. 97), Macmann assumes a rigid position like that of Neary, which reflects the tense conflict between obligation and impotence: "la pose est sans laisser-aller aucun, et n'était l'absence de liens on pourrait le croire maintenu par des liens, tant la pose est immobile et raide et faite de plans et d'angles nets, comme celle du colosse de Memnon" (p. 98). The source of compulsion here appears in the epithet for Memnon, "fils bien-aimé de l'Aurore" (p. 98). According to Greek mythology, the stone figure emits musical sounds at the first rays of dawn in response to the appearance of his mother Aurora. Thus, as an image for compelled creation, the Colossus presents impossible utterance evoked by a visual force. Struck by the light of morning, the statue must speak because of what it *sees*. Again, as in the image of St. Matthew, the compulsion is divine (Aurora was a goddess) and, consequently, not to be resisted. But here the inadequacy of the artist seems even greater than before. Made of stone, the monument illustrates absolute paralysis. Yet Memnon must express; he must make the creative act required by his divine mother. That this image represents a portrait of the artist is suggested by later reference to Macmann's poetic efforts (pp. 167-168) and by a strikingly similar allusion to the Egyptian colossus in Proust's *Contre Sainte-Beuve*: "Et déjà touché par ce rayon de soleil matinal, j'ai sauté à bas du lit, j'ai fait mille danses et gesticulations heureuses que je constate dans la glace, je dis avec joie des mots qui n'ont rien d'heureux, et je chante, car le poète est comme la statue de Memnon: il suffit d'un rayon de soleil levant pour le faire chanter." [43] Further evidence can be found, too, in Beckett's own works where "the petrified pose of ancient Egypt" [44] characterizes Murphy bound to his rocking-chair, Hamm riveted to his wheelchair, and even the hero of *L'Innommable* who cannot lift his hand from his knee. Describing the paradox of his situation, the Unnamable says: "C'est moi qui écris, moi qui ne puis lever la main de mon genou" (p. 28). Still, the image of Matthew and the angel persists, too, making it as noteworthy

[43] M. Proust, *Contre Sainte-Beuve* (Paris: Gallimard, 1954), 83.
[44] Mayoux, "Samuel Beckett and Universal Parody", 84.

as the allusion to Memnon. In fact, the Unnamable refers to the earlier image directly in the passage on paralysis cited above. "Je suis Mathieu et je suis l'ange", he writes (p. 28), describing in a minimum of words the anguish of feeling simultaneously the extremes of human impotence and divine imperative. Clearly, then, both the image of the demanding voice and that of the compelling light are essential to an understanding of the artist's obligation. Further examination of the prominent role they play discloses the source of that obligation.

Important throughout the fiction, the image of the voice comes to dominate the scene in the later, more self-conscious works. As Germaine Brée notes, "Tous les personnages de Beckett... à partir de Watt, sont aux prises avec cette voix.... [sont] habitès de voix." [45] Describing their general effect, Onimus writes: "si inconsistantes soient-elles, ces voix suffisent pour rompre la paix de l'innocence et créer l'angoisse." [46] Subject to the ramblings of "a little voice", Watt is perplexed, for he "never knew quite what to make of this particular little voice, whether it was joking, or whether it was serious" (*Watt*, p. 91). In "L'Expulsé", the narrator-hero hearkens to the declatations of a similar voice: "une voix me disait, C'est la lande de Lunebourg qu'il vous faut" (*Nouvelles*, p. 19). Both Mercier and Camier hear little voices, though each seems to be addressed by a quite different one from that of his companion: "La petite voix implorante, dit Camier, qui nous parle parfois de vies antérieures, la connais-tu? [-] Je la confonds de plus en plus, dit Mercier, avec celle qui veut me faire croire que je ne suis pas encore mort.... [-] Ce serait un organe analogue, dit Camier, qui depuis vingt-quatre heures va chuchotant, Le sac! Votre sac!" (*Mercier et Camier*, pp. 94-95). The power of the voice grows in the trilogy of novels where it begins to dictate to the narrator-heroes. Referring to its influence, Onimus shows how the later heroes are indirectly 'spoken through' as they are forced to record or repeat the words of the voice: "Cette voix nous traverse. Nous parlons sous sa dictée, nous 'citons', nous cessons d'être nous-mêmes." [47] Molloy, for example, says: "J'écoute et m'entends dicter.... Et j'écouterais encore ce souffle lointain, depuis longtemps tu et que j'entends enfin, que j'apprendrais d'autres choses encore.... Mais... je ne l'aime pas, ce souffle lointain, et même je le crains.... c'est un son qui n'est pas comme les autres" (*Molloy*, pp. 59-60). Unlike any other sound, the strange voice is not easily understood: "la petite voix... que j'avais mis si longtemps à comprendre, car il y avait

---

45   Brée, "L'Etrange monde des 'grands articulés'", 88-89.
46   Onimus, *Beckett*, 89.
47   Onimus, 69.

longtemps que je l'entendais. Et je la comprenais peut-être de travers,
mais je la comprenais et c'était là la nouveauté" (p. 90). Still, both Molloy
and Moran come to rely upon the instructions conveyed to them by their
respective voices. Molloy "obeys only the imperatives delivered by his
inner voice"; and when "abandoned by his voice [he] sinks down in his
ditch, awaiting further imperatives".[48] Though Moran describes his voice
as one which is "assez ambigue et qui n'est pas toujours facile à suivre,
dans ses raisonnements et décrets" (*Molloy*, p. 204), he claims to understand and to obey it (p. 204). Further, he reveals that he is committed to
following this voice and that he is totally dependent upon its pronounce-
ments: "Et j'ai l'impression que je la suivrai dorénavant, quoi qu'elle m'en-
joigne. Et que lorsqu'elle se taira, me laissant dans le doute et l'obscurité,
j'attendrai qu'elle revienne, avant de rien faire" (p. 204). Silence on the
part of the voice paralyses the hero who can only act at its bidding. Thus,
Sapo, Malone's first persona, responds in a way similar to that of Molloy
and Moran when his guiding voice is stilled: "Et quand il s'arrêtait ce
n'était pas pour mieux penser, ou pour mieux regarder son rêve, mais
c'était simplement que la voix qui lui disait d'avancer s'était tue" (*Malone*,
pp. 57-58).

   For the two author-heroes of *Molloy*, the significance of the voice cannot be underestimated, since it is responsible for their creative activity.
Indeed, it is the "mysterious voice which... [guides] both Moran and
Molloy through the wilderness to their existence as writers".[49] Compelled
to follow "the voice that bids him write",[50] every narrator-hero actually
depends upon the dictates of his voice for his very existence. But as the
heroes become more and more self-conscious, their penetrating lucidity
discerns in the voice an image which merely represents some other force:
"Mais c'est entièrement une question de voix, toute autre *métaphore* est
imprope" (*L'Innommable*, pp. 77-78; my emphasis); "c'est uniquement
une question de voix, tout [*sic*] autre *image* est à écarter" (p. 123; my
emphasis). Testifying to its effect on him, the anonymous creator refers
to it as "cette voix qui m'a dénaturé" (p. 130). Thoroughly obsessed by it,
he contrives for its source "l'image d'une grande bouche idiote, rouge,
lippue, baveuse, au secret, se vidant inlassablement, avec un bruit de
lessive et de gros baisers, des mots qui l'obstruent" (p. 212). But soon the
voice appears totally disembodied. Declares the last author-hero of the
Textes: "il n'y a personne, il y a une voix sans bouche" (p. 215). In *Com-*

48   Cohn, *The Comic Gamut*, 156.
49   Kern, "Moran-Molloy", 189.
50   Kern, "Dionysian Poet", 33-34.

ment c'est the hollow voice is virtually all that remains: "Contradictions deny the separateness of the two beings [the narrator and Pim], and even question the existence of any being; only a voice, 'quaqua,' asserts its own meaninglessness through space and time."[51] Endlessly taking dictation at the command of a mysterious voice, the protagonist mutters repeatedly the phrases "je cite" and "je le dis comme je l'entends" (p. 9 and passim). Still the voice itself is only a metaphor for something else, and the authority granted to it in the fiction invests other aural forms in the plays. Here, though "the inciting croaking voice"[52] of Croak in *Words and Music* and the voice of the Opener in *Cascando* recall the persistent presence of the voice in the novels, the compelling force expresses its will in *Happy Days* by ringing "the bell for waking and the bell for sleep" (p. 21). These bells "being rung by somebody... mechanize what remains vestigially a voice".[53] Similarly, the ever present sound of the sea in *Embers* compels Henry's endless soliloquy. But in the short mime *Acte sans paroles II*, the authority invests a goad, making the compulsion to act felt as an implacable prodding; and finally, in the coincident piece *Play*, the irresistible force "directs the inquisitorial spotlight",[54] coercing utterance in a manner like that illustrated by the image of Memnon.

Before going on to consider the details of this second key image, however, we must call attention to one last essential aspect of the voice – its inner origin. Clearly helpful in the quest for the source of compulsion, repeated allusions to the internal nature of the voice indicate a similar kind of origin for the compelling force itself. As early as *Murphy* the dictating voice issues from within. In the asylum, for instance, one finds paranoids "feverishly covering sheets of paper with complaints against their treatment or verbatim reports of their inner voices" (pp. 167-168). In fact, the voice seems to be a universal characteristic of the Mercyseat inmates (whom Murphy envies), for even Dr. Killiecrankie "had some experience of the schizoid voice" (p. 185). Difficult to comprehend (as Molloy and Moran would agree), this particular kind of voice "was not like a real voice, one minute it said one thing and the next minute something quite different" (p. 185). Mr. Endon, Murphy's favorite patient, gives great weight to the dictates of his voice. When it makes known a preference for suicide by apnoea, he puts his entire confidence in its judgment. Though this kind of death would be most difficult to achieve, "he

51 Hassan, *The Literature of Silence*, 170.
52 Kenner, "Progress Report", 62.
53 *Ibid.*; cf. the whistle in *Acte sans paroles I*.
54 Kenner, "Progress Report", 62.

said his voice would not hear of any other method" (p. 185)[55] Further, a description of this particular patient's voice reveals its continuous presence: "His inner voice did not harangue him, it was unobtrusive and melodious, a gentle continuo in the whole consort of his hallucinations" (p. 186). Like Mr. Endon, Watt listens to "an inner discourse"[56] and in one instance even hears "a voice urging him... to do away with himself" (*Watt*, p. 73). In "L'Expulsé" an aside suggests that the voice which speaks of the Lunebourg heath is actually that of the hero addressing himself; "je ne me suis pas beaucoup tutoyé", says he after citing the voice's words: "C'est la lande de Lunebourg qu'il vous faut" (*Nouvelles*, p. 19). For Molloy and Moran, the authority which at first seems alien soon becomes more and more familiar and is finally acknowledged as a part of their being. Thus, Molloy near the end of his tale speaks frankly of "une voix interne" (*Molloy*, p. 134) whose will he might have been able to do if *le dehors* (p. 133) had not thwarted him. Even the problem of arranging his stones provides an occasion for disclosing the presence of inner clamor, since the solution makes itself felt as an internal chant: "Cette proposition, qui se mit soudain à chanter au dedans de moi, comme un verset d'Esaïe, ou de Jérémie" (p. 108). Moreover, this biblical allusion recalls the image of Matthew and the angel. Molloy's most valuable revelation as to the nature of the sounds he hears comes before his story is half finished. Telling how he hears the strange "souffle lointain", Molloy declares that he will no longer listen to it; but he finds that it is by nature inescapable: "c'est un son qui se met à vous bruire dans la tête, on ne sait comment, ni pourquoi. C'est avec la tête qu'on l'entend, les oreilles n'y sont pour rien, et on ne peut l'arrêter, mais il s'arrête tout seul, quand il veut" (p. 60). The sound originates, then, within him, and is perceived exclusively by the mind. Furthermore, it has a will of its own; Molloy has no control whatever over it. Consequently, though he would prefer not to listen to it, he has no choice: "Que je l'écoute ou ne l'écoute pas, cela n'a donc pas d'importance, je l'entendrai toujours, le tonnerre ne saurait m'en délivrer, jusqu'à ce qu'il cesse" (p. 60). Moran, too, finds that he listens to an inner voice, one which communicates with him directly, one with which he has an intimate rapport: "Et la voix que j'écoute, je n'ai pas eu besoin de Gaber pour me la transmettre. Car elle est en moi et elle m'exhorte à être jusqu'au bout ce fidèle serviteur que j'ai toujours été, d'une cause qui n'est pas la mienne, et de remplir patiemment mon rôle jusque dans ses

---

[55] In the French translation, *Murphy* (Paris, 1965), 135: "Sa voix intérieure s'opposait à toute autre méthode."
[56] Fletcher, *The Novels*, 66.

dernières amertumes et extrémités" (p. 204). The mysterious and alien Youdi "has dissolved into an interior voice".[57]

The hero of *L'Innommable* early declares that he is not compelled to speak by some external agent: "Personne ne m'y oblige [à parler]" (p. 55). But he does describe how he is tyrannized by an uncontrollable inner (though strangely foreign) voice: "Elle sort de moi, elle me remplit, elle clame contre mes murs, elle n'est pas la mienne, je ne peux pas l'arrêter, je ne peux pas l'empêcher, de me déchirer, de me secouer, de m'assiéger" (p. 40). Later in his story he clearly proposes to believe that the voice he hears originates somewhere within himself, and must be at least in some measure his own: "Supposer notamment dorénavant que la chose dite et celle entendue soient de même provenance.... Situer cette provenance en moi, sans spécifier où" (p. 211). In one of the *Textes*, the hero listens intently for an inner voice: "l'oreille à l'affût d'une voix qui ne soit pas d'un tiers" (p. 160).[58] For the narrator of *Comment c'est*, the obsessive voice appears first without and then within: "voix d'abord dehors quaqua de toutes parts puis en moi quand ça cesse de haleter" (p. 9). He experiences it as fragmented, alien expression: "bribes d'une voix ancienne en moi pas la mienne" (p. 9). Yet at the very end of his tale he claims it as his own: "moi oui ma voix à moi oui pas à un autre non à moi tout seul" (p. 176). Represented by the inner voice, the compulsive force comes from within the artist; and the artist is dependent upon it for the drive and inspiration necessary to create. "One cannot sing", says Winnie, "just like that, no. (*Pause.*) It bubbles up, for some unknown reason" (*Happy Days*, p. 57). The creative urge originates at an as yet unspecified spot within the mind of the creator where the work itself has its roots. As Ruby Cohn notes, "with Beckett as with Mallarmé, 'le chant jaillit de source innée, antérieure à un concept.'"[59]

To determine precisely the source of the creative compulsion within the artist, let us consider now in detail the implications of the Memnon image. For the statue, the light of dawn represents an irresistible command; the son, though made of stone, must acknowledge his mother's presence. Indeed, the very first indications of her coming evoke a spontaneous musical tribute from him. But this kind of compulsion varies significantly from that of the voice. It is perceived, not by the physical or mental ear, but by the eye; it is a visible sign conveyed through the eye to the mind from which

[57] Cohn, *The Comic Gamut*, 156.
[58] In the English translation, *Stories and Texts for Nothing*, 95-96: "the ears straining for a voice not from without".
[59] Cohn, *The Comic Gamut*, 5.

it draws instant expression. To understand how eye and mind are related and how their rapport contributes to our knowledge of the inner source, we must examine the references and images in which visual perception and mental activity appear linked. In *More Pricks Than Kicks*, the narrator indicates a direct relationship between the eyes and the mind: "What were the eyes anyway? The posterns of the mind" (p. 90). As windows opening onto the mental scene, the eyes reflect the mind's content and condition. They are the traits essential to facial expression. Thus, Worm in his original form reveals no mental state at all: "Il n'est qu'un tas informe, sans visage capable de refléter l'histoire d'un tourment" (*L'Innommable*, p. 143). But the mysterious "ils", who are anxious for him to endure the suffering of the complete human being, insist upon his possessing an eye: "Dans le tas un oeil, hagard, chevalin, toujours ouvert, il leur faut un oeil, ils lui voient un oeil" (p. 143). Once the eye opens, all the turmoil of one's inner state becomes visible; and those who take sadistic pleasure in examining another's torment avidly pursue the traces of inner pain through the eye: "cet oeil, c'est là où il faut chercher" (p. 172). In the short piece "Dans le cylindre", the eyes are subject to detailed examination, even if they be closed: "Il est défendu évidemment de refuser le visage ou toute autre partie du corps au chercheur qui en fait la demande et qui peut sans crainte de résistance écarter les mains des chairs qu'elles cachent et soulever les paupières pour examiner l'oeil." [60] While making its investigation, the eye of the *chercheur* acts as perceiver of that which his victim's eye reveals. Thus, the eye's active role comes to light here. The eye as intense perceiver virtually dominates the scenario *Film*, which according to Alan Schneider "was once titled *The Eye*".[61] Indeed, the film begins with a close-up of an eye opening and staring straight ahead.[62] Easily interpreted as "the symbol of perception",[63] the eye here represents at a deeper level of understanding the "regard intérieur",[64] the inner organ of perception which probes the mind. The role of the inner eye becomes increasingly prominent in the later works. In the *Textes*, for example, one hero speaks of being on the alert, "les yeux exorbités derrière les paupières" (p. 160). Similarly, the narrator of *Comment c'est* makes frequent reference to his habit of closing "les yeux pas les bleus les autres derrière" (p. 11 and passim).

---

[60] "Dans le cylindre", 24.
[61] Schneider, "On Directing *Film*", 65.
[62] *Film*, 9.
[63] Federman, "*Film*", 49.
[64] Onimus, *Beckett*, 43.

Throughout the fiction visual activity is constant and intense. Its scope is often limited, but it gains power from this sharp focus. As early as *Mercier et Camier* the fixed stare characterizes the hero's face: "Les yeux gris pâle [de Mercier] regardaient fixement devant eux, comme avec effroi."[65] This same expression of unwavering attention reappears in *Malone meurt* where both Sapo and Macmann display it: "Au milieu des tumultes, à l'école et dans sa famille, il restait immobile à sa place, souvent debout, et regardait droit devant lui de ses yeux clairs et fixes comme ceux d'une mouette" (pp. 31-32); "Les yeux à peine plus bleus qu'un blanc d'oeuf fixent l'espace devant eux" (p. 109). In *L'Innommable*, the author-hero suffers a sort of visual paralysis, for he must stare before him without blinking "comme un grand-duc dans une volière" (p. 12): "les yeux... ne peuvent plus se fermer... pour me reposer de voir et de ne pouvoir voir ou simplement pour m'aider à dormir, ni se détourner, ni se baisser, ni se lever au ciel, tout en restant ouverts, mais sont contraints, centrés et écarquillés, de fixer sans arrêt le court couloir devant eux, où il ne se passe rien, 99% du temps" (p. 27). Calling attention to the painful effect of this visual strain, the hero speaks of the tears which stream down his cheeks (p. 12) and tries to imagine how his eyes must look: "Ils doivent être rouges comme des charbons ardents" (p. 27). As for Worm, although he has but one eye, he endures much the same discomfort as his creator: "laissons-lui cet oeil aussi, c'est pour voir, ce grand oeil farouche noir et blanc, humide, c'est pour pleurer, pour qu'il prenne l'habitude... il n'en fait rien, il le garde ouvert, l'oeil reste ouvert, c'est un oeil sans paupières, pas besoin de paupières ici, où il ne se passe rien, ou si peu, il pourrait les rater, les infréquents spectacles, s'il pouvait le fermer, on le connaît, il ne l'ouvrirait plus. Les larmes en jaillissent presque sans arrêt" (pp. 148-149). Unable to close his eye, Worm "ne peut pas le détourner non plus, ni le baisser, ni le lever, il reste braqué sur le même petit champ toujours, exclu des bienfaits de l'accommodation" (p. 152). The image of the eye returns in the later short fiction where, for example at the end of "Bing", nothing remains but an "oeil noir et blanc mi-clos" (*Têtes*, p. 65). Moreover, the close rapport between eye and mind is everywhere significant. Invoking sleep to rest his weary eyes, the narrator-hero of *Comment c'est* develops the image of coals introduced by the Unnamable: "viens éteindre ces deux vieux charbons qui n'ont plus rien à voir et ce vieux

---

65 Fletcher, "Sur un roman inédit", 140; cited from a copy of the original typescript, this passage does not appear in the edition of the novel published in 1970 by Editions de Minuit.

four détruit par le feu et dans toute cette guenille... le peu de sensation qu'elle garde encore de ce qu'elle est" (pp. 44-45). Posterns of the mind, the eyes serve as the connecting link between the outer and inner worlds. It is through them that the mental oven is heated, is driven to function. But as has been shown, the eyes can also probe the interior of the mind itself, and can thus use the mental condition as fuel for the mind's own consumption. The mind of the self-conscious artist appears, then, self-consuming, impelled to destroy itself through the relentless activity of the inner eye.

Further images reinforce this impression by illustrating what Kenner calls the eye's "rhetoric of tyranny".[66] Assuming the form of intense searchlights, the eyes of malevolent *chercheurs* torment the Unnamable and Worm: "ils me surveillaient à l'aide d'un projecteur" (*L'Innommable*, p. 63); "Et ces lumières, ce sont peut-être celles qu'ils braquent sur lui, de temps en temps, pour se rendre compte des progrès qu'il fait" (p. 140; "leurs longues lampes... leurs puissantes lampes, allumées, braquées sur le dedans", p. 160). Clearly the powerful 'eyes' of the anonymous observers are focused upon the inner being where all one's deepest sufferings can be discovered. In *Play*, the probing of a single spotlight compels the three characters to speak of their past woes and finally to question the nature of their ruthless tormentor. Describing it at first as a "mere eye",[67] the male protagonist believes a moment later that the spotlight is looking for something in his face: "Some truth. In my eyes" (p. 61). But he soon rejects this analysis and concludes that it is but "Mere eye. No mind" (p. 61). Finally, he wonders: "Am I as much as... being seen?" (p. 61). The "unique inquisitor" (p. 62) is, in fact, only a light which makes the three players visible. In itself it performs a very ordinary function; yet through its effect on the characters it reveals much, for "when a bright light focuses on them, they respond according to the promptings of their consciousnesses. Their bright inquisitor asks nothing, but by its glaring vacancy compels human thought to fill the void."[68] The three speakers interpret the light as consciousness of self persistently searching for the truth of one's situation. The spotlight simply embodies the self-perception which in reality functions from within the mind. Thus, the compelling force, though represented by an external device here, has an inner origin, as one of the two women finally realizes: "Nothing being asked at all. No one asking me for anything at all" (p. 56). One perceives only "the penetrating

---

[66]   Kenner, "Progress Report", 62.
[67]   *Play*, 60; referred to hereafter in the text with the appropriate page number in parentheses.
[68]   Moore, "Some Night Thoughts", 537.

light"[69] of one's own inner perception. Still, though not alien, its power is something to be reckoned with.

Represented in earlier works as unendurable brightness, constant self-perception is always merciless. In *Mercier et Camier* a sunny day has painful connotations: "From a sky of pitiless blue the sun darts its ardent rays" (p. 8). Even the night seems too bright for the narrator of *Comment c'est*: "après le soleil la lune lumière toujours jour et nuit" (p. 105). There is no letup; the light of self-consciousness is always lit. Winnie in *Happy Days* suffers endlessly, for in her world day and night are literally one. Only the ringing of the authoritative bells gives meaning to time. Unable to escape the incessant brightness by crawling into a hole (as Willie does), Winnie, imprisoned in the earth, is pitifully exposed to both the unabating elements and her own lucidity. "Against the great sun that shines upon her", writes Edith Kern, "(or is it against the scorching light of her own understanding?) her parasol is but a touching picture of inadequacy."[70] Indeed, there can be no protection from the blazing light of lucidity. Like the color white, brilliant light suggests "la transparence totale du regard intérieur, une nudité écrasante, une brûlure solaire, l'absence de toute ombre protectrice, de toute trace de souillure vivante".[71] Furthermore, particularly in the case of Winnie, it would seem that "la vie est destinée à se dessécher, à se purifier dans le brasier de la lucidité".[72] Even in one of the most recent pieces of fiction, "Lessness", the dazzling illumination of emptiness remains: "Little void mighty light four square all white blank planes all gone from mind."[73] Recalling how the mind of the narrator-hero is stripped in the attempt to achieve pure consciousness,[74] one can see that this image represents the activity of intense self-consciousness in an emptied mind. Circumscribed in scope, the consciousness of the diminished Beckettian hero can perceive only the mental scene, and, in effect, only itself, since every other mental faculty has been eliminated. Thus, the light in the image functions as consciousness, for "la conscience, comme l'affirmait déjà Monsieur Teste, plonge ses racines dans la clarté, se nourrit de lumière mais c'est une lumière 'froide,' qui brûle sans réchauffer".[75] More, the sense of identity itself assumes the form of light; as Esslin notes, "Our own consciousness, our awareness of ourselves is a small pool of

[69] Dukore, "Beckett's Play, *Play*", 21.
[70] Kern, "Beckett's Knight of Infinite Resignation", 51.
[71] Onimus, *Beckett*, 51.
[72] *Ibid.*
[73] "Lessness", 36.
[74] See Chapter 4.
[75] Onimus, *Beckett*, 51-52.

light surrounded by a vast outer darkness."[76] One thinks of Krapp as an example of this image, for he and his machine "occupy a circle of bright light surrounded by darkness".[77] Pursuing his past and present selves in the light, Krapp seeks to evade himself through the drinks he takes in the darkness. For him, "light means identity and consciousness"[78] and though he moves back and forth from light to darkness, he can never remain long in the realm of self-evasion. The darkness can never overwhelm the pool of light, for one "cannot extinguish the light of consciousness".[79] To obliterate the brightness, one would have to destroy oneself. Speaking to the spotlight in *Play*, one of the women says: "Quand tu t'éteins – et moi avec."[80] Her use of the familiar form of address underlines the intimate rapport between herself and the light. It is an essential part of her being – her very awareness of being. When it fails, she too will cease to exist.

Intricately combined in a final series of images, the inner eye and the penetrating light illustrate together the intensity of consciousness in the narrator-hero. Responding to his own question "Et dans le crâne est-ce le vacuum?" (*Malone*, p. 87), Malone describes how he lets go his hold on exterior reality by closing his eyes: "Et si je ferme les yeux, les ferme vraiment, comme ne le peuvent les autres, mais comme moi je le peux, car il y a des limites à mon impuissance, alors quelquefois mon lit se soulève et vogue à travers les airs, au gré des remous, comme un fétu, et moi dedans" (p. 88). He seeks to escape in this way not only his physical handicaps but also, if only temporarily, his own self-perception. Providing more details of this unusual kind of voluntary blindness, he continues: "Ce n'est pas une question de paupières heureusement, c'est comme qui dirait l'âme qu'il faut aveugler, cette âme qu'on a beau nier, perçante, guetteuse, inquiète, tournant dans sa cage comme dans une lanterne dans la nuit sans ports ni bateaux ni matière ni entendement" (p. 88). Both perceiving eye and probing illumination, the searchlight here acts as consciousness itself, as awareness of being, undeniable self-perception. With his attention barred from outside distractions, Malone can perceive only his own 'mindscape'. Consequently the inner eye, referred to here as the soul, discerns about it nothing but emptiness, the immaculate void of the hero's stripped mind. Further, like the ever vigilant beam from the lighthouse, Malone's self-perception never weakens in intensity or persistence. End-

[76]   Esslin, "Godot and his Children", 140-141.
[77]   Tindall, *Samuel Beckett*, 44.
[78]   *Ibid.*
[79]   Glicksberg, "Samuel Beckett's World of Fiction", 45.
[80]   *Comédie*, 21; in the English original, *Play*, 53: "When you go out – and I go out."

lessly surveying the barren horizon of his mind, its piercing watchfulness continuously perceives nothingness and absence, its own principal attributes. Moran, describing his inner state, uses similar images when referring to the mind: "Je me promenais dans mon esprit, lentement, notant chaque détail du labyrinthe, aux sentiers aussi familiers que ceux de mon jardin et cependant toujours nouveaux, déserts à souhait ou animés d'étranges rencontres.... Incompréhensible esprit, tantôt mer, tantôt phare" (*Molloy*, p. 164). Perceiver and perceived, the concentrated consciousness necessarily plays the double role of sea and searchlight. Recurring in the *Textes*, this image represents finally all of experience for the author-hero: "c'est comme un morceau de mer, sous le phare qui passe, de mer qui passe, sous le phare qui passe" (p. 204). Never constant, consciousness cannot fix upon itself; watery surface or rotating beam, it is forever changing, forever moving. Still, pictured as ever watchful eye or inextinguishable light, it seems a likely source for the creative compulsion. The artist, like Memnon, must respond to the light of his own self-perception. His intense self-consciousness never ceases to perceive and pursue its own terrible nothingness; and this dreadful inner vision gives rise to the overwhelming urge to speak. Self-perception, then, demands utterance; self-consciousness commands expression.

Before one can determine the rapport between self-perception and expression, however, one must first define clearly the inner source of the compelling voice. Though it seems to serve, as the inner eye or light, the function of impelling creative activity, one cannot assume that the voice is simply one with the visual images and that, consequently, it arises from the same inner source. Still, abundant evidence indicates that indeed the voice does spring from consciousness. Referring to his efforts to gain Murphy's attention through speech, Ticklepenny defines the voice as "the vocal stream issuing from the soul through the lips" (*Murphy*, p. 85). Two pages later the narrator reinforces the importance of this definition by echoing the poet: "It is hard to say where the fault lies in the case of Ticklepenny, whether with the soul, the stream or the lips, but certainly the quality of his speech is most wretched" (p. 87). Applying the reference in *Murphy* to *L'Innommable*, Ross Chambers speaks of "the voice issuing from the soul of the Unnamable".[81] This interpretation of the inner source appears justified when one considers further images from the earlier novel. Analysing Miss Dew's failure to tempt the sheep with her lettuce, the narrator speculates: "Car Mademoiselle Dew, n'étant pas l'Amour, ne pouvait se vanter de ne faire qu'un avec ce qu'elle dispensait, et elle

[81] Chambers, "Beckett's Brinkmanship", 155.

croyait que son insuccès venait de ce qu'il résonnait quelque part dans les sombres tréfonds de la conscience ovine une voix leur disant qu'elle, Mademoiselle Dew, n'était pas de la laiture."[82] Finally, Murphy himself, hearkening to a voice when he is face to face with Mr. Endon (pp. 249-250), responds in reality to an inspiration, an impelling mental force acting from within. At the conclusion of the hero's brief, compulsive speech, the narrator remarks: "That was the whole extent of the little afflatulence" (p. 250). As in the lighthouse image in *Malone meurt*, the soul represents one's sense of identity, one's awareness of being, one's consciousness of self. The creative compulsion issues from it, making itself felt as an inner voice which demands outer expression. Thus, the two principal images for the compelling force have similar though clearly distinct roles in the creative experience: the inner eye perceives and the inner voice communicates that perception. The vision takes on the form of works as it is transmitted to the writer.

That the voice does in fact originate in consciousness, that is it indeed the voice of consciousness itself, appears undeniable in the later novels. Molloy, for instance, speaks of a sound which seems to coincide with life: "cette rumeur qui se lève à la naissance et même avant... cet insatiable *Comment faire? Comment faite?*" (*Molloy*, p. 12). As Dieter Wellershoff says, "always... inside him a voice keeps talking, a voice that cannot stop".[83] One with existence, having begun its babble even before birth, the inner voice accompanies Molloy in his extreme old age and decrepitude. When he is little more than consciousness of self, the voice remains. Clearly, then, it can have no source but consciousness. In response to this same sort of rumor he tells his story: "En fait je ne me disais rien du tout, mais j'entendais une rumeur, quelque chose de changé dans le silence, et j'y prêtais l'oreille, à la manière d'un animal j'imagine, qui tressaille et fait la mort. Et alors, quelquefois il naissait confusément en moi une sorte de conscience, ce que j'exprime en disant, Je me disais, etc., ou, Molloy, n'en fais rien, ou, C'est le nom de votre maman? dit le commissaire, je cite de mémoire" (p. 135). Coincident with existence, the voice of consciousness steadily pursues its course and so compels the conscious being to speech. Describing his mother's condition, Molloy refers to "ce babil cliquetant, qui ne devait s'arrêter que pendant ses courts instants d'inconscience" (p. 24). A respite from the agony of forced expression comes only with unconsciousness, when for a moment the inner eye is blinded and, consequently, the inner voice stilled. Even Lousse, Molloy's

---

[82] *Murphy* (Paris, 1965), 76.
[83] Wellershoff, "Failure of an Attempt at De-Mythologization", 94.

overbearing hostess-warden, talks incessantly: "Et elle n'arrêtait pas de parler" (p. 72). Indeed, her constant babbling gives him the impression that "plus rien n'existât que cette voix monotone" (p. 71). But, as noted earlier, Molloy comes to rely on his own inner voice which remains with him to the very end. As Patrick Bowles explains it, "Molloy in his limbo of disintegration, listens to a voice, that speaks to him... that seems to be somewhere in him, enjoins him to do certain things, and it is this voice, deprived in the end of a subject and talking exclusively of its own existence and how it is able to talk, and the nature of this activity, that with Molloy becomes the reassuring thing on which his existence rests."[84] Moran, too, relies greatly upon his inner voice. Describing his first experience of it, he reveals its source: "Ce que j'entendais, dans mon for intérieur sans doute, à l'acoustique si mauvaise, c'était une première syllabe" (p. 174).[85]

The close rapport between the eye of consciousness and the voice appears in L'Innommable, where the tormentors' lamps produce both light and sound. Looking forward to a time when these may no longer disturb the dark stillness, the narrator says: "Mais les lampes sans servants ne brilleront pas toujours, au contraire, elles s'éteindront, peu à peu, sans servants pour les recharger, *elles se tairont*, à la fin" (pp. 160-161; my emphasis). The babbling voice depends upon the perceiving eye; bereft of perception it would be stilled. As long as one is conscious, however, a steady stream of words fills the mind; and one is compelled to give utterance to them. Describing the plight of the Unnamable, Onimus writes: "je ne puis me taire et je ne me tairai jamais, tant que j'aurai les yeux ouverts. C'est une fatalité de ma conscience."[86] One with consciousness, the inner voice is ever present and seems to go on forever, since consciousness cannot conceive of its own nonbeing. In fact, the voice itself represents consciousness, for it is "une voix qui ne s'arrête jamais" (p. 168), a vital sign which verifies that consciousness is functioning. In the Textes, the experience of the voice dates from the very beginning of the author's existence and is conceived as going on forever: "ce sont les mots qu'elle emploie, qui a toujours parlé, qui parlera toujours" (p. 216). For the narrator of Comment c'est, who realizes that he exists only in words, the voice is the source of life itself: "la voix quaqua d'où je tiens ma vie ces bribes de vie en moi" (p. 137); "d'elle que je tiens tout" (p. 153). Later he proposes to "en finir avec cette voix autant dire cette vie" (p. 173). At the very end,

---

[84]   Bowles, "How Samuel Beckett Sees the Universe", 1011.
[85]   In the English translation, Molloy (New York, 1965), 112: "What I heard in my soul I suppose, where the acoustics are so bad".
[86]   Onimus, Beckett, 69.

though he denies most of what he has just said, he insists that the voice is his own: "moi oui seul oui avec ma voix oui mon murmure... ma voix... à moi tout seul" (p. 176). Deprived of everything else, he is still conscious and the persistent voice whose dictation he utters comes from within himself. Expression, then, is existence for this narrator-hero; were he no longer to speak, his silence would indicate that consciousness itself had gone at last. The inner voice, evidence of consciousness, compels the outer voice, sign of life. As the narrator of "Assez" explains the relationship between himself and his muttering companion, "Hors de portée de sa voix j'étais hors de sa vie" (*Têtes*, p. 34). Reinforcing the intimate connection between the voice (inner and outer) and existence, the radio plays demonstrate how the human voice reaches out of "the interiority of a human person, with the thrust of [one's] uniqueness, expressing, pressing out, so much as may be... that sense of [being]"[87] which belongs to no other. Speaking of *Embers* in particular, Kenner says: "the second radio play... summarizes for the ear the internal world from which reaches the unique voice."[88] Indeed, in those works which are meant to be perceived through the ear alone the vital link between speaking and being is evident. Here more clearly than ever "existence and expression coalesce amorphously but eternally".[89]

The voice, then, is a comprehensive image for the creative compulsion, for it represents not only the irresistible prodding of self-consciousness but also the kind of expression which the compelling force demands of the Beckettian hero. According to Esslin, "the voice, the insistent, storytelling voice, is the most characteristic and the most consistent of Beckett's images, the one which most completely sums up the artist".[90] Welling up from inner depths, "the spontaneously emerging voice... is the [writer's] raw material".[91] Attentive to his own inner voice, the narrator-hero conceives everything in words, creates with words, and exists only in the words he himself expresses. In fact, verbal perception is so basic to the writer that he encounters difficulties in attempting to conceive of any other kind of inspiration. Calling attention to the difference between pictorial and verbal perception, Beckett writes: "Nous avons affaire chez Abraham van Velde à un effort d'aperception si exclusivement et farouchement pictural que *nous autres, dont les réflexions sont tout en murmures*, ne le

[87]   Kenner, *A Critical Study*, 183.
[88]   *Ibid.*
[89]   Cohn, *The Comic Gamut*, 144.
[90]   Esslin, "Looking for Beckett", 923.
[91]   Esslin, "Introduction", 11.

concevons qu'avec peine, ne le concevons qu'en l'entraînant dans une sorte de ronde syntaxique, qu'en le plaçant dans le temps." [92] For the author, consciousness consists of words. As Proust explains it, "le talent d'un grand écrivain, [ce] n'est qu'un instinct religieusement écouté au milieu du silence, imposé à tout le reste, un instinct perfectionné et compris." [93] Alone with consciousness of self, one perceives the essential truth of one's condition. Alluding to Proust's experience, Onimus speaks of this consciousness of being as the "*je* profond, dont on peut capter élusivement la présence dans le silence, dans la solitude, quand on est couché au fond d'un réduit capitonné, d'une chambre de liège, à l'écoute des voix intérieures".[94] Yet, as Mme Lamont notes, "monologue, dialogue, pour Beckett il n'y a qu'une seule voix".[95] Though sometimes perceived as an indistinct *rumeur* (*Molloy*, p. 12) and sometimes as a choir (*Watt*, pp. 33-35, 253-254), the inner discourse is most often attributed to a single voice, a voice which is clearly the expressive faculty of consciousness. Stripped of every other mental power and deprived of almost all physical faculties, the narrator-hero nevertheless continues to create, driven on by what can be nothing but intense self-consciousness. "What one senses through all Beckett's work", writes Mayoux, "are groping impulses, obscure, confused, inexplicable volitions, which animate the formless earthworm, impel the foolish mole, and move to spasms of illusory life the headless body of an eel. It is the presence of a temporal existence in these tatters of bodies without object, a special kind of ghost that hovers before him and before us, an obstinate and indestructible consciousness, a persistent voice which nothing seems able to silence completely, not even the extinction of its miserable body." [96] Robert Abirached, too, emphasizes the tenacity of the essential inner voice when describing the Beckettian hero: "en un mot, c'est un détritus d'homme ou de femme qui croupit avec détachement, mais l'essentiel subsiste en lui, cette voix qui couvre le bruit du monde, transcrite avec ses ratés et ses lapsus, annulant sans relâche ce qu'elle vient de prononcer, et qui est le souffle même de la conscience." [97] Voice and consciousness are inseparable; as long as one endures, the other must also. Thus, the narrator-hero, bereft of imagination, memory, and the means to busy himself with physical activity, be-

---

[92] "La Peinture des van Velde", 351-352; my emphasis.
[93] Proust, *Le Temps retrouvé*, *Œuvres complètes*, 7, pt. 2 (Paris: Nouvelle Revue Française, 1932), 45.
[94] Onimus, *Beckett*, 26.
[95] Lamont, "La Farce métaphysique", 105.
[96] Mayoux, "Samuel Beckett and Universal Parody", 90.
[97] Abirached, "La Voix tragique", 86.

comes the victim of his own self-consciousness, the unwilling audience for his own inner voice. As Mme Serreau writes, "L'homme reste seul, offert au néant, conscient seulement de ses souffrances indicibles et du néant qui les couronne. Et cette conscience c'est une voix, la voix de l'écrivain, celle de Beckett." [98]

[98]   Serreau, "Samuel Beckett", 99.

6. THE CIRCLE OF PERCEPTION AND EVASION

Inner eye and origin of the inner voice, consciousness is the source of the creative compulsion. The overwhelming, irresistible force which demands the impossible of the artist has its roots in the nature of consciousness itself. One cannot ignore the inner voice; on the contrary, one must do as it dictates in spite of one's inadequacy, for to hear and heed the voice of consciousness is a condition of being. As Olga Bernal explains, "Le discours se fera, la voix ne se taira pas tant qu'il y aura conscience... il n'y a qu'un seul moyen pour mettre fin au bavardage... et c'est la suppression de la conscience."[1] But consciousness cannot be suppressed, though every other faculty, both physical and mental, deteriorate and wither away. "Consciousness alone", says Mayoux, "crouching in the heart of being and refusing to rationalize action, escapes and endures."[2] Noting "the immaterial aspect of consciousness which incessantly renews itself in ever-recurring self-perception", Esslin goes on to say: "Consciousness cannot conceive of itself as nonexisting and is therefore only conceivable as unlimited, without end."[3] Unable to imagine the possibility of freedom from the tyranny of consciousness, Winnie laments: "There always remains something. (*Pause.*) Some remains. (*Pause.*) If the mind were to go. (*Pause.*) It won't of course. (*Pause.*) Not quite. (*Pause.*) Not mine" (*Happy Days*, p. 52). Echoing her, one of the women in *Play* twice expresses amazement at the persistence of consciousness: "How the mind works still!" (p. 54); "How the mind works still to be sure!" (p. 56). As Kenneth Hamilton observes, "the flux of life yields no certainties upon which consciousness can depend with security. Yet consciousness is not allowed to die".[4] Representing the seemingly immortal consciousness is the head, the essential part of every Beckettian hero. "Ma tête mourra en dernier",

---

1 Bernal, *Langage et fiction dans le roman de Beckett*, 193-194.
2 Mayoux, "The Theatre of Samuel Beckett", 145.
3 Esslin, "Introduction", 7.
4 Hamilton, "Negative Salvation in Samuel Beckett", 111.

predicts Malone (*Malone*, p. 208), whose death coincides precisely with his last utterances. In the *Textes*, too, the head remains long after the passing of the body: "la tête est en retard, sur le reste... ou bien elle continue toute seule, toute seule ses vieilles erres" (p. 197). For the hero of *Comment c'est*, nothing is left but the head and the voice which inhabits it: "après Pim plus que ça le souffle dans la tête plus qu'une tête rien dedans presque rien que le souffle" (p. 127); "en moi dans le caveau blancheur d'os des bribes" (p. 161). That the head, or consciousness which it represents, is the element upon which the hero's existence depends is clear from statements in the later fiction. As one hero in the *Textes* says, "le crâne, c'est là l'entendement, sans quoi nenni" (p. 144); and the narrator of *Comment c'est* elaborates: "l'âme est de rigueur l'intelligence aussi un minimum de chaque" (p. 17). Furthermore, it is precisely this mental equipment which outlasts even the means for its expression; as the Unnamable remarks, "l'âme [est] notoirement à l'abri des ablations et délabrements" (*L'Innommable*, p. 88). Of the head, he says: "voilà la partie de moi dont j'ai le mieux saisi et retenu la description" (p. 81). Even the anonymous creature described in "Bing" possesses a head: "Tête boule bien haute yeux bleu pâle presque blanc fixe face silence dedans (*Têtes*, p. 6 and passim).

Consciousness, then, enduring when all else has vanished, becomes the object of its own intense activity. With all exterior distractions removed, it has access only to itself. As a result, the existence of the diminished narrator-hero is concentrated in essential and incessant self-perception. This extreme experience of self recalls examples of the tendency toward self-contemplation in the earlier works. In "Le Calmant", for instance, the hero reports: "Tous les mortels que je voyais étaient seuls et comme noyés en eux-mêmes" (*Nouvelles*, p. 62). Describing a man with whom he converses briefly, the narrator says: "Vu de près il me semblait plutôt normal, enfin, à part cet air de reflux vers son centre que j'ai déjà signalé" (p. 63). In an attempt to explain this general kind of self-centeredness, Robert Torrance observes: "For modern man, more and more isolated, more and more forced inward upon himself, the physical world beyond him has come to seem increasingly unreal, contact with it increasingly impossible."[5] Still, is it not essentially the human condition itself which limits the scope of consciousness, permitting it to focus intently only upon the self? Even before losing all his faculties, the Beckettian man realizes that he is the center of his own perception. Malone, for example, avows: "Le large n'est plus éclairé que par reflets, c'est sur moi que mes sens sont braqués" (*Ma-*

---

[5] Torrance, "Modes of Being and Time in *Godot*", 94.

lone, pp. 20-21). Later in the *Textes,* where little remains but the vigilant eye of consciousness, one narrator speaks of seeing himself: "je me vois, vautré, les yeux fermés" (p. 131). The limited range of consciousness is felt most acutely in *Comment c'est.* His mind purged of memory and imagination, the narrator can only resign himself to "vivre donc sans visiteurs... sans autres histoires que les miennes autres bruits que les miens autre silence que celui que je dois rompre si je n'en veux plus c'est avec ça que je dois durer" (p. 16). Later he reinforces his resolution with the remark: "plus d'autre monde pour moi que le mien" (p. 39). The Beckettian hero, immured in the labyrinth of his own self-consciousness,[6] demonstrates "what happens to the mind when the mind has nothing to contemplate but its own symmetry".[7] Yet "self-perception is a basic condition of our being; we exist because, and as long as, we perceive ourselves".[8] According to Berkeley's dictum, "'*esse* is *percipi*,' that is, the very existence of corporeal objects consists in their being perceived".[9] Isolated from the perception of others, one must necessarily perceive himself if he is to exist; were he to lose the faculty for self-perception – consciousness – , he would cease to be. For the Beckettian creator, as has been shown, consciousness is the source of the creative compulsion, the source of the incessant inner voice which demands expression for what is perceived. Thus, when self-perception remains the only activity possible for consciousness, the voice requires the endless retelling of the self's own story, the endless reflection of the self's circumscribed condition. The compulsion to create, then, has its source in self-perception. Furthermore, since consciousness of self coincides with existence, compulsive creation is the main condition of the later heroes' experience. Even Murphy responds compulsively to self-perception. Looking deeply into Mr. Endon's eyes, "Murphy could see... in the cornea, horribly reduced, obscured and distorted, his own image"; and "seeing himself stigmatised in those eyes that did not see him", he is compelled to speak in spite of his natural reluctance to do so (*Murphy,* p. 249). Confronted with one's infinite gratuitousness, one has no choice. Thus, Winnie, deprived of access to her possessions in Act II, "is turned back upon herself... is driven to her 'story'".[10] The terrible revelations

---

6 Macksey, "The Artist in the Labyrinth", 243; cf. *Molloy,* 164: "Je me promenais dans mon esprit, lentement, notant chaque détail du labyrinthe, aux sentiers aussi familiers que ceux de mon jardin et cependant toujours nouveaux, déserts à souhait ou animés d'étranges rencontres."
7 Hassan, *The Literature of Silence,* 129.
8 Esslin, "Introduction", 3.
9 T. E. Jessop, *George Berkeley* (London: Longmans, Green & Co., 1959), 24.
10 Cohn, *The Comic Gamut,* 256.

communicated by the voice of self-perception cannot be ignored or forgotten. They demand expression so relentlessly that the later, more self-
conscious heroes can speak only of themselves and of their unbearable
situation. The result in *Comment c'est* is a startling self-portrait with
universal implications: "s'ils me voient je suis un monstre des solitudes"
(p. 16). Reduced to the essential human condition – perception of self – ,
the solitary narrator represents what all men are at the core. An isolated
creature whose only assurance of existence is his own self-consciousness,
this forlorn hero illustrates more forcefully than any of his predecessors
how man exists without a *raison d'être* and how ordinarily he seeks to
ignore the unfathomable nothingness at the center of being. The narrator
here, deprived even of light to see within himself, is aware of the great
emptiness with which he is immured: "la petite voûte... le petit caveau
vide fermé huit faces d'une blancheur d'os s'il y avait de la lumière une
flammette tout serait blanc" (p. 155). Speaking of his visit to New York,
Beckett remarks upon the look of great hostility which he saw in the faces
of men on the street: "But, of course, that's inevitable. It is the weight of
every man's fear and emptiness that produces this look. Somewhere he
must know that self-perception is the most frightening of all human observations. He must know that when man faces himself, he is looking into the
abyss."[11] To perceive the truth of one's condition, then, is a terrifying
experience. Yet, so long as one is conscious he must deal with self-perception. For the artist, the problem is an especially difficult one, since endless
self-perception brings with it the relentless compulsion to create, making
existence a continuous, agonizing struggle with the creative dilemma.

   Lucid self-consciousness is a constant source of suffering for the Beckettian hero. Dreading to discover the truth about himself, the Unnamable
avows: "la vérité enfin sur moi me ravagera" (*L'Innommable*, p. 127). Apparently frightened by what he sees within himself, Mercier stares fixedly,
"comme avec effroi".[12] Self-knowledge torments and overwhelms its pos-
sessor, for it constantly reminds him that he must die. As Jean-Marie Domenach says, "La connaissance est tragique en ce qu'elle nous révèle... des vé-
rités dont nous avions peur, qui prennent notre vie et peuvent la briser... le
savoir authentique nous rapproche de la mort."[13] Having its origin in the
mind, the intense agony of perception often takes the form of an unbear-

---

[11]   Beckett quoted by Gruen, "Nobel Prize Winner, 1969", 210.
[12]   Fletcher, "Sur un roman inédit", 140; cited from a copy of the original typescript,
this passage does not appear in the edition of the novel published in 1970 by Editions
de Minuit.
[13]   Domenach, *Le Retour du tragique*, 18.

able headache. Finding that he cannot continue the trek with Camier, Mercier denies that his legs or feet are to blame for his weakness. "C'est plutôt la tête", he asserts (*Mercier et Camier*, p. 175); and when Camier offers to help him walk, Mercier insists that such assistance would be of no use: "C'est dans la tête, je te dis, dit Mercier" (p. 175). As self-consciousness increases from one hero to the next, the cerebral affliction becomes more acute. In *Malone meurt*, the male nurse Lemuel suffers from "les affres de la réflexion": "Ecorché vif du souvenir, l'esprit grouillant de cobras n'osant ni rêver ni penser et en même temps impuissant à s'en défendre" (p. 177). Possessed by thought, compelled to experience the horrors which populate his mind, he reacts violently to lessen his mental torment: "La douleur physique, par contre, semblait lui être d'un précieux secours, et un jour, relevant la jambe de son pantalon, il montra à Macmann son tibia couvert de bleus, de cicatrices et d'écorchures. Puis sortant prestement d'une poche intérieure un marteau il s'en asséna, au beau milieu des anciennes blessures, un coup si violent qu'il tomba à la renverse" (pp. 177-178). The pain of the cure is but a dim reflection of that occasioned by the malady itself. Always keenly aware of the source of his distress, Lemuel applies his remedy where it seems most warranted: "Mais la partie qu'il se frappait le plus volontiers, avec ce même marteau, c'était la tête, et cela se conçoit, car c'est là une partie osseuse aussi, et sensible, et facile à atteindre, et c'est là-dedans qu'il y a toutes les saloperies et pourritures, alors on tape dessus plus volontiers que sur la jambe par exemple, qui ne vous a fait rien, c'est humain" (p. 178). Malone, too, comes to suffer intolerable headaches from which he thinks he may at last die: "Ma tête. Elle est en feu, pleine d'huile bouillante. De quoi vais-je partir enfin? D'un transport au cerveau? Ce serait le comble. Comme douleur, ma foi, c'est quasiment insoutenable. Migraine incandescente" (p. 189). In *L'Innommable*, both the narrator and his persona Worm experience "la tête qui peine" (p. 126), "le feu à la cervelle" (p. 128). Described by the epithet "thèque [treasure-house] du mal" (p. 137), a head is essential to Worm's existence and consequent suffering: "Il lui a poussé une tête, depuis l'oreille, pour qu'il enrage mieux.... La tête est là, collée à l'oreille, remplie de rage seulement.... C'est un transformateur, où le bruit se fait rage et épouvante, sans le secours de la raison" (p. 141). Sudden, blinding rages afflict the narrator of "From an Abandoned Work", who says of them: "No, there's no accounting for it, there's no accounting for anything, with a mind like the one I always had, always on the alert against itself" (p. 141).

In the drama, too, the pain of self-perception is clearly felt as originating

within the head. Taunting the protagonist in the television play *Eh Joe*,
the voice of a woman speaks of his mind as "that penny farthing hell...
where you think this [her voice] is coming from"; and she continues:
"That's where you heard your father... Isn't that what you told me?...
Started in on you one June night and went on for years... On and off...
Behind the eyes."[14] Here the inner voice is dramatized. Indeed, it is the
only speaker in the play. Haunted by the people in his past, the helpless
hero can do nothing but undergo the harangues which their memory stirs
up in his mind. In *Happy Days*, Winnie enveloped by the glare of her lucid
self-consciousness, seems to suffer even more than most other Beckettian
heroes. Compelled into consciousness by the ruthless bell for waking, she
dares not drift off to sleep before the bell for sleep rings. If she does seek
refuge in unconsciousness before the appointed hour, the bell for waking
prevents her escape. Its piercing wound is like the penetrating gaze of the
inner eye; and she perceives it as a sharp, deep pain: "The bell. (*Pause*.)
It hurts like a knife. (*Pause*.) A gouge" (p. 54). Tormented by this same
kind of unwavering self-consciousness, O in the scenario *Film* concentrates
all his energy in the effort to shake off painful lucidity. When at last,
apparently successful, he falls asleep in his rocking chair, he must suffer
as brutal an awakening as Winnie. The gaze of his own self-perception
pierces his sleep, and he is compelled to confront himself.[15] His face reveals
the painfulness of the experience, for it bears "an expression only to be
described as corresponding to an agony of perceivedness" (p. 16). Having
carefully eliminated one by one all other possible perceivers, O is left
alone with the only perceiving eye which he cannot veil – the inner eye of
consciousness. He is forced, in the end, to submit to that very pain which
he has tried so earnestly to avoid throughout the film. Paralysed by the
penetrating gaze of self-perception, he cannot turn away from the truth
of his condition. The face which he beholds reveals with poignant accuracy
the nature of his anguish: "It is O's face (with patch) but with very different expression, impossible to describe, neither severity nor benignity, but
rather acute *intentness*. A big nail is visible near left temple" (p. 47).[16]
Surely there could be no more striking image for the agony of self-perception, for the incessant throbbing pain which plagues so many of
Beckett's heroes.

Yet the artist-hero prefers the pain of lucidity to the illusory comfort

---

[14]   *Eh Joe*, 37.
[15]   *Film*, 41-45; referred to hereafter in the text with the appropriate page number in
parentheses.
[16]   Beckett's emphasis.

of willful blindness. Indeed, the suffering which comes from self-perception is one with the creative compulsion, for "it is pain that presses silence
into speech and presses speech back into silence".[17] Alone and removed
from distractions, the artist is especially vulnerable to this kind of suffering,
since it is "in silence and in stillness [that] the pain of being may be felt".[18]
For the Beckettian heroes, as we have seen, the inner vision of one's truth
demands utterance; "cruelly aware of what is happening to them",[19] they
must talk. But, though it involves a never-ending agony, expression compelled by suffering is highly valued by the narrator of *Comment c'est*:
"pour des comme nous... plus de nourriture dans un cri voire un soupir
arraché à celui dont le silence est le seul bien ou dans la parole extorquée
à qui enfin avait pu en perdre l'usage que n'en offriront jamais les sar-
dines" (p. 173). Though only minimal evidence of consciousness, still a
cry or sigh gives the creator-hero something to be going on with; and this
he must have, since his existence depends entirely upon his continued creation. Even the most incapacitated of creators responds to the pain of self-
perception. In fact, those whose faculties are fewest experience the keenest
self-awareness. As J. R. Moore says of them, "Outrageous suffering
stings them into action, however limited their capacities may have become."[20] The notion that suffering is important to artistic creation is not
new, however. Proust considered the creator's agony essential to art. For
him, the greatness of a work of art depends upon the intensity of suffering
at its source: "on peut presque dire que les oeuvres, comme dans les
puits artésiens, montent d'autant plus haut que la souffrance a plus
profondément creusé le coeur."[21] Paradoxically, sorrow and pain serve
the artist, for they lead him to truth: "Les chagrins sont des serviteurs
obscurs... des serviteurs atroces, impossibles à remplacer et qui par des
voies souterraines nous mènent à la vérité et à la mort."[22] As Beckett
himself writes in *Proust*, "Suffering... opens a window on the real and is
the main condition of the artistic experience" (p. 16). Torn by the dilemma
of obligation and impossibility, relentlessly pursued by terrifying self-
perception, the artist-hero knows little else but anguish. Still, his experience is valuable since it culminates in the revelation of the truth – the
unbearable truth of the human condition. Overwhelmed by his inner vi-

---

[17] Hassan, *The Literature of Silence*, 173.
[18] Hassan, 182.
[19] Pronko, *Avant-garde*, 43.
[20] Moore, "Some Night Thoughts", 537.
[21] Proust, *Le Temps retrouvé, Œuvres complètes*, 7, pt. 2 (Paris: Nouvelle Revue
Française, 1932), 65.
[22] Proust, *Le Temps retrouvé*, 67.

sion, the artist is compelled to give utterance to the voice of his consciousness. The result, according to Onimus, is startling: "Ce balbutiement des
origines a un effet foudroyant: il détruit instantanément les décors de la
culture et laisse pour un instant la lumière pénétrer l'abîme."[23] Yet,
having seen the truth, one instinctively withdraws from it, tries to forget it.
Speaking of the usual reaction to van Velde's paintings, Beckett writes:
"Car c'est bien de cela qu'il s'agit, de ne plus voir cette chose adorable et
effrayante, de rentrer dans le temps, dans la cécité, d'aller s'ennuyer
devant les tourbillons de viande jamais morte et frissonner sous les peu-
pliers."[24] Rejecting that art which reveals the dreadful inescapability of
human nothingness, man turns to illusions – the illusions of immortality
and of enduring natural beauty. Even the artist-hero who is aware of the
value of lucidity seeks a means of escape. As one narrator says after a fall
in the street, "Je ne perdis pas connaissance, moi quand je perdrai connaissance ce ne sera pas pour la reprendre" (*Nouvelles*, p. 74). The Unnamable,
speculating on the reason for Worm's tears, suggests: "peut-être qu'il
pleure, pour ne pas voir" (*L'Innommable*, p. 149). In a still later work, the
hero's remedy for self-perception recalls that of the bruised and battered
Lemuel: "There was a time I tried to get relief by beating my head against
something, but I gave it up" ("From", p. 141). In fact, of the Beckettian
heroes scarcely a one does not invent some means to escape self-consciousness.

Just as painful awareness of one's condition appears in all Beckett's
works, so "the flight from self-perception is one of the recurring themes of
his writing".[25] Face to face with the unbearable truth of oneself, one senses
an enormous "besoin de s'irréaliser",[26] one wants to escape the tyranny
of self-perception and to provoke "la déroute de sa conscience".[27] Like the
willingness to accept ready-made concepts rather than to think for oneself,
the pursuit of self-evasion is "a protective habitual gesture in every man's
continuing primitive project of bad faith, that spontaneous, almost involuntary determination of our being not to know."[28] Any distraction at
all will do as long as it serves to draw man away from himself, "to occupy
him, to amuse him, to help him forget his own pitiable condition".[29]

---

[23]   Onimus, *Beckett*, 17.
[24]   "La Peinture des van Velde", 353.
[25]   Esslin, "Introduction", 4.
[26]   Emile Benveniste, "Le jeu comme structure", *Deucalion* 2, (1947), 167.
[27]   Roger Caillois, *Les Jeux et les hommes: le masque et le vertige* (Paris: Gallimard,
1967), 103.
[28]   Rickels, "Existential Themes in Beckett's *Unnamable*", 146.
[29]   Pronko, *Avant-garde*, 38.

Formulating briefly the escapist philosophy, the narrator of "Le Calmant" declares: "Ce n'est pas moi... mais profitons, profitons" (*Nouvelles*, p. 63). Lying unnoticed in a crowded street, he is at peace: "J'étais bien, abreuvé de noir et de calme, au pied des mortels" (p. 74). In the same way, Mercier and Camier bear each other's company so as not to have to endure alone the struggle with self-perception: "Certes il fallait de la force pour rester avec Camier, comme il en fallait pour rester avec Mercier, mais moins qu'il n'en fallait pour la bataille du soliloque" (*Mercier et Camier*, p. 131). Their efforts to avoid self-contemplation appear to be successful, for near the end of their story Camier observes: "Au fond... on s'est parlé de tout sauf de nous" (p. 206). Interrupting his tale at an early point, Molloy shows his goal to be like that of his predecessors: "Dire que je fais mon possible pour ne pas parler de moi" (*Molloy*, p. 17). Aware of his own past efforts at self-evasion, Moran sees that in his work as a detective he filled his days with frantic, futile activity "dans le seul but de s'étourdir, de pouvoir ne pas faire ce qu'il avait à faire" (*Molloy*, p. 188). Entirely lucid with regard to his present creative activity, Malone admits: "Tout est prétexte, Sapo et les oiseaux, Moll, les paysans, ceux qui dans les villes se cherchent et se fuient, mes doutes qui ne m'intéressent pas, ma situation, mes possessions, prétexte pour ne pas venir au fait, à l'abandon, en levant le pouce, en disant pouce et en s'en allant, sans autre forme de procès, quitte à se faire mal voir de ses petits camarades" (*Malone*, p. 195). Having declared at the outset his intention to tell himself stories in order not to think about his dying, Malone leaves no doubt that he speaks "dans le but de tromper la solitude d'un esprit qui tourne à vide avant l'arrêt final".[30] The Unnamable makes a similar confession, saying that "tout ce qu'il a inventé... était déguisement et faux-semblant, création misérable pour se masquer son histoire à lui, la seule qui mériterait d'être racontée".[31] Recalling the words of Camier and Molloy, the motto which would suit this hero is: "De nobis ipsis silemus" (*L'Innommable*, p. 86). Further, he claims that his inner voice has nothing to say about himself: "Donc rien sur moi. C'est-à-dire aucune relation suivie. De faibles appels, tout au plus, de loin en loin. Ecoute-moi! Reviens à toi!" (p. 100). As Mahood in the jar, he experiences a blissful moment of near nonbeing: "Et souvent je parvenais à ne pas broncher, jusqu'au moment où, n'étant plus, je ne me voyais plus. Instant vraiment exquis" (p. 118). Destined to have some sort of existence, even the creature Worm will learn to flee from himself: "Qu'il découvre tout seul les baumes

---

30 Nadeau, "Samuel Beckett ou le droit au silence", 1275.
31 *Ibid.*

de la fuite de devant soi.... Qu'il ne compte plus que sur lui pour pallier
ce qu'il est, sans qu'il y soit pour rien" (p. 165). In the *Textes*, one hero
while speaking of his keepers reveals the kind of relief he himself would
seek: "Jouent-ils aux cartes, un peu, aux boules, *pour se reposer la tête*,
ont-ils droit à la récréation?" (p. 167; my emphasis). With a similar aim
in mind, the narrator of "From an Abandoned Work" describes how he
tries to ward off the barrage of his uncontrollable thoughts: "I strive with
them as best I can, quickening my step when they come on, tossing my
head from side to side and up and down, staring agonizedly at this and
that, increasing my murmur to a scream, these are helps" (p. 144). Almost
any exterior activity will help a little to alleviate self-perception, and anything at all is better than nothing – the nothing which inner vision constantly reveals. Thus, the narrator of *Comment c'est* says of his story: "ces
détails de préférence à rien" (p. 41).

In their efforts to escape nothingness, the Beckettian heroes depend
above all upon words. According to Mme Serreau, life for them is a weary
game "où les mots irremplaçables comme le sang, demeurent le dernier
recours et le dernier courage".[32] Holding on to existence through creation,
these 'players' must at the same time protect themselves from consciousness. Their defense lies in building "a screen of words between themselves
and nothingness",[33] between themselves and their doom, a "fabric of
words whose every syllable is a second gained on eternity".[34] In the drama,
words construct "the simulacrum of a parlor game to fill the otherwise
unendurable void".[35] As William Tindall observes, "no longer a way of
communicating – for that is impossible – talking together, generally at
cross-purposes, is 'occupation... recreation.' Any talk will serve: telling
stories, even contradiction or abuse."[36] Prone to frantic babbling, Vladimir and Estragon agree to control their impulsive talk so as to play at
conversation: "En attendant", suggests Gogo, "essayons de converser
sans nous exalter, puisque nous sommes incapables de nous taire." "C'est
vrai", agrees Didi, "nous sommes intarissables" (*Godot*, p. 105). Yet they
know why they cling to talk: "C'est pour ne pas penser" (p. 105). Fleeing
before the awful truth of their gratuitousness, the two must create an
existence for themselves through their prattle. Satisfied with the result of
their efforts, Gogo says: "On trouve toujours quelque chose, hein, Didi,

[32] Serreau, "Samuel Beckett", 90.
[33] Pronko, *Avant-garde*, 53.
[34] Grossvogel, *Four Playwrights and a Postscript*, 122.
[35] Grossvogel, *Four Playwrights*, 100.
[36] Tindall, *Samuel Beckett*, 10.

pour nous donner l'impression d'exister?" (pp. 116-117). Later Didi, pleased with the relief afforded by their exchange of insults, exclaims: "Comme le temps passe quand on s'amuse!" (p. 128). Passing the time is their principal aim; unable to divert themselves by leaving the desolate spot where Godot has said he will meet them, they have only each other to help put aside the real misery that gnaws at them. While they wait, "they must 'meubler' the void of time and thus prevent the ennui of inanition and the realization of the pain of their physical suffering and loneliness".[37] Anxious to lose himself in feverish activity, Molloy, too, speaks of filling up time: "poursuivons, faisons comme si tout était surgit du même ennui, meublons, meublons, jusqu'au plein noir" (*Molloy*, p. 19). For the hero who depends upon the spoken word, however, the process of self-evasion necessarily involves the presence of another; "la parole vit de l'autre ...le personnage veut un frère... il est le lieu d'un couple."[38] The need to utter words implies the need for a receptive ear. As Janvier explains it, "Parler, mais à quelqu'un. De quelqu'un. Cette nécessité... éclaire l'oeuvre tout entière, depuis *Watt* jusqu'à *Oh les beaux jours*."[39] Totally dependent on Willie's presence, Winnie declares repeatedly that she could not bear "to be alone, I mean prattle away with not a soul to hear" (*Happy Days*, pp. 20-21). As long as he responds, if only infrequently, she feels reassured that something of what she says is being heard. "That", she admits, "is what enables me to go on, go on talking that is" (p. 21). Without his presence, she would be unable to speak, unable to escape the pain of being for even a moment: "what would I do, what *could* I do... between the bell for waking and the bell for sleep? (*Pause*.) Simply gaze before me with compressed lips.... Not another word as long as I drew breath, nothing to break the silence of this place" (p. 21). Afraid above all to be alone with her helplessness, "she owes her happy days"[40] to Willie. As Ruby Cohn says of him, "In spite of his limitations as a conversationalist, his *presence* protects her from becoming Hamm, whose final words are spoken into the silence, or Krapp, who speaks only to his tape recorder. Intermittently but dependably, Willie protects Winnie from the solipsistic self she calls her 'wilderness.'"[41] Indeed, her repeated references to a future moment when Willie will no longer be there to hear her reveal how truly frightened she is of complete solitude: "another

---

[37]   Radke, "The Theater of Samuel Beckett", 60.
[38]   Janvier, *Pour Samuel Beckett*, 69.
[39]   Janvier, 69-70.
[40]   Cohn, *The Comic Gamut*, 257.
[41]   *Ibid*.

time when I must learn to talk to myself a thing I could never bear to do such wilderness" (p. 27); "I say I used to think that I would learn to talk alone. By that I mean to myself, the wilderness" (p. 50). Dark and dreadful, the real horror of her situation is too forbidding to be faced alone. Deprived of her listener, she would doubtless be overwhelmed by the truth within her, that is, by her own lucidity. Paralysed and thoroughly imprisoned, especially in Act II, "there is nothing for Winnie to do but talk, for speech (with her, as with so many others in Beckett's plays and fiction) – when there is another person to talk to – is a way of creating a kind of camp-fire, about which one can huddle by way of staving off the surrounding wilderness." [42] Even when one is alone, speech can help. As Hamm says, "Puis parler, vite, des mots, comme l'enfant solitaire qui se met en plusieurs, deux, trois, pour être ensemble, et parler ensemble, dans la nuit" (*Fin de partie*, pp. 92-93). To cover the silence of one's own nothingness, to veil from sight the inner abyss, one must speak. "Il faut parler", writes Abirached, "jusqu'à en perdre le souffle pour être bien sûr d'exister, puisque toute autre activité humaine est interdite aux enlisés, mais... le simulacre rend présent ce qu'il imite: Winnie ...se crée amoureusement, une à une, les illusions nécessaires pour subsister; il suffit de rompre le silence pour que tout redevienne possible." [43] He continues: "La parole, chez Beckett, c'est le miracle et la prérogative de l'âme: rien de pédant dans cette souffrance exprimée, mais l'enfantin, l'immémorial désarroi de l'être devant le monde et devant soi-même." [44]

One's misery can be forgotten, then in the game of conversation, in talk. "But", according to Mayoux, "artistic creation too is a game, a pastime, a diversion in the Pascalian sense." [45] Whether spoken or written, the word remains the principal means for self-evasion. In the fiction, storytelling serves to divert the narrator-hero from his agony. For example. the hero of *Premier amour* interrupts his narrative to muse: "Mais pourquoi ces détails? Pour retarder l'échéance" (p. 37). In "Le Calmant", the narrator admits from the outset that he intends to tell a story in order to forget his own decomposition: "j'ai trop peur ce soir pour m'écouter pourrir.... Je vais donc me raconter une histoire, je vais donc essayer de me raconter encore une histoire, pour essayer de me calmer" (*Nouvelles*, p. 41). Apparently, he habitually turns to storytelling for relief from self-perception, having been accustomed to the tranquillizing effect of fiction

---

[42]   Scott, *Samuel Beckett*, 122.
[43]   Abirached, "La Voix tragique", 87.
[44]   Abirached, 88.
[45]   Mayoux, "Samuel Beckett and Universal Parody", 86.

since his childhood: "il faut ce soir que ce soit comme dans le conte que mon père me lisait... pour me calmer" (p. 46). An adventure story is what he prefers, something that will occupy and excite his mind, that will effectively draw his attention away from himself. Once involved in his own uneventful tale, the hero indulges in reveries to escape the desolateness which he has only just created. Having arrived at the harbor of the deserted town in his story, he dreams of escape by freighter: "Et je pourrais peut-être me glisser à bord d'un cargo en partance, inaperçu, et partir loin, et passer au loin quelques bons mois, peut-être même une année ou deux, au soleil, en paix, avant de mourir" (p. 50). Tempering his ambition, he then changes his story to provide a more accessible source of evasion. The empty city suddenly fills with a crowd: "Et sans aller jusque-là [à partir en voyage] ce serait bien le diable, dans cette foule grouillante et désabu-sée, si je ne parvenais pas à faire une petite rencontre qui calmât un peu ou échanger quelques mots avec un navigateur par exemple, mots que j'emporterais avec moi, dans ma hutte, pour les ajouter à ma collection" (pp. 50-51). A conversation with a strange sailor would furnish him with words to turn over and over in his mind – words which might help him when again he seeks to tell a story. But what is most striking about both the projected voyage and the improbable meeting is that they constitute evasions within an evasion. While telling a story, the narrator – hero of his tale – imagines still other stories which have as their setting the fictional context of the first. Near the end of his narrative he tries to find diversion in the creatures which briefly populated it: "Quoi encore? Ah oui, mon butin. J'essayai de penser à Pauline, mais elle m'échappa, ne fut éclairée que le temps d'un éclair, comme la jeune femme de tantôt. Sur la chèvre aussi ma pensée glissait désolée, impuissante de s'arrêter" (p. 72). A possible source of further evasion, his own fictional beings are too volatile to serve him as he would like. They slip in and out of his mind, scarcely leaving a trace. In his tale he returns home with some assurance of his own existence: "je remportais chez moi la quasi-certitude d'être encore de ce monde-là aussi, dans un sens" (p. 60), but without gaining much to be going on with. Near the beginning of his narrative Molloy, too, acknowledges his need for stories: "Ce dont j'ai besoin c'est des histoires, j'ai mis longtemps à le savoir" (*Molloy*, p. 16). Careful not to waste his resources, he queries: "Décrirai-je la chambre? Non. J'en aurai l'occasion peut-être plus tard. Quand j'y chercherai asile, à bout d'expédients, toute honte bue" (p. 24). The room where he will eventually come to rest presents a diversion for him too, but he will save it as material for exposition until the moment when he has exhausted every other possibility. To distract himself from self-contemplation, he proposes to keep his mind occupied: "se poser des questions... n'importe quoi qui vous empêche de perdre le fil du songe" (pp. 73-74). He must do this, he says: "afin de me croire toujours là.... J'appelais ça réfléchir. Je réfléchissais presque sans arrêt, je n'osais pas m'arrêter" (p. 74). Similarly, "le petit maigre" in *Malone meurt* "se posait des questions à voix basse, réfléchissait, y répondait" (p. 206). Without such distractions the mind would surely turn inward and gnaw away at itself. To prevent this kind of agonizing self-consciousness, Molloy invents problems for himself, asks himself questions, and tells his story.

Like the hero of "Le Calmant", Malone declares from the start that he intends to divert himself from his moribund condition by telling stories: "On va pouvoir m'enterrer, on ne me verra plus à la surface. D'ici-là je vais me raconter des histoires, si je peux" (*Malone*, p. 9). Of this project Tindall says: "Telling stories to himself is the best way to pass the time, and... the best of games." [46] Having apparently failed in previous attempts to attain a measure of tranquillity through his fictions, Malone feels assured that now he will succeed: "Cette fois je sais où je vais. Ce n'est plus la nuit de jadis, de naguère. C'est un jeu maintenant, je vais jouer. Je n'ai pas su jouer jusqu'à présent" (p. 9). In the midst of his ramblings he interrupts himself to wonder why he goes on talking; but soon he remembers: "Ah oui, c'est pour me désennuyer. Vivre et faire vivre" (p. 37). Prolonging his existence by his creative efforts, Malone produces at the same time a variety of creatures whose tales keep him busy. Yet he "doubts whether he can lose himself in his creations", [47] and he realizes that their existence depends entirely upon his own. Referring to them as "ceux que j'ai appelés à mon secours", he speaks near the end of wanting to place them once more in his notebook "afin qu'ils meurent avec moi" (p. 191). As Ruby Cohn explains, "Malone has moments of hope that these fictional parodies will lead away from himself.... But the hope wanes as he continues to compose." [48] Then in "a final effort to free himself from himself", [49] Malone creates Macmann who practices the same kind of evasion through illusion as does his creator. Pretending that the rain which is drenching him will soon stop, Macmann reveals his close kinship to Malone, who remarks: "C'est là en effet le genre d'histoire qu'il s'est raconté toute sa vie, en se disant, Il est impossible que ça continue encore longtemps" (p. 122). No stranger to this kind of self-deception, Malone implicitly avows

[46]   Tindall, *Samuel Beckett*, 28.
[47]   Cohn, *The Comic Gamut*, 157.
[48]   Cohn, 127.
[49]   Cohn, 128.

his own weakness for fictions. His life "a dreary waiting for death",[50] he seeks to evade the truth of his helplessness; but his stories have done no more to hasten the end of his misery than does Macmann's unwarranted optimism to stop the rain. Still, for the Beckettian hero words are the only recourse.

The attraction of storytelling is so great for the Unnamable that he confesses: "je glisse déjà, avant d'être à la dernière extrémité, vers les secours de la fable" (*L'Innommable*, p. 43). He speaks of his creature Mahood as a source of evasion: "Tiens, je vais me raconter une histoire de Mahood, pour me reposer" (p. 45); and later tells how, as Mahood, his story provides entertainment for his children: "les vieux racontaient ma vie, aux enfants ensommeillés. Ça faisait veillée de chaumière" (p. 64). The secret of escape through creation he reveals still later: "Du moment qu'on peut dire, Un autre est en route, tout va bien" (pp. 133-134). One must avoid the first-person singular at all costs; one must speak of another, some third person, any *other* – anyone but oneself. In this way, one can continue to maintain one's existence in words without being paralysed by fearful self-perception. As one hero in the *Textes* admits, "C'est comme ça que j'ai tenu, jusqu'à l'heure présente" (p. 134). The narrator of "From an Abandoned Work", compelled for a moment to mention his present misery, reverts instinctively to the past which offers him ample means for escape: "No, back to that far day, any far day" (p. 143). Similarly, the protagonist in *Comment c'est* depends upon 'little scenes' to give him material for development: "pour continuer... pour le pouvoir quelques petites scènes" (p. 103). When no exterior distraction presents itself, when one can no longer seek relief outside oneself, the inventions of the fading imagination provide one last oasis before the barren desert of self-consuming consciousness. Thus, in Act II "reduced to moving her facial muscles and vocal chords, Winnie creates again".[51] "What now?" she asks; and then replies: "There is my story of course, when all else fails" (*Happy Days*, p. 54). Henry, too, in *Embers* turns to storytelling for relief from his inner vision; but his 'wilderness' is represented by the sound of the sea. To drown out this sound, which in its persistence is comparable to the inner voice of consciousness, he "tells himself sad stories about the past".[52] Storytelling then, is the last recourse for protagonists of drama and fiction alike.[53] In fact, it is the constant remedy employed by the ra-

---

[50]   Glicksberg, "Samuel Beckett's World of Fiction", 39.
[51]   Cohn, "Play and Players", 48.
[52]   Tindall, *Samuel Beckett*, 40.
[53]   Cf. also Hamm, Dan Rooney, and Krapp.

tional mind to explain away the meaninglessness of existence, to blot out
distressing insights into the self, to veil the inevitability of death, As Mme
Lamont observes, "Irrémédiablement voués à la solitude... nous nous
berçons d'histoires pour passer le temps entre deux abîmes."[54]

Evasion always fails, however, for self-perception is inescapable. Even
O, the most frantic evader of all, finds his efforts doomed. Though he
eliminates all other perceivers, he cannot blind the inner eye of consciousness. "*Esse est percipi*", writes Beckett in the introduction to *Film*; "all
extraneous perception suppressed, animal, human, divine, self-perception
maintains in being. Search of non-being in flight from extraneous perception breaking down in inescapability of self-perception" (p. 11). Summarizing the action in the scenario as "an implacable hunting down",[55]
Kenner goes on to say that the film "is about the self-scrutiny, the agonizing ultimate confrontation no Beckett being can evade".[56] In his description of O's final efforts, Onimus notes: "Bref tout espèce de regard, tout
espèce de reflet doit disparaître. Afin de pouvoir s'oublier totalement, de
pouvoir échapper à soi, ne plus se voir, détruire son passé, il déchire une
liasse de vieilles photos: sera-t-il enfin libre, évadé du cercle de la conscience?"[57] The answer, of course, must be negative. One cannot leave
the circle of consciousness in life. As Winnie knows so well, the brief
moments of "bienheureuse inconscience"[58] cannot last. What O's experience demonstrates, then, is that "plus on cherche à se fuir plus s'affirme
l'intuable fantôme: c'est le moi décollé de lui-même dont le regard s'allume
quand tombe la nuit des sens."[59] Inexhaustible, always available, consciousness is "le point sensible par lequel on a prise sur la créature".[60] A
condition of our very being, self-perception is inescapable. As Sypher
puts it, "Man cannot alienate himself from his own consciousness."[61]
Alone with our self-consciousness, we are like the characters in *Fin de
partie* "enfermés dans un lieu funèbre, dans un camp de la mort",[62] where
"escape frustrated is a picture turned against the wall, windows beyond
reach".[63] For those who have seen the truth of their situation "tout le

---

54 Lamont, "La Farce métaphysique", 110
55 Kenner, "Progress Report", 69.
56 Kenner, 71.
57 Onimus, *Beckett*, 44.
58 Onimus, 104.
59 Onimus, 44.
60 Onimus, 104.
61 Sypher, *Loss of the Self*, 7.
62 Onimus, *Beckett*, 123.
63 Grossvogel, *Four Playwrights*, 110.

reste... n'est que du 'cinéma' pour gens heureux".[64] Hence, the painter, described by Hamm (*Fin de partie*, pp. 62-63), whose gaze penetrates beneath the superficial beauty before him sees aright. He is not mad, "celui qui, dans ce paysage radieux, n'aperçoit qu'un vestige de fête, un voile d'illusions masquant le désert de cendres".[65] Likewise, wedded forever to self-perception, the Beckettian hero knows that the anguish of being cannot be evaded, that indeed "the human condition is self-reflection".[66]

This realization is overwhelming for the author-hero who, though he seeks self-evasion in the creation of fictions, inevitably speaks only of himself and his misery. Momentarily a diversion, artistic creation leads back always to self-contemplation, self-exploration. As Madden, in *Mercier et Camier*, describes the artist's experience of unsuccessful evasion, "On se croit tranquille, bien à l'abri des fâcheux, mais pardon. Car voilà le vieux Madden qui s'amène, au dernier moment. Le train prend de la vitesse, on est enfermé avec lui, rien à faire" (p. 61). Like all diversions, those that Mercier and Camier themselves experience are "de courte durée", and the heroes are soon "frappés par leur situation" again (p. 207). Aware of the futility of attempts at self-evasion, Mercier remarks to his companion at one point: "Va-t-on jeter le peu de nous qu'il nous reste dans l'ennui des fuites et les rêves d'élargissement?" (pp. 149-150). Similarly, Moran says of his efforts to postpone setting out: "Tortillements inutiles" (*Molloy*, p. 163). In the *Nouvelles*, the narrator-heroes are even more aware of the futility of evasion. For example, one advises: "Alors il ne faut pas penser à certaines choses, à celles qui vous tiennent à coeur, ou plutôt il faut y penser, car à ne pas y penser on risque de les retrouver" (p. 12). Later this same protagonist suggests that even in death one cannot gain release from self-consciousness: "Mais ça va vite chez nous, le dernier voyage, on a beau presser le pas, le dernier fiacre vous lâche, celui de la domesticité, fini le relâche, les gens revivent, regare à vous" (pp. 25-26). Unable to take refuge in his "douleurs" as he is accustomed to do, the hero of "Le Calmant" resigns himself to his failure with the reminder: "Petit à petit tu reviens à toi" (p. 71). The powerful persistence of self-perception appears on the following page where he describes his inability to take an exit when one appears: "Ainsi j'allais, dans l'atroce clarté enfoui dans mes vieilles chairs, tendu vers une voie de sortie et les dépassant toutes, à droite et à gauche, et l'esprit haletant vers ceci et cela et toujours renvoyé, là où il n'y avait rien" (p. 72). In spite of himself, he is drawn toward his own nothing-

---

64 Onimus, 123.
65 *Ibid.*
66 Driver, "Beckett by the Madeleine", 25.

ness, toward the abyss at the center of being. In the same way, Molloy speaks of "l'angoisse du retour... à l'absence peut-être" (*Molloy*, p. 63). Of the simultaneous attraction and repulsion he feels toward this absence, he says: "il faut y retourner, c'est tout ce que je sais, il ne fait pas bon y rester, il ne fait pas bon la quitter" (p. 63). In the midst of his story about Macmann, Malone interrupts the narrative to report: "On est venu. Ça allait trop bien. Je m'étais oublié, perdu.... Ça allait. J'étais ailleurs. Un autre souffrait. Alors on est venu. Pour me rappeler à l'agonie" (*Malone*, p. 178). Having enjoyed the distraction of storytelling for a time, he is compelled by some anonymous force to abandon the game, to return to reflections on his own condition. Creating fictions, then, fails to give permanent relief from self-perception. As Molloy observes, "On n'invente rien, on croit inventer, s'échapper, on ne fait que balbutier sa leçon, des bribes d'un pensum appris et oublié, la vie sans larmes, telle qu'on la pleure" (*Molloy*, p. 46). Malone, too, knows the ineffectiveness of self-evasion through fiction: "Car j'ai beau me raconter des histoires, au fond je n'ai jamais cessé de me croire vivant de la vie de l'air de la terre, même les jours abondant en preuves du contraire" (*Malone*, pp. 110-111). Moreover, he realizes that every word he speaks reveals in some measure his own story: "je n'ai pas à réfléchir, ni avant ni après, je n'ai qu'à ouvrir la bouche pour qu'elle témoigne de ma vieille histoire" (p. 116). Of his experience, Ruby Cohn writes: "On the face of it, nothing would seem safer than the dull, mock-naturalist descriptions of Mrs. Lambert sorting her lentils, and finally giving up impatiently, but she, like Malone's other fictions, leads back to himself, whom he half-heartedly, ironically, attempts to convert to a spring-board back to fiction."[67] Later she summarizes these observations: "Through his willful invention of fictions, the aged Malone is led circuitously but inevitably back to his absurd cosmos, on the one hand, and to his absurd self, on the other.... he is continually jolted back to himself and to the senseless mystery of the cosmos."[68] Even though he carefully establishes an order for his narratives, his "design yields in practice to disorderly shifting about among his... distractions, all of which, however, are centered upon himself, directly or indirectly; for himself is his problem".[69] Paradoxically, the attempt to divert oneself through storytelling is inextricably bound up with the involuntary recital of one's misery. In his study of this paradox, Janvier notes that "le mouvement qui porte l'être à parler, à écrire, semble coïncider avec celui qui permet de se

---

[67] Cohn, *The Comic Gamut*, 144.
[68] Cohn, 157.
[69] Tindall, *Samuel Beckett*, 27.

fuir ou si l'on veut de s'occuper... mobilisation de la conscience pour un travail qui le détourne de la contemplation solipsiste".[70] He continues: "En même temps, la nécessité du jeu, ici, n'empêche pas de sentir que, las d'écrire, l'écrivain est fatigué de s'en aller de lui, ou ne se quitte plus avec 'la même avidité' ou enfin revient à lui brièvement."[71] In effect, then, "Ecrivant, il s'écrit.... Il se quitte, mais c'est pour revenir à lui."[72] Hence, in the case of Malone: "Du jeune Saposcat au vieux Macmann, nous nous approchons de Malone. Malone, racontant autre chose que lui, se raconte et, partant, s'approche de lui-même."[73] As Glicksberg sees it, "What he writes about is the story of the degrading helplessness of the human animal before death overcomes him."[74] His fictions reunite him with himself, reveal his misery.

But it is the very medium of storytelling – language – more than any other factor that leads the creator back to self-consciousness. It plays, in fact, a dual role, as does fiction itself, for "le langage est ce qui m'éloigne de moi, et ce qui me suscite en moi. Sa pente, à laquelle je cède, est en même temps glissement incontrôlable vers ma vérité."[75] In *L'Innommable* there is evidence of this "langage qui vient à la recherche de l'être".[76] Repeatedly the narrator declares the futility of storytelling.[77] No matter what he may do to flee himself, he is his own destination: "où que j'aille je me retrouve, m'abandonne, vais vers moi, viens de moi, jamais que moi" (p. 204): "il n'y a pas d'autre écurie que moi, pour moi" (p. 233). Beneath the masks of his creatures, he finds himself lurking: "cette petite créature aux nombreux déguisements allant et venant, passant de l'ombre à la lumière, faisant son possible, cherchant le moyen, de rester parmi les vivants, de passer à travers, ou, enfermé, regardant par la fenêtre le ciel toujours changeant, c'est ça ne plus pouvoir me perdre" (p. 215). Finally, like Malone he admits that to speak is to say oneself: "je ne peux parler que de moi" (p. 240). Throughout the later fiction, too, the self-conscious artist acknowledges his plight and recognizes that there is no way out for him, since to use language is to give utterance to one's inner voice. For example, one hero avows: "on a beau être distrait" (*Textes*, p. 132). Another abandons all hope of evasion: "unhappiness like mine, there's

---

[70] Janvier, *Pour Samuel Beckett*, 68.
[71] *Ibid.*
[72] Janvier, 71.
[73] *Ibid.*
[74] Glicksberg, "Samuel Beckett's World of Fiction", 39.
[75] Janvier, *Pour Samuel Beckett*, 72.
[76] Janvier, 78.
[77] For examples, see, *L'Innommable*, 200, 203, and 210.

no annihilating that" ("From", p. 144). Still another refers repeatedly to coming back to himself: "je reviens à moi à ma place dans le noir la boue" (*Comment c'est*, p. 31); "je venais de revenir à moi dans une souspréfecture tropicale" (p. 52). In the plays, too, storytelling fails to result in effective self-evasion. Henry's stories, for example, "ne font que le parler lui-même".[78] In much the same way, Winnie reveals her misery in the two stories she tells herself (*Happy Days*, pp. 41 ff.). According to Domenach, "plus elle parle, et plus elle s'enfonce en proclamant son émerveillement, plus elle a peur et plus elle bavarde.... 'Tirer sa journée' à l'aide de ce monologue fait de futilités et de citations, c'est l'arracher au néant, et s'y engloutir en même temps."[79] Fiction, paradoxically, conveys fact. While inventing a fiction, one inevitably speaks of himself, tells his own story, for, composed of words, "lies... are germinal, even of the truth".[80] As Beckett says: "Avec les mots on ne fait que se raconter. Eux-mêmes les lexicographes se déboutonnent. Et jusque dans le confessional on se trahit."[81]

For the lucid Beckettian hero, then, existence is a closed circle of self-perception, flight, and inevitable return to self: "rejeter brutalement le voile, apercevoir le vide et aussitôt créer de nouvelles illusions pour échapper au vertige."[82] But, although the narrator reaches for his "calmant habituel",[83] although he interposes "une fiction entre le néant et son angoisse",[84] the words which at first screened him from the truth soon unveil that truth in all its appalling aspects. Though they try through continuous speech to "faire taire en eux la pensée",[85] the narrator-heroes only succeed in expressing the terrifying thoughts they would evade. They are caught "dans une histoire sans issue" (*Mercier et Camier*, p. 101) – their own existence; and their thoughts continue forever along the same old route. As Moran describes it: "Je pensais beaucoup à moi. C'est-à-dire que j'y jetais un coup d'oeil, fermais les yeux, oubliais, recommençais" (*Molloy*, p. 245). Unable to endure self-perception for any length of time, yet at the same time incapable of suspending perception indefinitely, the mind moves without pause between self-consciousness and illusory diversions. Aware of this movement in his own narrative, Malone writes: "J'ajoute mainte-

---

78 Janvier, 127.
79 Domenach, *Le Retour du tragique*, 273-274.
80 Gerard, "Molloy becomes Unnamable", 319.
81 "La Peinture des van Velde", 349.
82 Onimus, *Beckett*, 71.
83 *Ibid.*
84 *Ibid.*
85 Onimus, 122.

nant ces quelques lignes, avant de me quitter à nouveau" (*Malone*, p. 63).
Anticipating but one more flight into fiction later in his story, he predicts:
"Car je ne ferai plus peut-être qu'un seul voyage, dans les longues galeries
que je connais, avec mes petits soleils et lunes que j'accroche et mes poches
pleines de cailloux pour représenter les hommes et leurs saisons, plus
qu'un seul, c'est ce que je me souhaite. Puis reviendrai ici, à moi, c'est
vague, pour ne plus me quitter, plus me demander ce que je n'ai pas" (pp.
116-117). Again it is the word that is most instrumental in maintaining the
circle of escape and return: "elle [la parole] décrit le nouveau voyage qui
emmène loin de soi puis y ramène, elle dit en même temps une approche
et une fuite, elle indique le combat dont la personne est devenue le lieu."[86]
The circular process described by Janvier is a continuous and inescapable
one for the author-hero: "Raconter pour survivre, revenir à soi guéri
d'illusions, repartir vers les autres par le pouvoir des mots, glisser lentement vers le centre: c'est dans ce va-et-vient, dans cette évolution que
s'exécute l'immobile et secret travail qui emprunte, pour se faire, le
secours du voyage par d'autres êtres."[87] It is as though the writer were
two: "Quelqu'un demeure et s'enfonce, en même temps quelqu'un s'est
échappé et se libère. La contradiction sentie, il n'empêche qu'elle est
assumée tout entière et Malone se l'avoue, désignant ainsi nettement le
dépit du moi-seul-non-résigné vers les autres, échos libres, prêts à parler
pour lui, de lui."[88] Thus, Malone invents tales "to distract him from his
true condition",[89] but all the while his central creatures "grow nearer
[himself] as he makes ready to die, the very idea of character nearly dis-
pensed with".[90] For the narrator of *L'Innommable*, too, creation takes the
form of circular motion. Proposing to tell himself a story about Mahood
"pour me reposer", he resigns himself at the same time to the inevitable
return to truth which must follow the respite: "Puis, retapé, je m'attaque-
rai à nouveau à la vérité, avec des forces centuplées" (p. 45). Speaking of
this endless circular activity, David Grossvogel observes: "The grim fun
of Beckett derives from this vicious circle, from the obstinacy with which
the human urge conjures mirages whereby to maintain itself."[91] Yet he
stresses the lucidity of the creator-heroes as he continues: "But the characters of Beckett are not fooled: they know that they are seeking only a
brief diversion and are, even so, conscious of the crudeness of their decep-

---

[86] Janvier, *Pour Samuel Beckett*, 65.
[87] Janvier, 68-69.
[88] Janvier, 69.
[89] Bowles, "How Samuel Beckett Sees the Universe", 1011.
[90] *Ibid.*
[91] Grossvogel, *Four Playwrights*, 102.

tion... their concentration on the game breaks down frequently. At such moments, abruptly, their words have another ring. There is no longer a game being played, they are fully steeped in horror, and their words suggest a gamut of reactions from the sarcasm of lucidity to the outcry of anguish that rises from depths that are beyond any vision." [92] Thus, in Beckett's universe "self-perception maintains in being" (*Film*, p. 11) and compels through suffering the revelation of its dreadful truth.

[92] Grossvogel, 102-103.

7. THE NEED FOR SELF-KNOWLEDGE

The self-conscious artist caught up in the throes of creation must create a portrait of the artist suffering the agony of his dilemma. The work of art will be a self-portrait, an attempt at self-definition. As Janvier reminds us, "D'autre part, il n'est possible que de se nommer, que de s'écrire."[1] Using language, one has no choice. Even the cabman in "L'Expulsé" can speak of nothing but his life: "A travers la table il me parla de sa vie, de sa femme, et de sa bête, puis encore de sa vie, de la vie atroce qu'était la sienne" (*Nouvelles*, p. 31). In the same collection, the hero of "La Fin" refers to the story he might have told as a "récit à l'image de ma vie" (p. 123). The trilogy presents the self-conscious writer who, according to Tindall, "miserably sits or lies, creating his own image".[2] Moran, for example, "becomes Molloy, [is] a moribund bum writing of moribund bums."[3] It is Malone, however, who is most recognizable as a spinner of tales. Perfectly lucid with regard to his creative project, he says of the stories he plans to tell: "Ce seront des histoires ni belles ni vilaines, calmes, il n'y aura plus en elles ni laideur ni beauté ni fièvre, elles seront presque sans vie, comme l'artiste" (*Malone* p. 9). Producing a portrait of himself in Macmann, who is a poet, Malone reveals in the course of his writing "the nature and process of literary creation"[4] as he experiences it. One cannot invent or describe another without giving a description of oneself. As the hero of *Comment c'est* reasons, "si le 814 336 décrit au 814 335 le 814 337 et au 814 337 le 814 335 il ne fait en définitive que se décrire soi-même" (p. 146). He himself has no creative resource other than self-consciousness: "moi dire moi pour dire quelque chose pour dire ce que j'entends quand ça cesse de haleter" (p. 42). The same is true for the storytellers in the drama. Hamm, for example,

---

[1]   Janvier, *Pour Samuel Beckett*, 73.
[2]   Tindall, *Beckett's Bums*, 3.
[3]   Tindall, *Beckett's Bums*, 10.
[4]   Tindall, *Samuel Beckett*, 27.

in his chronicle creates a protagonist who, like himself, is "lord of a life-less earth, and sole custodian of its dwindling supplies".[5] The self-conscious artist tells simply how it is with him. Yet all art, according to Proust, "is necessarily subjective, the reflection of a unique internal world",[6] for the only reality to which we have access resides in individual consciousness. It is the artist, moreover, who is haunted by penetrating self-perception and who is compelled to give expression to his inner voice – indeed, whose very existence is bound up with constant self-scrutiny in creation. In short, "the artist, to be true to his vocation, must confine himself to the faithful reflection of his changing self".[7]

Thus, the self-conscious artist produces inevitably a never-ending series of self-portraits. But relentless self-consciousness is not the only force responsible for his compulsive activity. In addition to the obligation to express created by his inner voice, the Beckettian hero feels a need to express. As Sypher puts it, "He has a need to utter something."[8] According to Domenach, it is "le besoin de signifier, le goût inextinguible des mots". [9] Yet, as Esslin notes, this need "is not dictated by any idea of utility to others".[10] The author-hero does not seek to communicate anything, for he knows that communication is impossible. "There is no communication", writes Beckett in *Proust*, "because there are no vehicles of communication. Even on the rare occasions when word and gesture happen to be valid expressions of personality, they lose their significance on their passage through the cataract of the personality that is opposed to them" (p. 47). Prefabricated, language, as we shall see later, is inadequate to the task of communication. Groping to understand himself, the hero could scarcely imagine conveying a reliable message to another. "The notion that we can express to our deaf selves", says Steiner, "let alone communicate to any other human beings, blind, deaf, insensate as they are, a complete truth, fact, sensation – a fifth, tenth, millionth of such aforesaid truth, fact, or sensation – is arrogant folly. James clearly believed the thing was feasible, so did Proust and Joyce.... Now the park gates are shut, top hats and rhetoric moulder on empty benches. Saints above, sir, it's hard enough for a man to get up stairs, let alone *say* so."[11] As Harvey explains it: "Both the isolation of the artist and his unintellect-

---

[5] Cohn, *The Comic Gamut*, 230.
[6] Beebe, *Ivory Towers and Sacred Founts*, 233.
[7] Esslin, "Introduction", 3.
[8] Sypher, *Loss of the Self*, 150.
[9] Domenach, *Le Retour du tragique*, 278.
[10] Esslin, "Introduction", 10.
[11] Steiner, "Of Nuance and Scruple", 164.

ual pursuit militate against 'communication' with his audience.... He is compelled toward making... more in order to relieve inner tensions than to express himself. The need to communicate with his fellow man is at the very most a secondary, peripheral concern."[12]

The author-hero writes not so much to convey meaning to another as to find relief for some vague inner discomfort. In the novels one finds references to such unspecified distress. Watt, for example, depends upon language to exorcise the uneasiness he feels when confronted with absurd occurrences at Knott's. When successful, he turns "a disturbance into words, he [makes] a pillow of old words, for a head" (*Watt*, p. 117). In the case of later heroes, the nature of the inner tension is not so clear. Mercier and Camier are impelled to set out on their trip "par un besoin tantôt clair, tantôt obscur" (*Mercier et Camier*, p. 8). Macmann, too, feels the necessity to come and go "pour des raisons obscures et connues qui sait de Dieu seul" (*Malone*, p. 133). In the critical essays, however, the source of the mysterious need to create begins to appear. Although in one of these essays he describes the forces of genesis as "d'absurdes et mystérieuses poussées vers l'image... d'obscures tensions internes",[13] Beckett provides additional information in this and other pieces which clarifies the artist's motives. One does not, then, have to conclude with Harvey that the creative act is undertaken with a "lack of motive".[14] On the contrary, one must examine the indications which together reveal the nature of the artist's one great need – the need to see.

Harvey himself seems aware of this need and appreciates to some extent its importance. In fact, he describes the artist as "a being whose deepest need is to see".[15] Yet he fails to note the essential rapport between the need to see and the creative act. In his lengthy essay on the painters van Velde, Beckett refers repeatedly to the central role of this need in creation. For example, in describing Bram van Velde's paintings he speaks of "la chose seule, isolée par le besoin de la voir, par le besoin de voir".[16] One page later he again mentions this need, attributing to it the painter's greatest originality: "C'est justement en l'idéalisant [l'étendue] qu'il a pu la réaliser avec cette objectivité, cette netteté sans précédent. C'est là sa trouvaille. Il la doit à un besoin tendu à l'extrême de voir clair".[17] It is his manner of seeing that makes van Velde's work unique, and it is his urgent

---

[12] Harvey, "Life, Art, and Criticism", 551.
[13] "La Peinture des van Velde", 350-351.
[14] Harvey, "Life, Art, and Criticism", 554.
[15] Harvey, 548.
[16] "La Peinture des van Velde", 352.
[17] "La Peinture des van Velde", 353.

need to see clearly that compels him to create. In his own words, he asks
for nothing more than to see: "Au fond, c'est tout ce que je demande,
rester spectateur. Que m'importe le reste!"[18] Thus, the artist whose task
is to make visible the invisible, to "cleanse for us the doors of perception",[19] feels in himself an overpowering need to see, to perceive, to
know. "Se peut-il", queries the Unnamable, "que je sois la proie d'une
véritable préoccupation, comme qui dirait un besoin de savoir?" (*Innommable*, p. 14). But the artist cannot know, just as he cannot create. His inability to meet the need to see matches his impotence before the obligation
to express. As always he is caught between an irresistible compulsion and
the limitations which his condition imposes upon him. He seeks "to know
the unknowable, to see the unseeable"[20] through his creative experience.
Further, nothing "outside the artist's own need... would make his struggle
comprehensible".[21] His work exists only as a response to his need. It is,
writes Beckett, "l'oeuvre considérée comme création pure, et dont la
fonction s'arrête avec la genèse".[22] Demanding the impossible, the artist
feels "the overwhelming need that cannot be justified to speak out, to
grope for light in a darkness that will never be lifted".[23] Uncertainty is the
only certainty in the Beckettian universe where no solutions ever appear,
where all remains veiled by a gray atmosphere. But irrational as it may be,
the artist yields to his need, that need which Beckett defines perhaps most
clearly in his essay on Denis Devlin: "the need that is the absolute
predicament of particular human identity".[24] Compelled to create in
anguish by the weight of incessant self-consciousness, the Beckettian
artist feels at the same time a need to know even more about himself than
the penetrating inner eye can disclose. Driven on by this need for self-
knowledge, he produces an art "that condenses as inverted spiral of
need",[25] that becomes ever more demanding as it bores deeper into the
self. For example, Malone reports: "Et je sens même une étrange envie me
gagner, celle de savoir ce que je fais, et pourquoi, et de le dire" (*Malone*,
pp. 34-35). Preoccupied with self-knowledge, the Unnamable, too, feels
the need to see himself clearly:: "Il ne suffit pas que je sache ce que je
fais, il faut aussi que je sache comment je suis" (*L'Innommable*, p. 57).

---

[18]   "Paroles de Bram van Velde", *Derrière le Miroir* 11-12, 13.
[19]   Morse, "The Ideal Core of the Onion", 29.
[20]   Harvey, "Life, Art, and Criticism", 549.
[21]   Gerard, "Molloy becomes Unnamable", 318.
[22]   "La Peinture des van Velde", 349.
[23]   Glicksberg, "Samuel Beckett's World of Fiction", 43.
[24]   "Denis Devlin", 290.
[25]   *Ibid.*

Circumscribed within the confines of his mind, the Beckettian hero discovers that he is a stranger to himself; but armed with the only cognitive tool remaining to him – self-perception – "he must strive to know".[26] Paradoxically, the artist is forced to explore the most terrifying domain of all – the inner abyss. What others instinctively flee, what he himself seeks to evade through storytelling – the nothing at the center of being – draws him near in spite of himself. Moreover, he is driven to this dreadful inner quest by a need which he can never satisfy but whose service he can never abandon. Just as the compulsion to express the inner vision endures as long as consciousness itself, so does the need to know the ever changing self burden the artist throughout his life. For him, all experience is dominated by "the struggle of the mind to know itself".[27]

The search for identity appears throughout the novels, becoming more urgent in the later works where creator and creature often merge into one. Alluding to this confusion, Ruby Cohn writes: "At this late stage of human history, when man cannot decipher his identity from the comic complexity of fictions and words, he nevertheless is compelled to seek that identity."[28] The importance of having an identity is implicit in the experience of one early hero who must prove who he is in order to receive an unspecified sum of money. Of his interview with the lawyer involved, he reports: "Il s'assura de mon identité. Cela dura un bon moment" (*Nouvelles*, p. 29). But in the trilogy, no hero is certain of who he is. Unable to remember his name when questioned at the police station (*Molloy*, p. 31), Molloy later describes his habitual alienation from himself: "la sensation de ma personne s'enveloppait d'un anonymat souvent difficile à percer" (p. 45). In *L'Innommable* the problem is even worse, for the hero, who insists that he has never seen or met himself and can therefore not identify himself (p. 228), is harassed by inquisitors who reproach him for his lack of identity: "à votre âge, être sans identité, c'est une honte" (p. 184). However, since the interrogators are fictional, since they are the creation of the narrator-hero himself, the situation is rather one of self-reproach by "an author agonising with himself about the nature of his own identity".[29] Yet, "being committed to his fictional role, the creator-hero is compelled to go on, if only to attain a semblance of identity and authenticity".[30] Indeed, it is "the urgent need to define self which stimu-

---

[26]   Glicksberg, "The Lost Self in Modern Literature", 527.
[27]   Harvey, "Life, Art, and Criticism", 548.
[28]   Cohn, *The Comic Gamut*, 296.
[29]   Davin, "Mr. Beckett's Everymen", 39.
[30]   Federman, *Journey to Chaos*, 186.

lates such feverish, though inconclusive, verbal and mental activity"[31] in all the later fiction. As Frederick Hoffman remarks, "The Beckett man is engaged restlessly in an undiminished effort to define himself."[32] Every successive work is but a continuation of one "continual exercise in self-definition".[33] Peopled by characters who lack a traditionally detailed identity, these tales present what Glicksberg calls "picaresque ghosts in a nameless region, wandering lost in a fugue of wretched and invariably futile self-awareness, seeking an identity or an illumination of meaning that forever eludes them".[34] Still, these nameless creators "are constrained to speak out, [for the] self seeks to confess, to be known, to proclaim its identity".[35] Indeed, all expression, all art, represents an effort at self-revelation. For Esslin, it is "the raising of the problem of identity itself"[36] which matters most in Beckett's works. Describing the quest for man's identity as "totally fearless, dedicated and uncompromising", he concludes that it is "in the last resort a religious quest in that it seeks to confront the ultimate reality".[37] In fact, what the Beckettian hero seeks is the elusive center of the self, the utter essence of his sense of selfhood. Thus, the "ritual of self-identification which each of Beckett's monologuists goes through"[38] is doomed to go on forever. To seize upon consciousness of self remains an impossible task, yet the author-hero must continue the vain pursuit, he must keep on saying words in a futile effort to stumble upon his identity. "For", writes Wellershoff, "to talk means to stand outside oneself; he who does not possess himself and remains concealed from himself is compelled to talk";[39] and he continues later: "Only he who has attained to his own identity can be silent, only when thinking has reached reality, will it come to a stop."[40] Clearly, then, the need to see into oneself, as much as the persistence of self-perception, compels creative activity, drives the artist to create in the search for self-knowledge.

The need to see or know fixes upon the self because no other object is accessible to the mind. Reduced to consciousness of self-consciousness, the Beckettian hero, confined in his activities to self-contemplation, practices unremitting solipsism. Finding that the self can be aware of nothing but

---

[31] Radke, "The Theater of Samuel Beckett", 58.
[32] Hoffman, *Samuel Beckett*, 113.
[33] Scott, *Samuel Beckett*, 75.
[34] Glicksberg, "The Lost Self", 535.
[35] Glicksberg, 538.
[36] Esslin, "Godot and His Children", 138.
[37] *Ibid.*
[38] Friedman, "The Novels of Samuel Beckett", 57.
[39] Wellershoff, "Failure of an Attempt at De-Mythologization", 92.
[40] Wellershoff, "Failure of an Attempt at De-Mythologization",101.

its own experiences and states, the solipsist comes to believe that nothing exists or is real but the self. Subscribing to the *"esse* is *percipe"* of Bishop Berkeley, a solipsist such as Murphy denies the reality of the exterior world. Alone in "the only world that has reality and significance, the world of [one's] own latent consciousness" (*Proust*, p. 3), one is forever imprisoned in self-consciousness. He can truly perceive nothing but himself. Quoting Proust, Beckett writes: "'Man... is not a building that can receive additions to its superficies, but a tree whose stem and leafage are an expression of inward sap'"; and he continues: "We are alone. We cannot know and we cannot be known. 'Man is the creature that cannot come forth from himself, who knows others only in himself, and who, if he asserts the contrary, lies'" (*Proust*, pp. 48-49). Our inability to know "entails our impotence over all things except what goes on inside our heads".[41] All Beckett's heroes live firmly immured in their minds, all are solipsists like Murphy. For them, "the only certain evidence of being is the individual's experience of his own consciousness".[42] Hence, "knowledge begins with consciousness".[43] But the knowledge available through consciousness never goes beyond the self. "Consciousness can know only itself", writes Hassan; "this is the condemned epistemology of Beckett.... The solipsism of mind reduces all its activities to a closed game."[44] The only reality is that represented in the mind, that which the eye of consciousness reveals; and "this reality that suffering makes accessible to us is... only the reality of ourselves: our solitude remains the central fact."[45] Still, he who seeks his own inner essence finds that all else is insubstantial. As Mayoux explains it, "When all fabrications of what we call civilization, all objective structures, are rejected as illusory, when all worldly activity is viewed as vain, useless, ridiculous, nothing remains but the consciousness of ourselves, and the forms of expression which we can give to that consciousness."[46] The stripped hero discovers, then, that the self is all that matters. The experience of existence is nothing more or less than "the experience of the self";[47] and the author-hero learns that the voice he hears is a metaphor of his self. All the same, the Beckettian hero resists self-contemplation, flees self-perception. Only after he has tried every escape route imaginable does he come to accept that "the preoccupation... with his own self is primary".[48]

[41] Fletcher, *Samuel Beckett's Art*, 134.
[42] Esslin, "Introduction", 9.
[43] Cohn, *The Comic Gamut*, 13.
[44] Hassan, *The Literature of Silence*, 207.
[45] Mayoux, "Samuel Beckett and Universal Parody", 88.
[46] Mayoux, "The Theatre of Samuel Beckett", 142.
[47] Rickels, "Existential Themes in Beckett's *Unnamable*", 136.
[48] Erickson, "Objects and Systems in the Novels", 120.

"What must concern him," writes J. C. Oates, "is himself alone, and there remains only the blackness of self, 'short of all its accidents'; here there is metaphysical chaos, no dimensions, no time, no relatives, no absolutes beyond the fluctuating absolute of the 'I' which continues on but which finds no rest because there is no final answer."[49] Cruelly aware of his situation, the "hermetically self-sealed solipsist"[50] endures ruthless introspection, for his mind "in mad lucidity, gnaws away like a galvanized mouse at the trivial underpinnings of man's logical existence".[51] Indeed, he has no choice; the Beckettian hero must seek to know himself. As Milton Rickels observes. "The clairvoyant vision of the intellect is not comfortable or easy; in seeking to know the self, it is seeking to know the only thing it can know."[52]

The need to see is a need to see within oneself, for inner vision is the only kind of vision possible. The solipsist can perceive only the internal world of his mind. The limits of perception appear in *Murphy* where the hero delights in the life of the mind. Describing Murphy's peculiar kind of seeing, the narrator says: "before he could see it had to be not merely dark, but his own dark. Murphy believed there was no dark quite like his own dark" (p. 91). Distinct from "the vision that depends on light, object, viewpoint, etc.", Murphy's vision is of the kind "that all those things [light, etc.] embarrass" (p. 90). Further reference to seeing in the dark occurs in *Watt*: "The problem of vision, as far as Watt was concerned, admitted of only one solution: the eye open in the dark" (p. 232). Similarly, the hero of "La Fin" advises: "Il ne faut pas fermer les yeux, il faut les laisser ouverts dans le noir, telle est mon opinion" (*Nouvelles*, p. 116). Later the Unnamable declares: "Que tout devient simple et clair, quand on ouvre l'oeil sur le dedans" (*L'Innommable*, p. 114). For the artist, inner vision is the only valid kind of perception available; without it he could create nothing of value. As Proust says, "Ne vient de nous-même que ce que nous tirons de l'obscurité qui est en nous et que ne connaissent pas les autres." To create, one must acknowledge "le sens artistique, c'est-à-dire la soumission à la réalité intérieure". Later he goes on to say: "les vrais livres doivent être les enfants non du grand jour et de la causerie mais de l'obscurité et du silence." [53] The outer world of illusions and distractions has nothing at all to offer the artist. Fully aware of his inability

---

[49]   Oates, "The Trilogy of Samuel Beckett", 164.
[50]   Jerome Stone cited in Pronko, *Avant-garde*, 43.
[51]   *Ibid.*
[52]   Rickels, "Existential Themes in Beckett's *Unnamable*", 145.
[53]   Proust, *Le Temps retrouvé, Œuvres complètes*, 7, pt. 2 (Paris: Nouvelle Revue Française, 1932), 26, 29, 50.

to know anything but himself, he pursues what knowledge he can derive from introspection. Writing of Bram van Velde's paintings, Beckett describes the creative perception as "une prise de vision... une prise de vision tout court"; and he specifies the kind of vision involved: "une prise de vision au seul champ qui se laisse parfois voir sans plus... au champ intérieur." Developing this theme further, he insists upon the ultimate importance of inner vision: it is in the "boîte crânienne" "qu'on commence enfin à voir, dans le noir. Dans le noir qui ne craint plus aucune aube. Dans le noir qui est aube et midi et soir et nuit d'un ciel vide, d'une terre fixe. Dans le noir qui éclaire l'esprit."[54] Thus, Beckett replaces the traditional image of knowledge – light – with its opposite – darkness. Paradoxically, this latter element can light up the mind; it is the blacklight of inner vision which makes possible the only kind of perception worthy of the artist. In another essay on the van Veldes, Beckett describes Bram's vision as a tightly sealed internal world: "parmi les masses inébranlables d'un être écarté, enfermé et rentré pour toujours en lui-même, sans traces, sans air, cyclopéen, aux brefs éclairs, aux couleurs du spectre du noir." The painter's terms are those "du dedans, l'obscurité, le plein, la phosphorescence".[55] As Harvey notes, "the daylight world is a realm of blindness"[56] for the artist. Only in turning to the dark inner world of the mind can he have any hope of glimpsing the ultimate reality, the essence of his own existence. Needing above all to know himself, he must "move from traditional representations of the exterior world to the metamorphosed objects of the mind".[57] Yet, because it is constantly changing, his own self will forever elude him. He will never be able to terminate the search for self. Nonetheless, as a result of his dilemma, out of "this need and impossibility of knowing once and for all arises the work of art, an anguishing oscillation between painfully inadequate alternatives".[58]

Traditionally, the artist's unique powers of perception make him a sensitive observer, who sees things that are invisible to those ruled by habit. Ever on guard against the superficial and the illusory, the artist combats inauthenticity, especially in himself. As Ruskin says: "All [men] are partly encumbered and crusted over with idle matter; only, if they have real life in them, they are always breaking this bark away in noble rents, until it becomes, like the black strips upon the birch tree, only a witness

---

[54]   "La Peinture des van Velde", 352.
[55]   "Peintres de l'empêchement", 7.
[56]   Harvey, "Life, Art, and Criticism", 548.
[57]   *Ibid.*
[58]   Harvey, 549-550.

of their own inward strength."[59] For Beckett (as shown in Chapter 2), "destruction of bourgeois smugness and the dulling power of habit is the prerequisite of true existence and of artistic creation".[60] The artist, compelled to probe beneath surfaces, cannot accept the ready-made formulas and pat answers which habit and convention provide for others. He must be uncompromising in all things, but above all in his attempts to know himself. Like Proust, he must "look behind the surface of the ego, behind voluntary to involuntary memory, behind will and desire to conscious perception".[61] Examined thus closely by the unflinching gaze of the artist, "l'existence se dévoile telle qu'elle est: dur atome de présence dans le noir de la liberté absolue et de l'universelle contingence".[62]

To achieve this kind of essential vision, however, one must penetrate deeply into the interior of the mind, one must undertake what Mme Serreau calls "ce cheminement vers les profondeurs".[63] The obsession with depth (already noted in Chapter 1) is here again of major importance, for only by descending within himself can the artist attempt to satisfy his need to know. Images of the interior descent appear as early as *Murphy* (with the image of the Great Auk, p. 193) and reappear throughout the fiction. In *Premier amour*, the hero speaks of how his thoughts approach nothingness "comme par des marches descendant vers une eau profonde" (p. 39). A diversion for him in the past, the woman Anne no longer occupies his mind, leaving him free and ready once more to endure "les descentes lentes vers les longues submersions dont j'étais depuis si longtemps privé, par sa faute" (pp. 45-46). The narrator of "La Fin" seems to have reached his destination when snug in his lidded canoe he remarks: "il m'arrivait de vouloir déplacer le couvercle et sortir du canot, sans le pouvoir, tant j'étais paresseux et faible, et bien *au fond* là où j'étais" (*Nouvelles*, p. 119; my emphasis). Molloy, too, is at home in the depths, though he has not reached the end of his descent: "Le fond", he writes, "c'est mon habitat, oh pas le fin fond, quelque part entre l'écume et la fange" (*Molloy*, p. 19). Indeed, he cannot arrive at any one of his avowed destinations (his town, his mother's room) without going by way of the interior: "Et pour y accéder [à la ville] il fallait passer par l'intérieur, du moins moi je ne connaissais pas d'autre chemin" (p. 115). For the author-hero, there is no other way to self-knowledge, as Moran discovers to his

---

[59]   Ruskin quoted in Beebe, *Ivory Towers and Sacred Founts*, 149.
[60]   Kern, "Beckett and the Spirit of the Commedia Dell'Arte", 265.
[61]   Frye, "The Nightmare Life in Death", 443.
[62]   Onimus, *Beckett*, 53.
[63]   Serreau, "Samuel Beckett", 116.

dismay: "Que l'homme est peu d'accord avec lui-même, mon Dieu. Moi qui me flattais d'être pondéré, froid comme du cristal et aussi pur de fausse profondeur" (*Molloy*, p. 174). To deny the existence of interior depths does not help. On the contrary, one must accept the challenge of their hidden mysteries, though the descent be fraught with peril. Emphasizing the anguish and futility of this experience, Federman writes: "the French creator-hero descends time after time into the depths of Hades (his own consciousness) to bring back an identity which repeatedly eludes him."[64] The heroes themselves seem aware of some unutterable horror lurking in the depths of the self. Murphy, for example, tries to control the emptying of his mind (which is compared to the unreeling of a spool), for "it was his experience that this should be stopped, whenever possible, before the deeper coils were reached" (*Murphy*, p. 252). Referring to the inner regions as "infernales profondeurs" (*Molloy*, p. 121), Molloy describes their hellish aspect in greater detail as follows: "l'intérieur, tout cet espace intérieur qu'on ne voit jamais, le cerveau et le coeur et les autres cavernes où sentiment et pensée tiennent leur sabbat" (p. 12). Still, there are more specific indications as to the nature of what one finds deep within oneself. Citing a conversation he had with Beckett, Harvey reports: "He spoke of depths where all is mystery and enigma. 'We don't know what our own personality is.' It certainly has little to do with the surface self, with that 'existence by proxy' in the macrocosm. Somewhere perhaps, Beckett believes, is an 'abortive self,' a being somehow stunted, undeveloped, but more real, more authentic than the public man, who seems closer to the second or third person than to the first."[65]

The close rapport between Molloy and Moran demonstrates this sense of duality. Moran "amidst the tidiness and triviality of his little world... has, from time to time, uneasy intimations of a life within himself that is deeper and darker and less rational than that of the simple diurnal self with whom he customarily has dealings."[66] Edith Kern shows that inner self to be Molloy, the one for whom Moran searches with such pain and persistence. Speaking of Molloy, she writes: "More than a mission... he is a part of Moran and sporadically asserts himself."[67] A terrifying inner presence, "Molloy appears as a chimera that haunts and possesses [Moran]." In this light, "Moran's quest for Molloy (who is a secret part of himself) resembles the task which Yeats had set for each man, and the

---

[64] Federman, *Journey to Chaos*, 183.
[65] Harvey, "Life, Art, and Criticism", 556.
[66] Scott, *Samuel Beckett*, 63.
[67] Kern, "Moran-Molloy", 185.

poet in particular: to seek out the 'other self, the antiself or antithetical self' and indeed to become –'of all things not impossible the most difficult' – that other self."[68] Stressing the complexity and potential hazards of this quest, Miss Kern continues: "not merely a departure from the confines of the familiar, not merely a metamorphosis, [Moran's journey] represents a descent into his own subconscious where dwells Molloy – a *via dolorosa* into Molloy's immense universe of uncertainty and absurdity."[69] Of primary importance to the artist's search for the essential in existence, this agonizing quest for self involves the caustic removal of all surfaces. In the case of Moran, the "destruction of the body and the senses is a further stripping away of all that is contingent in order to bare that which is essential". There is no other route to the mother's room, metaphor for "the core of artistic existence".[70] Thus, Moran descends into the depths of his being "to embrace there his antithesis as man and as poet".[71] In the end he is changed, and yet "he is more sure of his identity than ever before":[72] "Et pour tout dire je continuais à me reconnaître et même j'avais de mon identité un sens plus net et vif qu'auparavant, malgré ses lésions intimes et les plaies dont elle se couvrait" (*Molloy*, p. 263). But Moran is not the last hero to explore the inner depths. The Unnamable speaks of "un monde à moi, dit aussi intérieur", and of the only possible abandon being "en dedans" (*L'Innommable*, p. 212). For the narrator of *Comment c'est*, the interior descent is endless, the depths bottomless: "j'ai dû glisser on est au plus bas c'est la fin on n'est plus on glisse c'est la suite" (p. 27). Recalling the image of the mind as sea, the words of Ada in *Embers* suggest the acute silence of the inner world: "It's [the sound of the sea is] only on the surface, you know. Underneath all is as quiet as the grave. Not a sound. All day, all night, not a sound."[73] The surface sound only serves to cover by its presence the terrifying silence at the center of being.

In the essay on Proust, Beckett refers directly to the interior regions as the only place where the true self can be found. Describing the depths as "that ultimate and inaccessible dungeon of our being to which Habit does not possess the key" (*Proust*, p. 18), he goes on to say that "here, in that 'gouffre interdit à nos sondes,' is stored the essence of ourselves... the pearl that may give the lie to our carapace of paste and pewter" (pp. 18-19).

[68] Kern, 186.
[69] Kern, 187.
[70] Kern, 189.
[71] Kern, 187.
[72] Hamilton, "Boon or Thorn? Joyce Cary and Samuel Beckett on Human Life", 440.
[73] *Embers*, 114.

It is here "where any truth that may be in us lies hidden",[74] "où se con-
servent, par delà le réseau des habitudes mortes, les secrets de la vie authentique".[75] According to Proust himself, the writer must seek to see "ce
qu'il y a au fond", to know "ce qui se passe au fond de lui".[76] In *Le Temps
retrouvé* he goes into greater detail concerning the artist's task: "Ce
travail de l'artiste, de chercher à apercevoir sous de la matière, sous de l'ex-
périence, sous des mots quelque chose de différent." The task of the artist,
then, is to make visible the invisible, to reveal the truth which the depths
conceal: "En somme, cet art si compliqué est justement le seul art vivant.
Seul il exprime pour les autres et nous fait voir à nous-même notre propre
vie, cette vie qui ne peut pas s' 'observer,' dont les apparences qu'on observe ont besoin d'être traduites, et souvent lues à rebours, et péniblement
déchiffrées." The work of abstract intelligence and of habit, "c'est ce
travail que l'art défera, c'est la marche en sens contraire, le retour aux
profondeurs, où ce qui a existé réellement gît inconnu de nous qu'il nous
fera suivre".[77] In short, one must "descendre au delà du monde des apparences".[78]

For Beckett, this descent is essentially a solitary journey which the artist
must make in order to know what little he can of himself. Writing in
Proust, he says: "the only possible spiritual development is in the sense
of depth. The artistic tendency is not expansive, but a contraction. And
art is the apotheosis of solitude" (p. 47). One page later he describes the
artist's path as a downward spiral boring into the self: "The only fertile
research is excavatory, immersive, a contraction of the spirit, a descent.
The artist is active, but negatively, shrinking from the nullity of extracircumferential phenomena, drawn into the core of the eddy" (p. 48). With-
drawing from surfaces, the creator must attempt to coincide with his own
essence, with the intangible nothingness at his core. He must strip away
the outer husk to get at the dark absence beneath; and Beckett makes
plain early in his essay what the artist should receive in recognition of his
efforts: "the heart of the cauliflower or the ideal core of the onion would
represent a more appropriate tribute to the labours of poetical excavation
than the crown of bay" (pp. 16-17). Yet one can expect no reward for one's
quest. After all, the "descent into the self is the only authentic activity for
the unutterable condition which is Being";[79] and it is without end.

---

74 Torrance, "Modes of Being and Time", 94.
75 Onimus, *Beckett*, 25.
76 Proust, *Contre Sainte-Beuve* (Paris: Gallimard, 1954), 365 and 366.
77 Proust, *Le Temps retrouvé*, 48.
78 Proust, *Le Temps retrouvé*, 51.
79 Rickels, "Existential Themes in Beckett's *Unnamable*", 137.

Relentlessly, the Beckettian heroes are compelled to take the plunge, to submerge themselves in their own inner formlessness in order to find the true self, the essence of existence. Describing this descent, Claude Mauriac writes: "Beckett fait aller ses personnages, spéléologues d'eux -mêmes, toujours plus loin à travers les bas-fonds intimes. Descente aux enfers de l'être qui n'en finit pas, car le plongeur trouve indéfiniment d'autres zones souterraines. Sa quête est de la réalité fondamentale qui demeurerait, une fois détruit ce qui est accessoire en l'homme."[80] The evolution in the works (as analysed in Part I) reflects the inward and downward spiralling search for self. Ever more self-conscious and more nearly self-coincident, the novels and plays seem to seek their own essence. In his description of this movement, Fletcher writes of Beckett's work: "it prefers to plunge downwards rather than swim abroad, to know itself more thoroughly than to explore the world about. As Proust has it, and as Beckett would agree, the artist moves in the only direction open to him: into himself, in search of a starker, poorer, but more universally valid self."[81] The evolution in the works, then, parallels the quest for identity which the creator must make. But the dual path of creation and self-knowledge is not an easy one to follow; and the artist submits to the difficulty and distress it occasions only because he is compelled to do so. The obsession with inner depths is bound up with the need to know, the need to accomplish "une descente en direction de la pointe (inaccessible) de l'enfer intime où l'absolu de l'existence confine au néant".[82]

Constrained though he is to probe his inner essence, the artist remains reluctant to do so, for he dreads to encounter the *néant* which he feels lurking within him. An insurmountable obstacle to his progress, fear of the truth prevents him from casting off the last veil, from reaching the deepest depths. Forever to be fathomed, these depths of being offer to view "cette réalité fondamentale qui se propose sans cesse à nous mais dont sans cesse une épouvante nous écarte, que nous refusons de voir et où nous devons sans cesse nous efforcer de ne pas sombrer, qui n'est connue de nous que sous la forme insaisissable de l'angoisse."[83] Apprehension thus thwarts all attempts to reach the self. Calling attention to this paralysing terror, Chambers describes it as "une force invisible, une peur, une angoisse, qui nous retient sur le seuil qui nous sépare de nous-même, et qui nous prive à jamais du calme que nous rêvons"; and he continues:

[80] Mauriac, "Samuel Beckett", 86-87.
[81] Fletcher, *The Novels of Samuel Beckett*, 232.
[82] Onimus, *Beckett*, 36.
[83] Bataille, "Le Silence de Molloy", 387.

"Cette force, sur laquelle Beckett reste très discret, semble bien être le sentiment du néant, la conviction intime où nous sommes qu'au centre de nous-mêmes il y a... un vide intérieur rejoignant le vide extérieur."[84] To come upon this abysmal inner revelation would not be bearable. "Ne rien voir du tout", says one hero, "non, c'est trop" (Nouvelles, p. 117). With this and other similar indications Beckett "convinces us skilfully of the terrifying blank to which enquiry into personal identity may lead us".[85] Clearly, the artist's ability to see is not a blessing. As Harvey puts it, "'seeing' is by no means a joyous thing".[86] But needing to see, being cursed with inner vision, the artist must peer into the depths, though what he glimpses there is a frightening sight, is indeed the painful vision of man's nature and condition, the revelation of his own misery.

The essence of existence presents itself as an emptiness, as a hole in the center of being. Man appears as "an absence, a self stripped of ontological truth".[87] In the words of Iris Murdoch: "The individual seen from without is a menace, and seen from within is a void."[88] Consciousness fixed upon itself perceives only nothingness, for being "constantly in flux and ever changing and therefore negative rather than positive, [it is] the empty space through which the fleeting images pass".[89] Thus, for the self-conscious artist inner vision reveals the void. Even in the early novels the heroes have intense experiences of nothingness. Murphy, for example, when gazing into Mr.Endon's eyes begins after a while "to see nothing, that colourlessness which is such a rare postnatal treat, being the absence... not of *percipere* but of *percipi*" (*Murphy*, p. 246). Yet "the positive peace", which Murphy derives from his encounter with "the accidentless One-and-Only, conveniently called Nothing" (p. 246), is not shared by Watt. Dwelling under the same roof with "the supreme embodiment of the unthinkable and the unspeakable, the very 'being of nothing'"[90] – Knott – , Watt is continually perplexed by the "presence of what [does] not exist, that presence without, that presence within, that presence between" (*Watt*, p. 45). In particular the Gall incident bothers him; but the narrator discloses in concluding his recital of that episode that "Watt learned towards the end of this [*sic*] stay in Mr Knott's house

---

84   Chambers, "Vers une interprétation de 'Fin de Partie'", 96.
85   Fletcher, *The Novels*, 214.
86   Harvey, "Life, Art, and Criticism", 551.
87   Glicksberg, "The Lost Self", 527.
88   Iris Murdoch, *Sartre: Romantic Rationalist* (New Haven, Conn.: Yale University Press, 1967), 73.
89   Esslin, "Introduction", 9.
90   Tindall, *Samuel Beckett*, 20; see *Watt*, 39.

to accept that nothing had happened, that a nothing had happened, learned to bear it and even, in a shy way, to like it" (*Watt*, p. 80). The experience of nothing which the heroes of the trilogy must endure is more intense, however, than Watt's and definitely more difficult to accept. With no exterior distractions available to divert them from their own inner emptiness, the author-heroes compulsively gaze upon the void within. Macmann, for example, stares fixedly at an unutterable sight before him: "Les yeux à peine plus bleus qu'un blanc d'oeuf fixent l'espace devant eux, qui serait alors le plein calme éternellement des abîmes" (*Malone*, p. 109). Similarly, the Unnamable describes how he is compelled to gaze continuously at a small space before him "où il ne se passe rien, 99% du temps" (*L'Innommable*, p. 27). Worm's fate resembles almost exactly that of his creator, for he too must contemplate with lidless eye a space "où il ne se passe rien, ou si peu, il pourrait les rater, les infréquents spectacles, s'il pouvait ciller" (p. 149). Later the hero, yearning to be able to locate himself, to describe the place where he exists, reveals instead how he perceives nothing tangible anywhere: "je ne sens pas d'endroit, pas d'endroit autour de moi"; and he continues, showing how he himself has no well-defined presence: "je n'arrête pas, je ne sais pas ce que c'est, ce n'est pas de la chair, ça n'arrête pas, c'est comme de l'air" (p. 230). But dissatisfied with the truth of nothingness which is the essence of being, he longs still for a more conventional identity: "l'endroit d'abord, après je m'y trouverai, je m'y introduirai, bien solide, au milieu, ou dans un coin" (p. 231).

All the same, in spite of himself, the Unnamable comes face to face with "that very centre of nothingness, that state of pure potentiality" [91] which is consciousness at the core of the self. As Mayoux says, "Here, what Beckett makes us see with a horrible intensity is this inner space, not a screen but a sort of formless pit with indistinguishable walls, lit by a grey, brain-colored light... anguished, shifting, vertiginous, haunted like Milton's Chaos with the phantoms of the future." [92] Yet this dreadful nothingness is "[la] réalité la plus certaine de l'homme". [93] At the end of the quest for self "il n'y a plus que le néant", [94] because consciousness intent upon itself encounters no thing. In the trilogy, then as J. C. Oates remarks, "we have only the self-conscious 'I' and the progressive movement inward to zero, in this case the primary zero which is the first and in a very important sense the final state of the individual's existence"; the 'I' "moves in-

[91]   Esslin, "Samuel Beckett," 142.
[92]   Mayoux, "Samuel Beckett and Universal Parody", 81.
[93]   Nadeau, "Samuel Beckett, l'humour et le néant", 694.
[94]   Nadeau, "Le chemin de la parole au silence", 64.

ward to a frank, brutal... consciousness of its own essence".[95] Indeed, the confrontation with the hollow self is frightful; as Mayoux puts it: "Terrible is the awareness that takes possession of man in his solitude – that he exists for nothing." [96] Self-knowledge is above all an encounter with the inevitability of death, with the utter gratuitousness of existence. As one can see in modern tragedy, "ce qui compte, ce n'est pas ce qui est affirmé, c'est ce qui manque, quelque chose a été égaré quelque part".[97] Deprived even of the hope of fulfillment, the contemporary tragic hero experiences life as an infinitely gaping void, as a burdensome, empty wait for death. In *Godot*, for example, we have "a pattern of uncertainties and questions, an action demonstrating the absence of action";[98] nothing happens, making the play "a lucid testimony of nothingness"[99] as it is experienced in life. In the face of the nothingness about them, the pathetic heroes try every evasion imaginable, only to return each time to their misery and their meaningless wait for the unknown. Compelled like them to confront the eery emptiness at the center of existence, the artist yet feels drawn to the hollowness within himself. In his pursuit of it, he creates, and in creating he comes ever closer to his essence. The creative experience becomes, then, "un dévoilement sans fin, voile derrière voile, plan sur plan de transparences imparfaites, un dévoilement vers l'indévoilable, le rien, la chose à nouveau".[100]

[95] Oates, "The Trilogy", 160.
[96] Mayoux, "The Theatre of Samuel Beckett", 146.
[97] Domenach, *Le Retour du tragique*, 269.
[98] Esslin, "Godot and His Children", 132.
[99] Pronko, *Avant-garde*, 30.
[100] "Peintres de l'empêchement", 7.

8. THE QUEST FOR SELF THROUGH CREATION

As the dominant theme of the artist-centered novel, the quest for self is intimately bound up with the creative act. For Proust, the true self of the artist presents itself only in his works: "le moi de l'écrivain ne se montre que dans ses livres." This is "le moi qui a attendu pendant qu'on était avec les autres, qu'on sent bien le seul réel, et pour lequel seuls les artistes finissent par vivre", the 'I' which compensates for the inferior self who predominates in society.[1] Although Proust stresses "the disparity between what an artist appears to be in person and what he is in his art"[2] in order doubtless to explain his own personality, the intense study he makes in his work of the artist's vocation and experience indicates that, in fact, he achieves at least some measure of "self-discovery through narration".[3] In Beckett's fiction quest of self and creative activity are inseparable. Having resolved to tell himself a story, the narrator of "Le Calmant" begins by comparing his fictional introduction to a setting forth: "A moi maintenant le départ, la lutte et le retour peut-être" (Nouvelles, p. 47). In the trilogy, too, quest and creation are closely interwoven. Molloy tells of his search for his mother's room, and Moran recounts his efforts to find Molloy – his own inner self. The latter example is especially revealing, since one can trace as they occur the symptoms which reflect the author-hero's metamorphosis. Moran's quest "becomes a discovery of self",[4] and his narrative continues the quest of which it is the report. Describing his feelings at the moment of recital, he says at one point: "je suis davantage celui qui découvre que celui qui narre" (Molloy, p. 205). Even seemingly insignificant details which he recalls about his adventure yield some self-knowledge. For instance, he writes of one encounter: "Il me demandait

---

[1] Proust, *Le Temps retrouvé, Œuvres complètes*, 7, pt. 2 (Paris: Nouvelle Revue Française, 1932), 165, 163, 157-158.
[2] Beebe, *Ivory Towers and Sacred Founts*, 233.
[3] Cohn, *The Comic Gamut*, 223.
[4] Tindall, *Samuel Beckett*, 23.

du pain et je lui proposais du poisson. Tout mon caractère est là" (p. 227). The discovery of self through creation becomes more evident still in *Malone meurt* where the paralysed hero cannot by any means undertake a voyage. Here "the writing is the adventure",[5] the story is the quest. Proposing early to examine himself from time to time as he spins his tales, "Malone is the first Beckettian hero [who deliberately seeks] to know himself through writing fiction."[6] "A chaque menace de ruine", he writes, "je m'arrêterai pour m'inspecter tel quel" (*Malone*, p. 26). Yet he does not really desire to do this; he admits in fact: "C'est justement ce que je voulais éviter" (p. 26). But there is no other way to keep going: "Mais c'est sans doute le seul moyen. Après ce bain de boue je saurai mieux admettre un monde où je ne fasse pas tache" (p. 26). He must speak of himself for his thoughts are occupied with nothing else: "Quelque part dans cette confusion la pensée s'acharne, loin du compte elle aussi. Elle aussi me cherche, comme depuis toujours, là où je ne suis pas. Elle non plus ne sait pas se calmer" (p. 21). Later he avows that indeed he has resigned himself to writing "afin de savoir où j'en suis" (p. 61). Even his personae are a means to self-discovery: "Je me glisse dans lui [Macmann], dans l'espoir sans doute d'apprendre quelque chose" (p. 96). As Tindall explains it: "At once personal and impersonal, Malone's stories are also ways of discovery through dramatic projection, and, by distancing his horrors, of protecting himself from them. Sapo and Macmann are masks or 'homunculi,' under whose changing names Malone seeks his own identity."[7]

The Unnamable, too, seeks to know himself through his fictions; but he is dissatisfied with the meager results he gets: "leurs douleurs ne sont rien à côté des miennes", he complains, "rien qu'une petite partie des miennes, celle dont je croyais pouvoir me détacher, pour la contempler" (*L'Innommable*, p. 33). On the very next page, he describes these same personae as "inexistants, inventés pour expliquer je ne sais plus quoi" (p. 34). Unable to penetrate to the self through them, he forgets why he created them in the first place. The close rapport between searching for the self and creating appears even more clearly later in the novel where the verbs *raconter*, *chercher*, and *parler* become virtually synonymous: "racontant toujours, n'importe quoi, cherchant encore" (p. 201); "parlant toujours, cherchant toujours, en soi, hors de soi" (p. 202). Finally, he reveals that it is the voice which is searching for him – "elle est aveugle,

---

[5] Cohn, 117.
[6] Fletcher, *The Novels of Samuel Beckett*, 171.
[7] Tindall, *Samuel Beckett*, 29.

elle me cherche, dans le noir" (p. 254) – in order to tell him all: "la voix me
dira tout" (p. 255). Seeking to "penetrate behind linguistic and fictional
formulae to himself",[8] a self reduced to "a round, hard object with a
voice",[9] this author-hero only experiences increasing anguish at the impossibility of ever reaching his goal. Thus, in the trilogy "we start with
fiction and we end in the most ruthless self-revelation, the agony of a
soul in search of its own identity".[10] Creation and self-examination become inextricably meshed. In the *Textes*, the search for self through fiction
is even more of a problem than in *L'Innommable*. Lost in a maddening
web of words, the narrator-heroes persevere in the attempt to achieve
some kind of tangible identity. Recalling Malone, one says: "j'essaie de
me situer" (p. 195).

   Clearly, then, the exploration of the self comes to occupy a place of
primary importance in Beckett's fiction as the narrator-hero becomes ever
more self-conscious. Compelled to create, he is compelled at the same time
to contemplate how he creates and to try to determine why he does so.
Unable to answer these questions about himself without the aid of fictions,
he continues to create in order to satisfy his need to know. The result of
repeated efforts to probe ever more deeply into the creating self, the
evolution in the fiction is significant. Explaining what it reveals, Ruby
Cohn writes: "Through the years Beckett has hacked at his plots and
characters; he has decimated his sentences and the number of his words,
until he is left with a single protagonist in the generalized human situation,
an 'I' in quest of his 'I' through fiction, who is in quest of his 'I' through
fiction, who, etc."[11] But it is Esslin who perhaps better than anyone else
sums up the intricate, essential relationship between creation and self-
discovery: "To Beckett", he writes, "the novel is not an act of communication or storytelling, it is a lonely and dedicated exploration, a shaft driven
deep down into the core of the self. It is a self-contradictory, Quixotic...
attempt at expressing the inexpressible, saying the unsayable, distilling
the essence of being and making visible the still centre of reality."[12]

   Aware of their quest as they are of their creative efforts, the narrator-
heroes allude from time to time to the self they seek. In *Molloy*, Moran
abruptly refers to one – not Molloy – whom he has longed to see: "Et cet
Obidil dont j'ai failli parler, que j'aurais tellement voulu voir de près, eh

---

[8]   Cohn, "Still Novel", 49.
[9]   Cohn, 160.
[10] Esslin, "Samuel Beckett", 142.
[11] Cohn, 299.
[12] Esslin, "Samuel Beckett", 129.

bien je ne le vis jamais, ni de près ni de loin, et il n'existerait pas que je n'en serais que modérément saisi" (p. 251). But, a distant attraction, the Obidil may in fact be quite different from the authentic self which the later author-heroes describe variously as a home, as the place where they belong, as a being which needs them. Malone, for example, wondering why he sets out on his fictional sallies concludes that he does so only to return home afterward to himself: "Ce à quoi je voulais arriver, en me hissant hors de mon trou d'abord, puis dans la lumière cinglante vers d'inaccessibles nourritures, c'était aux extases du vertige, du lâchage, de la chute, de l'engouffrement, du retour au noir, au rien, au sérieux, à la maison, à celui qui m'attendait toujours, qui avait besoin de moi et dont moi j'avais besoin... que j'ai beaucoup fait souffrir et peu contenté, que je n'ai jamais vu" (*Malone*, pp. 37-38). Similarly, the Unnamable observes: "on se cherche dans la montagne et dans la plaine... on se veut dans son coin" (*L'Innommable*, p. 232), and he speaks of returning "là où je suis... là où je m'attends" (p. 157). Obsessed with finding his true self, this hero describes repeatedly the one he seeks: "celui qui a l'air fait pour moi et qui ne veut pas de moi, celui dont j'ai l'air de vouloir et dont je ne veux pas, au choix, je ne saurais sans doute jamais s'il m'engloutit ou s'il me vomit et qui n'est peut-être que l'intérieur de mon crâne lointain, où autrefois j'errais" (p. 31). Identifying himself directly with this other self, he writes: "je suis aussi cet impensable ancêtre dont on ne peut rien dire. Mais j'en parlerais peut-être, et des temps impénétrables où j'étais lui.... Oui, j'en parlerai peut-être, un instant, comme dans un écho, moqueur, avant de le rejoindre, celui dont on n'a pas su me séparer" (pp. 134-135). Having as its domain "l'impensable indicible" (p. 98), the authentic self is beyond the reach of thought and language. Still the hero must try to find this self with words – the only resource left to him: "il s'agit de lui qui ne sait rien, ne veut rien, ne peut rien... qui ne peut ni parler ni entendre, qui est moi, qui ne peut être moi, dont je ne peux parler, dont je dois parler" (p. 241). Ever more anxious to attain his true self, to be self-coincident, the Unnamable in the final pages of his story discovers what he must do: "me voilà l'absent, c'est son tour, celui qui ne parle ni n'écoute, qui n'a ni corps ni âme... il est fait de silence... il est dans le silence, c'est lui qu'il faut être, de lui qu'il faut parler, mais il ne peut pas parler, alors je pourrai m'arrêter, je serai lui, je serai le silence, je serai dans le silence, nous serons réunis, son histoire qu'il faut raconter, mais il n'a pas d'histoire, il n'a pas été dans l'histoire... il est dans son histoire à lui, inimaginable, indicible" (pp. 258-259). In searching for his authentic self, the narrator comes to see that the being in his depths is in fact unindentifiable. Dwelling outside the limits of knowledge and language, the deepest self evades discovery through fiction. Withdrawn into himself "as far from sense perception as possible, in an effort to find the real self back of all the outer images, to find his 'identity'",[13] the Unnamable cannot escape the final barrier between himself and his essence – the ever present thought process, the endless string of words.

In the *Textes* the struggle to be at one with the self continues, though it seems doomed forever to fail. One hero, for example, refers to the self as "le même inconnu que toujours" (p. 153). Another tells how he tries to achieve self-coincidence: "je cherche à être comme celui que je cherche, dans ma tête, que ma tête cherche, que je somme ma tête à chercher, en se sondant" (p. 160). At one point it even seems that the self speaks: "Je ne suis pas dans sa tête, nulle part dans son vieux corps, et pourtant je suis là, pour lui je suis là, avec lui, d'où tant de confusion" (p. 153). Apparently aware of the creator's efforts to be at one with him, this self continues: "Cela devrait lui suffire, m'avoir trouvé absent, mais non, il me veut là, avec une forme et un monde, comme lui, malgré lui, moi qui suis tout, comme lui qui n'est rien" (pp. 153-154). Unable to abandon the conventions of thought and language, the author-hero cannot strip away the last veil covering his essence. In *Comment c'est*, the search continues as the hero says "chercher le vrai homme" (p. 126). But the self remains forever undiscovered, for the artist lacks the equipment with which to detect it. To the question "parler peut-il mener à soi?"[14] the answer must be no. The author-hero cannot identify himself though his creations; on the contrary, "il ne peut qu'inventer d'autres personnages et d'autres histoires subsituts d'un moi et d'une histoire qui ne se peuvent raconter".[15] As Rickels puts it, "the project of discovering the authentic self is dreadful and austere".[16] Moreover, it is an impossible task which can never be completed. All the same, the artist is compelled to pursue the quest, for "all traveling is toward the self, all waiting is for the self, all escape is from the self".[17] Tyrannized by persistent self-consciousness, one cannot abandon the search. Finally, it seems that by itself "la quête, dépourvue d'objet, de réalité et de motifs, continue son cours imbécile et terrible",[18] driving the hero to ever greater and ever more futile efforts. An endless sentence that the artist can never serve out, the quest for self is experienced as the

13   Hamilton, "Portrait in Old Age", 162.
14   Janvier, *Pour Samuel Beckett*, 74.
15   Nadeau, "Le droit au silence", 1276.
16   Rickels, "Existential Themes in Beckett's *Unnamable*", 145.
17   Rickels, "Existential Themes", 134.
18   Nadeau, "Le droit au silence", 1276.

punishment for some mysterious crime, as the effect of an unalterable condemnation.

Together the obligation to express and the need to know oneself exert an enormous compulsive force which the artist perceives as a never-ending duty to make expiation. Of the Unnamable, Onimus writes: "Il lui faut parler et ce soliloque indéfini ressemble à un châtiment infernal: c'est le prix dont se paie la présence à soi-même!"[19] To illustrate the burdensome nature of the combined compulsion he feels, the creator-hero often speaks of it as a pensum imposed upon him since birth. "On m'a donné un pensum", says the Unnamable, "à ma naissance peut-être, pour me punir d'être né peut-être" (L'Innommable, pp. 46-47). Coincident with existence itself, the artist's burden of atonement represents his obligation to express and to seek self-knowledge through creation. As long as self-perception remains active, the overwhelming compulsion to create makes itself felt as a duty, the duty to atone for having come into existence. As early as his essay on Proust, Beckett compares "the life of the body on earth" to a pensum (Proust, p. 72) and describes the tragic figure as one who "represents the expiation of original sin, of the original and eternal sin of him and all his 'soci malorum,' the sin of having been born" (p. 49). In the early fiction, too, the theme of the pensum appears. Linking it to the creative act, the narrator of More Pricks Than Kicks exclaims in an erudite allusion: "Happy Infanta! Painted by Velásquez and then no more pensums!" (p. 51). For Mercier, it is simply a part of his condition which he calls "ma peine" (Mercier et Camier, p. 50) and "cette absurde peine" (p. 150), and which he proposes to deal with first by a purging (p. 50), later by accommodation (p. 150). Inescapable as self-consciousness, the ever present pensum is often experienced as a curse. Describing one moment in his quest, Moran writes: "Affaissé sur mon parapluie, la tête penchée comme sous une malédiction... je ne bougeais pas plus qu'une statue" (Molloy, p. 200). Overshadowed by the impossible demands of his very being, the author-hero considers life itself to be the expiation he must make ("ma leçon, ma vie", L'Innommable, p. 39). But the precise nature of his atonement is not clear. He does not know how to respond to the "termes mal compris d'une damnation obscure" (L'Innommable, p. 42). Gradually, however, the direct rapport between expiation and creation is established ("ce récit qu'on m'impose", L'Innommable, p. 203), and in the later fiction the hero recognizes that his duty to expiate involves the quest for self. For example, the Unnamable reflects: "Curieuse idée...

---

[19] Onimus, Beckett, 69.

celle d'une tâche à accomplir, avant de pouvoir être tranquille. Curieuse tâche, que d'avoir à parler de soi" (p. 48). As Janvier explains: "Il faut continuer: parler, ainsi, c'est satisfaire à ce pensum, à cette leçon qu'il faut réciter et dont le personnage fait parfois l'origine de son entreprise.... Le devoir, la leçon, le pensum, c'est la damnation ressentie... d'aller vers soi." [20]

Obsessed with his sense of a duty to perform in order to attain rest and silence, the narrator-hero of *L'Innommable* speaks repeatedly of his task: "il fallait parler seulement de moi, afin de pouvoir me taire" (p. 32); "dire qui j'étais, ce que j'étais, afin de pouvoir me taire, ne plus écouter" (p. 45); "[chercher] moyen de me rejoindre, là où je m'attends... ma seule chance de me taire, de parler un peu sans mentir... pour ne plus avoir à parler" (p. 70). Weary of having to speak on and on, the author is anxious to make atonement in order to earn "le droit au silence" (p. 38). But inadequately equipped (having only language to aid him), he cannot carry out his task. Between him and "le repos vivant, s'étend la même leçon que toujours (p. 38). His lesson is his life (the story of his life, of his misery) that he has tried to evade through fictions and that he must now try to discover by the same means. To be free from his obligation to speak, he must tell his own story, reveal the truth of his condition: "pour pouvoir m'arrêter, [des] mots à dire, [une] vérité à retrouver, pour pouvoir la dire, pour pouvoir m'arrêter" (*L'Innommable*, p. 54). He must define himself if he is ever to be silent; and until his words coincide with the truth of his inner being, he will have to go on speaking. Thus, "il s'agit de parler, il s'agit de ne plus parler" (p. 216). But progress toward silence is painfully slow, for one cannot speak of the self in spite of one's urgent need to do so: "C'est de moi maintenant que je dois parler... ce sera un commencement, un pas vers le silence, vers la fin de la folie, celle d'avoir à parler et de ne le pouvoir, sauf de choses qui ne me regardent pas, qui ne comptent pas, auxquelles je ne crois pas, dont ils m'ont gavé pour m'empêcher de dire qui je suis, où je suis, de faire ce que j'ai à faire de la seule manière qui puisse y mettre fin, de faire ce que j'ai à faire" (pp. 75-76). Beginning over and over again to try to speak only of himself in order to throw off his burden, the Unnamable never accomplishes his pensum and can only imagine how it will be in the future when at last he has said his piece: "C'est moi alors que je vomirai enfin" (pp. 76-77). Having abandoned "ce discours inutile qui ne m'est pas compté, qui ne me rapproche pas du silence d'une syllabe" (p. 41), he will achieve "le vrai silence, celui que je n'aurai plus à rompre"

[20]   Janvier, *Pour Samuel Beckett*, 78.

(p. 219) and will know the ideal state of entering "encore vivant dans le silence, pour pouvoir en jouir... pour me sentir qui me taisais, uni à tout cet air que moi seul agite depuis toujours" (p. 225). Only in silence and perfect immobility will he be at one with himself: "je parlerai de moi quand je ne parlerai plus" (p. 216); "dans le silence... ce sera moi" (p. 261). Frantically pushing on to reach this goal, he concludes his narrative with a summary of the pensum which remains to be said, of the goal which is yet to be reached: "il faut dire des mots, tant qu'il y en a, il faut les dire, jusqu'à ce qu'ils me trouvent, jusqu'à ce qu'ils me disent, étrange peine, étrange faute, il faut continuer, c'est peut-être déja fait, ils m'ont peut-être déjà dit, ils m'ont peut-être porté jusqu'au seuil de mon histoire, devant la porte qui s'ouvre sur mon histoire... si elle s'ouvre, ça va être moi, ça va être le silence, là où je suis, je ne sais pas, je ne sais pas, je ne le saurai jamais, dans le silence on ne sait pas, il faut continuer, je vais continuer" (pp. 261-262).

Similarly constrained to search for themselves through creation, the narrator-heroes of the *Textes* try to tell their own story in order to gain release from the obligation to express. Experiencing the creative compulsion as a pensum, one hero refers to his narrative as "ce devoir" (p. 180). Another shows how the telling itself reflects its punitive nature: "Et les oui et non ne veulent rien dire, dans cette bouche, ce sont comme des soupirs ponctuant une peine" (p. 189); and he goes on to describe his life as the serving of a prison sentence: "Et j'ai peut-être passé la moitié de ma vie dans les prisons de leur Etat, à purger les délits de l'autre moitié" (p. 194). Like the Unnamable, each author-hero here must find himself in words in order to be granted peace. Thus, one narrator is anxious to begin his story so that he may end it (p. 158). Another clearly acknowledges his need to identify himself: "parler tout seul, gentiment, sur bibi" (p. 198). Yet, as always, the task remains unfinished, incomplete, so that in the eleventh piece the hero admits: "Et je suis encore en route, par oui et par non, vers un encore à nommer, pour qu'il me laisse la paix" (p. 203). In *Comment c'est*, the same kind of expiation burdens the narrator, who defines his pensum at the outset: "raconte-moi encore finis de me raconter... ma vie dernier état" (p. 9). He recounts his life "as the penitential task that all Beckett's heroes perform".[21] Still, as shown in Chapter 4, he can never really tell 'comment c'est' because he cannot simultaneously relate and convey his reflections on the act of relating.

The primary importance of telling one's own story is dramatically evi-

---

[21]   Cohn, 296-297.

dent in *Play*. Here even after death the characters are compelled by self-perception to seek the truth of their past and present situations. Attempting to determine the purpose of the probing spotlight, one of the women remarks: "Penitence, yes, at a pinch, atonement, one was resigned, but no, that does not seem to be the point either" (p. 59). Uncertain of what the light demands, she formulates a theory that closely resembles interpretations of the expiation made by the heroes of the fiction: "Is it that I do not tell the truth, is that it, that some day somehow I may tell the truth at last and then no more light at last, for the truth?" (p. 54). Truth and its peace remain unattainable here too, however, for the play repeats itself,[22] indicating that the agony of trying to reach the true self goes on forever. The characters must undergo endlessly what Kenner calls the "Beckett ordeal, trying to tell the right story so as to be permitted peace".[23] Such is the plight of every author-hero, for whom "sin and punishment... meet in the impossible task of writing, describing, recounting, *creating*".[24] More detailed here, the dilemma involves the obligation to reach one's true self through expression and the impossibility of ever achieving that end. Art as evasion is replaced by art "as a kind of absurd but inescapable imposition, a 'pensum' exemplary of the absurd punishment that is our life".[25] Writing, in particular, is an onerous task which in the end seems totally futile. As Onimus describes it, "l'écriture... ne sera pour Beckett qu'un *pensum* imposé par une loi mystérieuse, une suite de mots éphémères par quoi l'homme, condamné à l'existence, est requis de se dire de se redire sans fin".[26] Thus, each author-hero presents "le spectacle d'un homme sans illusions qui, sachant sa tâche vaine, se sent condamné à la poursuivre jusqu'à son terme improbable".[27] Driven on by his obligation to find authentic reality, he can only move between "une parole vaine et un repos impossible".[28] There can be no rest, for the truth remains hidden somewhere beneath the words. Persistent effort, the relentless stripping off of one veil after another, brings one closer to the self, but "we can never reach the center itself".[29] Describing the "threshold situation" at the end of *L'Innommable*, Chambers defines the limit of approach to the self

[22] See indication, *Play*, 61: "*Repeat play*."
[23] Kenner, "Progress Report", 73.
[24] Mayoux, "Samuel Beckett and Universal Parody", 81; Mayoux's emphasis.
[25] Chambers, "Beckett's Brinkmanship", 152.
[26] Onimus, *Beckett*, 26.
[27] Nadeau, "Le droit au silence", 1273.
[28] Nadeau, 1274.
[29] Chambers, "Beckett's Brinkmanship", 156.

which the Beckettian hero achieves: "always on the brink but never able to cross it, unable to continue any longer and yet unable to stop and so continuing perforce, waiting endlessly in the faint hope that one day a door will unexpectedly open and we will have arrived."[30]

The duty to say the self seems particularly burdensome, then, because it can never be accomplished and, hence, is endless. One with existence, the compulsion to go on creating, to go on searching, makes life itself a painful obligation to continue doing whatever one must do. As early as *Watt*, the motif of compulsive, continuous activity appears. The hunchback Mr. Hackett, for example, cannot stand still. Finding his favorite bench occupied, he is forced to continue his walk: "he would not long remain motionless, for the state of his health rendered this unfortunately impossible. The dilemma was thus of extreme simplicity: to go on, or to turn, and return, round the corner, the way he had come" (*Watt*, pp. 7-8). Watt, too, is overshadowed, even while sitting down to rest on the way to Knott's, by the ever present need to go on: "He knew, as he did so, that it would not be easy to get up again, as he must, and move on again, as he must" (pp. 32-33). To assume that one's journey may have an end is only foolish, as the narrator of "La Fin" suggests: "je me trouvai dans les faubourgs, et de là aux vieilles erres ce n'était pas loin, au-delà du stupide espoir du repos ou de moindre peine" (*Nouvelles*, p. 105). The compulsion to create is felt continuously; it cannot be escaped, not even in time, for it weighs upon the author-hero without letup. One is not allowed to stop; as Molloy puts it, "il est interdit d'abandonner et même de s'arrêter un instant" (*Molloy*, p. 125). Telling what he knows of Molloy before setting out in search of him, Moran refers to his subject's continuous activity: "Il était toujours en chemin. Je ne l'avais jamais vu se reposer" (p. 175). Later speaking of his own report, he indicates that his labor is endless by comparing himself to Sisyphus (p. 206). For Malone, the need to continue reflects the need to keep on living, to cling to existence through creation: "l'essentiel... c'est que ...je continue à tenir dans cette chambre" (*Malone*, p. 114). Even Macmann comes to understand the importance of persevering. Having made the mistake of lying down on the ground during a torrential rainstorm, he is amazed at himself for his lack of foresight: "Et au lieu de s'étonner de cette pluie si violente et si longue, il s'étonnait de ne pas avoir compris, dès les premières gouttelettes, qu'il allait longuement et violemment pleuvoir, et qu'il ne fallait pas s'arrêter et s'étendre, mais au contraire continuer tout droit devant soi, aveuglément, en pressant

[30] *Ibid.*

autant que possible le pas" (p. 125). Obessed with his pensum, as shown above, the Unnamable makes repeated mention of the need to pursue it, to go on: "Continuer, puisqu'il le faut" (*L'Innommable*, p. 200); "je dois continuer" (p. 217); "continuer, c'est un circuit, un long circuit, je le connais bien" (p. 252). Describing the enormity and endlessness of his task, he says: "Rien ne pourra jamais m'en dispenser, il n'y a rien, rien à découvrir, rien qui diminue ce qui demeure à dire, j'ai la mer à boire, il y a donc une mer" (p. 55). Aware that he cannot escape this infinitely long expiation, the narrator admits to himself the boundless nature of the work before him. In the end, he seems as far as ever from his goal since he closes with the words: "il faut continuer je vais continuer" (p. 262). Yet, like Dante's proud ones, the creator hero "can no more".[31] Weary, talked out, he feels the impossibility of saying one more word. But he must go on, and, taking up from where *L'Innommable* left off, the first words of the *Textes* record the continued struggle: "je n'en pus plus, je ne pus continuer" (p. 127). Again the refrain *il faut continuer* appears (p. 200), and the ceaseless talking is termed *l'interminable délire* (p. 199). Time and place compose a limitless expanse, as one hero's query reveals: "peut-il y avoir ailleurs à cet ici infini?" (p. 169). Later another narrator recalls how the atonement must last as long as he does: "J'ai toute la journée, pour me tromper, pour me rattraper, pour me calmer, pour renoncer, je n'ai rien à craindre, mon billet est valable à vie" (p. 178). There is no end in sight either for the hero of "From an Abandoned Work". Compelled to speak, he recounts days drawn from his past; but though he is anxious to get through the telling, the conclusion of one 'day' calls for the getting on to another: "But let me get on now with the day I have hit on to begin with... on with it and out of my way and on to another" (p. 140); "So on to this second day and get it over and out of the way and on to the next" (p. 145); "But let me get up now and on and get this awful day over and on to the next" (p. 147). Existence itself seems endless in *Comment c'est*, where the hero speaks of Pim as "increvable frère" (p. 91) and declares: "je vais rester là oui collé contre lui oui à le martyriser oui éternellement oui" (p. 120). His own suffering and that of his victim must go on forever; as he remarks at one point near the end, "ça ne finit jamais" (p. 159).

The heroes of the fiction are not the only ones to know endless agony. Clov, in *Fin de partie*, is anxious to stop 'playing' and to leave Hamm's

---

[31]   Dante Alighieri, *Purgatorio*, ed. and trans. by John D. Sinclair (New York: Oxford University Press, 1961), 137.

abode. But when he implores, "Cessons de jouer!" Hamm replies, "Jamais!" (p. 102). Finally, resigning himself to his fate, Clov declares: "Bon,
ça ne finira donc jamais, je ne partirai donc jamais" (p. 108). Here existence itself is "une longue agonie vécue par des misérables qui attendent
une fin qui ne vient jamais, et qui ne saurait être pire qu'elle".[32] In *Play*,
too, the torment is endless, for the characters, victims of persistent self-
perception, are "condemned to rearticulate forever"[33] the story of their
lives. The suffering and effort required to keep going here are compared
by one of the women to the enormous task of "dragging a great roller,
on a scorching day. The strain... to get it moving" (p. 57). Describing this
situation, Fletcher writes: "As their 'inquisitor' probes, as the spot fixes
on each of their almost featureless faces in turn, they recite their piece, *da
capo* indefinitely. Theirs is indeed a 'world without end,' and that is their
tragedy." Speaking of the other plays, he continues: "Hamm can never
die. Clov never leave, Godot never come, just as the Voice of *Cascando*
can never hope for 'no more stories... sleep.' There is no end to the punishment inflicted on man for having been born."[34] In the same way, the
author-heroes must continue to search for themselves through creation,
for there is no choice. Life itself is "a pain that will not end".[35] There is
nothing else to be done but to keep on going. Unable ever to find the self,
to say the truth of self, one can never fulfill the expiation. "On s'analyse
sans fin", says Onimus, "mais plus on cherche à s'identifier plus on s'égare
dans le labyrinthe.... En s'obstinant à forer sa voie vers un centre qui la fuit
toujours, la conscience ne réussit qu'à éliminer ses différences spécifiques,
elle se perd de vue à force de se chercher."[36] Life for the artist-hero is,
then, a pursuit of self, "the endless, hopeless task of pursuing an infinitely
receding *something* which – resisting definition and being inseparable
from what surrounds it – has the characteristics of *nothing*".[37] Unbearable
frustration, existence appears basically "as endless exile from and pursuit
of an infinitely unattainable self".[38] Saddled from birth with an impossible
task to do, the author-hero is indeed a kind of Sisyphus whose unceasing,
eternally repeated efforts are never enough to satisfy the requirement:
"Le Sisyphe beckettien n'est porteur que de lui-même, il redescend éter-

---

[32]   Boisdeffre, "Samuel Beckett ou l'au-delà", 683.
[33]   Kenner, "Progress Report", 76.
[34]   Fletcher, *Samuel Beckett's Art*, 72-73.
[35]   Glicksberg, "Samuel Beckett's World of Fiction", 41.
[36]   Onimus, *Beckett*, 45.
[37]   Chambers, "Beckett's Brinkmanship", 154.
[38]   *Ibid.*

nellement à la recherche de lui-même; d'où le thème si fréquent du recommencement."[39]

Bound forever to futility and frustration, the creator-hero in search of himself through fiction knows nothing but suffering. His existence, dominated by acute distress and anxiety, follows "the dolorous and necessary course" (*Proust*, p. 51) which is the lot of the Beckettian artist. Throughout the fiction, the agony of the hero grows, but at all times it is unbearable. The voyage of Mercier et Camier, for instance, is likened by Fletcher to a calvary.[40] Indeed, this same critic speaks of the evolution in the fiction as a "pente douloureuse" which in the end produces "l'Innommable au bout de son calvaire".[41] The torment he undergoes is bad enough; but he is capable of imagining an even worse torture, one like that of Prometheus, agonizing and meant to be eternal: "Et si je parlais pour ne rien dire, mais vraiment rien?... je me ferais grignoter moins vite, dans mon vieux berceau, et les chairs arrachées auraient le temps de se recoller, comme dans le Caucase, avant d'être arrachées à nouveau" (*L'Innommable*, pp. 31-32). Still, the suffering he endures could scarcely be worse: "C'est un supplice tarabiscoté, impossible à penser, à cerner, à sentir, à subir, oui, insubissable aussi, je souffre mal aussi... comme une vieille dinde mourant debout, le dos chargé de poussins, guettée par les rats" (p. 55). Worm, his creature, has no better fate: "Il n'a pas besoin de raisonner, seulement de souffrir, toujours de la même façon, jamais moins, jamais plus, sans espoir de trève, sans espoir de crève" (p. 165). In *Comment c'est*, the pain of creation is transferred as the narrator compels Pim to utter sounds in response to beatings and to answer questions which the hero carves into his back with the fingernail of his index finger (pp. 63-121). The creative process becomes a virtual martyrdom as the victim suffers the rigors imposed by his tormentor: "le cul à sang les nerfs à vif" (p. 89). Yet the combined efforts of the hero and Pim are somehow necessary, inevitable, for the narrator defines a couple as "deux étrangers qui s'unissent pour les besoins du tourment" (p. 147). Moreover, here in the dark and the mud, a cry is a sign of life: "la vie parce que ça crie c'est la preuve" (p. 148). As shown in Chapter 2, suffering is the only reality for those who have once eluded the grasp of habit. Fully aware of his misery, the self-conscious artist shows in his works that "creation and creator are conceivable, believable, only as aspects of anguish".[42] Indeed, the agony in-

---

[39] Onimus, *Beckett*, 45.
[40] Fletcher, *The Novels*, 115.
[41] Fletcher, "Beckett et Proust", 99.
[42] Cohn, 204.

creases so from one work to the next that in the end there seems to remain only a cry, a stripped suffering. Describing this evolution, Claude Mauriac writes: "Anéantissement progressif, si bien qu'à la fin il n'y a plus rien qu'une bouche qui se plaint. Pas même: une voix. Un être informe, impalpable, inexistant mais qui souffre." [43]

---

[43] Mauriac, "Samuel Beckett", 86.

9. MASKS

Torn between the obligation to create, the need to seek the truth, and the impossibility of accomplishing the creative act, of being at one with himself, the artist-hero suffers deeply and endlessly. Compelled by self-perception and the need to know himself, he is forever paralysed by his inability to express the inner vision, by his failure to find the self in words. Having examined the source of the compulsion he feels, let us consider now the nature of those obstacles which prevent him from achieving success, from fulfilling his expiation.

Bound to storytelling as a means of self-discovery, the author-hero finds, first of all, that his creatures, though meant to aid him in his search, only stand in his way or divert him from his purpose. Malone's fictions, for instance, are "devised to aid him in his understanding of the perplexing creature, man; he deals with his creatures as extensions of himself."[1] Yet, in the end he rejects them all as futile attempts to evade the truth of himself: "Tout est prétexte, Sapo et les oiseaux, Moll, les paysans, ceux qui dans les villes se cherchent et se fuient, mes doutes qui ne m'intéressent pas, ma situation, mes possessions, prétexte pour ne pas en venir au fait, à l'abandon, en levant le pouce, en disant pouce et en s'en allant, sans autre forme de procès, quitte à se faire mal voir de ses petits camarades" (*Malone*, p. 195). Anxious to have done with his pensum, the Unnamable repeatedly blames his creatures directly for having retarded his progress: "Ces Murphy, Molloy, et autres Malone, je n'en suis pas dupe. Ils m'ont fait perdre mon temps, rater ma peine, en me permettant de parler d'eux, quand il fallait parler seulement de moi, afin de pouvoir me taire" (*L'Innommable*, pp. 32-33). Referring to them as "ces souffre-douleurs" (p. 33) and as "quelques gentils damnés à qui accrocher mes gémissements" (p. 38), he speaks of himself lurking behind them as behind a screen or mask: "derrière mes homuncules... j'ai perdu mon temps, renié mes droits, raté

---

[1] Oates, "The Trilogy of Samuel Beckett", 163.

ma peine, oublié ma leçon" (p. 38). Describing how they distract him from himself, he says: "Suis-je vêtu? Je me suis souvent posé cette question, puis vite je parlais du chapeau de Malone, du manteau de Molloy, du costume de Murphy" (p. 35). Basile and the others in the present narrative he refers to as: "Inexistants, inventés pour expliquer je ne sais plus quoi. Ah oui, Mensonges que tout ça. Dieu et les hommes, le jour et la nature, les élans du coeur et le moyen de comprendre, lâchement je les ai inventés... pour retarder l'heure de parler de moi" (p. 34). Again he avows: "Superflu, petite âme toujours, l'amour je l'ai inventé, la musique, l'odeur du grosseiller sauvage, pour m'éviter. Des organes, un dehors, c'est facile à imaginer, d'autres, un Dieu, c'est forcé, on les imagine, c'est facile, ça calme le principal, ça endort un instant" (p. 36). Fictions divert him from the pain of being, but only momentarily. He must always come back to his unfinished task. Faced with it once again, he can only claim that his creatures are responsible for his plight. For example, of Mahood he says: "C'est lui qui me racontait des histoires sur moi, vivait pour moi, sortait de moi, revenait vers moi, rentrait dans moi, m'agonisait d'histoires.... C'est sa voix qui s'est souvent, toujours mêlée à la mienne, au point quelquefois de la couvrir tout à fait" (p. 44). He cannot speak the truth, then, because Mahood has gained control of him, has usurped his faculties: "Mais sa voix continuait à témoigner pour lui, comme tissée dans la mienne, m'empêchant de dire qui j'étais, ce que j'étais, afin de pouvoir me taire, ne plus écouter" (p. 45). Finally, he suggests that these fictions of his regularly deprive him of his identity: "Mahood. Avant lui il y en avait d'autres, se prenant pour moi. Ça doit être une sinécure passant de père en fils, à en juger par leur air de famille" (p. 56). As a means to self-knowledge, his creatures are completely inadequate; in fact, he comes to see them "as disguises of himself out of which he must define his own identity".[2] They are no more than veils to be torn away in the search for the authentic self. Speaking of how he is hidden beneath his fictions, he asks: "M'estime-t-on déjà suffisamment enduit de balivernes pour ne plus jamais pouvoir m'en dépêtrer ni faire un geste qui n'ait l'effet d'animer un plâtre?" (p. 77). Comparing himself to a masker, he continues: "Leurs attributs, il m'en ont chargé, et je les ai traînés, comme au carnaval, sous les missiles" (p. 77). But his is no ordinary costume; describing it as "ma carapace de monstre" (p. 77), he calls attention to the grotesqueness of so much falsity.

Suggesting repeatedly that he is the author of all the preceding novels,

---

[2] Oates, 164.

the Unnamable insists at the same time that the other author-heroes are
clearly distinct from him. In the very beginning he describes Malone, who
turns about him, as "étranger pour toujours à mes faiblesses" (p. 25).
Later he makes a formal denial of any identity between himself and previous heroes: "Je ne suis pas, est-ce besoin de le dire, ni Murphy, ni Watt, ni
Mercier, non, je ne veux plus les nommer, ni aucun des autres... qui m'ont
dit que j'étais eux, que j'ai dû essayer d'être, par force, par frayeur, pour
ne pas me reconnaître, aucun rapport" (p. 79). Questioning the validity of
all fiction, he asks: "Mais est-ce une vie, ça, qui se dissipe dès qu'on passe
à un autre sujet?" (p. 136). Still later in his story he continues to regret the
time lost with his inventions: "temps que j'ai perdu avec ces paquets de
sciure, à commencer par Murphy, qui n'était pas le premier, alors que je
m'avais moi, à domicile, sous la main, croulant sous mes propres peau et
os, des vrais, crevant de solitude et d'oubli, au point que je venais à douter
de mon existence" (p. 213). Yet he had no choice but to invent them, since
he has always been compelled to speak and has always been unable to speak
of himself directly. Admitting that he is responsible for creating Mahood
and the rest, the Unnamable says he did so "afin de pouvoir parler, puisqu'il fallait parler, sans parler de moi, je ne pouvais parler de moi, on ne
m'avait pas dit qu'il fallait parler de moi" (p. 223). Then, claiming that
the creatures themselves asked him to speak of them, he goes on to explain
why he decided to do so: "je croyais que ça m'arrangeait, puisque je n'avais
rien à dire, puisque je devais dire quelque chose" (p. 224). Aware of
the futility inherent in this evasion of his problem, the Unnamable nevertheless turns to fictions for relief even near the end of his narrative: "j'y
trouverai quelqu'un, je me mettrai dans lui, je dirai que c'est moi" (p. 233).
Thus, dependent on fictions to see him through his dilemma of having to
express and having nothing to say, the narrator-hero never achieves the
expiation required to attain peace. "For", writes Wellershoff, "narrative
now appears... as the most striking form of self-deception. In the narration
one puts on a costume, slides away from oneself, leaves oneself. Earlier
the hidden 'I' had told itself stories and persuaded itself they dealt with
itself.... It had seen itself as Molloy, Moran, Malone, and Macmann. But
these figures are *homunculi* who never existed. All the time there had existed
nothing but the talking 'I'... concealed... behind the fictions in which it
vainly searched for itself."[3] Yet there is no other way to the truth for the
creator-hero; at least, he can find no other solution to his dilemma. As
Gerard explains it: "The artist, who is concerned only with the truth, can

---

[3]   Wellershoff, "Failure of an Attempt at De-Mythologization", 101.

arrive at it only by means of a fiction. The creations of the Unnamable –
Molloy, Malone, Macmann and the rest – stand... not only as surrogates
of the Unnamable's non-existent personality, but as an illustration of this
tortuous irony in the artist's search for himself.... It does seem that it is
only by the adoption of a fictitious mechanism and the entry into a labyrinth that may never lead back to the self that the self can be found. It does
seem that it is only by the saying of words on other subjects... that the
words will be found which will discover the self and release it from its
torment." [4]

But words – the very medium for the writer's art – are not to be trusted.
Paradoxically, although they reveal much about oneself, one's words can
never convey anything beyond the surface personality. Indeed, having an
existence of their own, they screen one from oneself. As Molloy says of
his encounter with a shepherd, "Tout cela à travers une poussière étince-
lante et bientôt à travers cette bruine aussi qui chaque jour me livre à moi
et me voile le reste et me voile à moi" (*Molloy*, p. 42). The inner vision
provided by self-perception is distorted by conception, by the tissue of
words in which one attempts to seize it. Thus, storytelling, creating with
words, is "une convention qui veut qu'on mente ou qu'on se taise" (*Molloy*, p. 135), since it inevitably involves both fictions and words which
mask the self. Let us examine now more closely the basic obstacles language poses to expiation. Language cannot name the self, first of all, because words exist separately from those objects and ideas which they are
supposed to designate. Inadequate even to perform the everyday function
of referring to visible things, language proves to be an extremely unwieldy
tool for probing the inner depths, since the word itself always stands between the one who names and the thing he seeks to name. Moreover, words
are so laden with multiple meanings that one can never be certain of a
single word's definition. As the narrator in *Murphy* says, "In the beginning was the pun" (p. 65). Language inevitably exists separately from fact
and idea. "Signs of the intellect's representations of reality", writes Robert Klawitter, "language is still further removed from reality than thought.
Yet every man inevitably lives in a world his words create around him." [5]
Never identical with the object of its articulation, the word as it is spoken
or thought creates its own reality which it interposes between the conceiver
and the thing conceived. As Wellershoff observes, "language is the fundamental deception... a system of sounds devoid of content which moves
only within itself. Because the word is not the thing it indicates, one can

4   Gerard, "Molloy becomes Unnamable", 318-319.
5   Klawitter, "Being and Time", 7320.

believe one is speaking of something without possessing or understanding
it." The rapport between language and thing is, then, one of "pure non-
possession".[6] For Watt, this discovery about language is agonizing, since
he depends on words to unburden his mind of inexplicable occurrences:
"For to explain had always been to exorcize, for Watt" (*Watt*, p. 78). At
Knott's, however, both things and Watt's own condition elude language,
leaving him in great distress: "For Watt now found himself in the midst
of things which, if they consented to be named, did so as it were with
reluctance. And the state in which Watt found himself resisted formulation in a way no state had ever done" (p. 81). As an example of his plight,
"looking at a pot... or thinking of a pot... it was in vain that Watt said,
Pot, pot. Well, perhaps not quite in vain, but very nearly. For it was not a
pot, the more he looked, the more he reflected, the more he felt sure of
that, that is was not a pot at all. It resembled a pot, it was almost a pot, but
it was not a pot of which one could say, Pot, pot, and be comforted" (p.
81). In Mr Knott's house words no longer fit the things they are supposed
to name. Moreover, Watt, though not a permanent part of the Knott establishment, can no longer identify himself with linguistic formulae:
"Then, when he turned for reassurance to himself, who was not Mr
Knott's in the sense that the pot was, who had come from without and
whom the without would take again, he made the distressing discovery
that of himself too he could no longer affirm anything that did not seem as
false as if he had affirmed it of a stone" (p. 82). He cannot even be comforted by calling himself a man. Though he continues to think of himself as
one, "for all the relief that this afforded him, he might just as well have
thought of himself as a box, or an urn" (p. 83). Desiring always that words
be applied to his situation so that he might be tranquillized, Watt suffers
from the lack of "semantic succour" (p. 83) which he feels so keenly under
Knott's roof. Thus, he continues to make "agonized and agonizing efforts
to explain the world through language"[7] but inevitably fails to find a
language that will describe the reality which he experiences.

The language that used to serve him so well no longer functions here. It
is out-of-date, useless as an old coin. Still, "most often he found himself
longing for a voice ...to speak of the little world of Mr Knott's establishment, with the old words, the old credentials" (pp. 84-85). A similar nos-
talgia for an outworn language appears in *Happy Days* where Winnie, who
realizes that certain terms – particularly those having to do with time – no
longer apply to her situation, exults in what she calls "the old style" of

[6]   Wellershoff, "Failure of an Attempt at De-Mythologization", 102.
[7]   Cohn, *The Comic Gamut*, 87.

speech (p. 13 and passim). *Daily*, *day*, and *night* (pp. 13, 18, 44, and passim) describe nothing for her now. Caught forever beneath a scorching sun which never sets, she can only query: "May one still speak of time?" (p. 50). With reason or not, she does speak of time, of days and nights, for although these concepts have no real meaning, they are all she has to go on with. She is unable to replace them with new words that would describe her situation more accurately. Temporal distinctions seem to be meaningless too in *Fin de partie* where Clov remarks of the words *sommeil*, *réveil*, *soir*, and *matin*: "Ils ne savent rien dire" (p. 108). Similarly, the hero of *Comment c'est*, surrounded by utter darkness as Winnie by light, knows well that the language of the past has no value in his timeless world: "entendre jour le répéter le murmurer ne pas avoir honte comme s'il y avait une terre un soleil des moments où il fait moins noir plus noir" (p. 133); "pas de soleil pas de terre rien qui tourne le même instant toujours partout" (p. 136). There are no words for his miserable condition, so he must rely on those left over from another era.

Terms for time are not the only ones lacking, however. Existence itself escapes formulation. As Winnie says, "life… Yes, life I suppose, there is no other word" (*Happy Days*, p. 28). In the same way, the narrator of *Premier amour* describes his relationship with Anne: "Oui, je l'aimais, c'est le nom que je donnais, que je donne hélas toujours, à ce que je faisais, à cette époque" (p. 27). Not at all the right words for what they are supposed to designate, these linguistic tags do not satisfy the speakers who choose them. But there are no other words from which to choose. Equipped only with a language that is worn thin by universal application and bound up in endless connotation, the creator-heroes have small hope of ever saying what they really mean; and, as their anguish becomes ever more acute, as their condition steadily deteriorates, the language of a former time seems further and further removed from the reality they now know. For Molloy, the meaning of words is obscure (*Molloy*, p. 41), and he is unable to make himself understood by others (p. 128). In fact, he does not even comprehend what he says himself: "Et les mots que je prononçais moi-même et qui devaient presque toujours se rattacher à un effort de l'intelligence, souvent ils me faisaient l'effet d'un bourdonnement d'insecte" (p. 75). For him, words are simply a part of the general chaos of existence. He perceives them "comme des sons purs, libres de toute signification" (p. 74). Thus attuned to the independent existence of language, he finds conversation "indiciblement pénible" (p. 75). Having abandoned Watt's hope of finding names to fit things, Molloy has long accepted the fact that "la condition de l'objet était d'être sans nom, et inversement" (pp. 45-46).[8] Forever separated by an unbridgeable gulf, word and object go each its own way; one can never coincide with the other, for they occupy different realms – the one the intelligence, the other the world. Yet ideas, too, elude words, as the Unnamable discovers: "Appeler ça des questions, des hypothèses. Aller de l'avant, appeler ça aller, appeler ça de l'avant" (*L'Innommable*, p. 7). Echoing Molloy, he observes how words cannot be applied to his inner vision: "ces images sans nom que j'ai, ces noms sans images" (p. 247). In the *Textes*, the utter lack of rapport between language and phenomenon reflects the dilemma of the artist as it appears in the form of an impossible imperative: "Nommer, non, rien n'est nommable, dire, non, rien n'est dicible" (p. 203). One cannot create, one cannot name the self, for nothing is namable. The obligation to expiate through expression can never be met. In *Comment c'est*, words applied to objects do not stick (p. 74), and they always seem to say too much: "tous ces mots trop forts presque tous un peu trop forts" (p. 140); "ces mots ne sont pas assez faibles la plupart pas tout à fait" (p. 154). As Moran puts it, "tout langage est un écart de langage" (*Molloy*, p. 179). To say is to contradict reality: "C'est vite dit, et vite écrit, ne pas pouvoir, alors qu'en réalité rien n'est plus malaisé" (*Molloy*, p. 215). Words, then, convey nothing but themselves, are in effect empty, as Winnie realizes with such pain: "On the other hand, did I ever know a temperate time? (*Pause.*) No. (*Pause.*) I speak of temperate times and torrid times, they are empty words. (*Pause.*) I speak of when I was not yet caught – in this way – and had my legs and had the use of my legs, and could seek out a shady place, like you, when I was tired of the sun, or a sunny place when I was tired of the shade, like you, and they are all empty words" (*Happy Days*, p. 38). Present reality belies the past so completely that the very language of that other time has no further significance. Only the present is real, and for the agony of the present moment there are no words. Yet even if Winnie could find words to fit her misery, they would not serve, for, as Beckett writes in one of the critical essays, "chaque fois qu'on veut faire faire aux mots un véritable travail de transbordement, chaque fois qu'on veut leur faire exprimer autre chose que des mots, ils s'alignent de façon à s'annuler mutuellement".[9] Similarly, Malone observes: "Mais mes notes ont une fâcheuse tendance, je l'ai compris enfin, à faire disparaître tout ce qui est sensé en faire l'objet" (*Malone*, p. 162). Expressing the same idea, the hero of "Le Calmant" declares: "Tout ce

[8]   In the English translation, *Molloy* (New York, 1965), 31: "there could be no things but nameless things, no names but thingless names".
[9]   "La Peinture des van Velde", 352.

que je dis s'annule, je n'aurai rien dit" (*Nouvelles*, p. 43). Forever alienated from meaning, language can never function for the creator-hero. Though he is bound to it (since he has no other tool), "le langage... s'avère impuissant à représenter, à dire autre chose que des mots".[10]

   Language will not serve to define the self, then, because of its own identity. But even were it able to convey meaning, it would be inadequate to the demands the artist makes upon it, for it exists as a repository for society's general notions. It champions the collective, the impersonal, the familiar, and can say nothing of the individual, the personal, the unforeseen. An aid to habit, it provides general labels for almost any circumstance. At the appearance of some distressing or incomprehensible phenomenon, it quickly supplies an antidote to bewilderment and disbelief in the form of a cliché designed to 'civilize' the event, to somehow make it more palatable to the mind, less outrageous, and finally acceptable. Intended specifically to gloss over unpleasant realities, language forged by society has little to offer the artist whose main concern is to get beneath deceptive surfaces and to arrive at the truth no matter how disagreeable it may be. As Harvey explains, "language belongs to the practical world of surfaces, to the domain of intellect. It is an instrument poorly adapted to the exigencies of art."[11] Significantly, Beckett "describes his own language as a veil which must be torn asunder in order to get at the things (or the nothing) lying behind. 'Grammar and Style!' he writes scornfully... A mask.'"[12] Language is a mask because it does not belong to the writer who uses it. It is the product of others, made in accordance with their way of seeing, or not seeing, existence. Stressing the importance of this insight into language, Onimus writes: "Beckett avait découvert que l'homme est fait de mots et que ces mots ne sont pas à lui, qu'il n'existe que par les mots des *autres*. Quand il s'écoute c'est un discours étranger qui se fait entendre, un moi universel, un *je* collectif qui tendent à s'exprimer, une structure de stéréotypes verbaux."[13] Making this same discovery is painful for Watt, because he has always counted so heavily on the tranquillizing power of language. Once he can no longer find comfort in words, he can no longer escape the misery of his perplexing situation. As Warhaft explains it: "In Watt the acid of experience dissolves the verbal chain (by showing up its arbitrariness, its irrelevance, the fact that it is only a rationalization and not a reality) and leaves man face to face with the thing.

---

[10]   Bernal, *Langage et fiction*, 93.
[11]   Harvey, "Life, Art, and Criticism", 555.
[12]   *Ibid.*
[13]   Onimus, *Beckett*, 73-74.

Watt discovers that the word 'pot' no longer fits the thing pot, that 'man' no longer has any relation to his own self – that with which he has to deal. He has lost the semantic chains by which the world has always been artificially manipulated and is forced into the encounter with that world in itself."[14] Rather than being able to find truth through words, one must break away from language and the preconceptions it supplies if one is to learn anything about the human condition or oneself. Alien to Molloy, as it is indeed to all the narrator-heroes, language cannot begin to establish a rapport with him. "Toute conversation que nous pourrions avoir avec lui", observes Georges Bataille, "ne serait qu'un spectre, une apparence de conversation. Elle nous éloignerait, nous renvoyant à quelque apparence d'humanité, à autre chose qu'à cette absence d'humanité, qu'annonce l'épave se traînant dans la rue et qui fascine."[15] Keenly aware that the words he uses to carry out his pensum are those of others, the Unnamable struggles against the ready-made categories and concepts which are imposed upon him. Indeed, he seems to recognize that this prefabricated language is a major obstacle to the completion of his task, for he complains repeatedly: "rien que les paroles des autres" (L'Innommable, p. 55); "je n'ai que leur langage à eux" (p. 78); "peut-être que cette fois-ci encore je ne ferai que chercher ma leçon sans pouvoir la dire, tout en m'accompagnant dans une langue qui n'est pas la mienne" (p. 39). At one point he imagines that those who are responsible for the language he uses have expressly forced their words upon him in order to make him like themselves, to blur even further his identity: "M'avoir collé un langage dont ils s'imaginent que je ne pourrai jamais me servir sans m'avouer de leur tribu, la belle astuce" (p. 76). All the same, one cannot make the words of others conform to one's thought. As a result, the creator-hero finds his own words strange. Mrs. Rooney, for example, avows: "I use none but the simplest words, I hope, and yet I sometimes find my way of speaking very... bizarre."[16] Having no language of his own, the artist is compelled to use the poor tool society has made. In his efforts to see into the truth of himself, he has only the blinding, distorting, utterly inadequate formulae of others to aid him. Yet, all men are limited by such a language; one can ask with Mayoux, "who does not express himself in a foreign language?"[17]

Not surprisingly, then, communication of any kind is difficult, if not

---

[14]   Warhaft, "Threne and Theme in *Watt*", 14-15.
[15]   Bataille, "Le Silence de Molloy", 388.
[16]   *All That Fall*, 35; hereafter referred to in the text with the appropriate page number in parentheses.
[17]   Mayoux, "The Theatre of Samuel Beckett", 154.

impossible, for the Beckettian hero. Anxious to say a few words to a young boy he meets on his excursion, the narrator of "Le Calmant" makes a ludicrously futile effort: "Je préparai donc me phrase et ouvris la bouche, croyant que j'allais l'entendre, mais je n'entendis qu'une sorte de râle, inintelligible même pour moi qui connaissais mes intentions" (*Nouvelles*, p. 53). Explaining then that his *aphonie* is due to long periods of silence, he goes on later to note how, during a conversation with a strange man he meets, "les mots me revenaient petit à petit, et la façon de les faire sonner" (p. 66). Alien objects difficult to articulate, words are not of his being and consequently can help little in the search for self. Even more handicapped in his attempts to communicate, the hero of "La Fin" tries at one point to rely on facial expression but finds to his dismay that his visage will no longer assume the various masks necessary to his survival: "J'avais dû changer depuis mon expulsion du sous-sol. Le visage notamment avait dû atteindre sa climatérique. Le sourire humble et naïf ne venait plus, ni l'expression de misère candide.... Je les appelais, mais ils ne venaient plus. Masque de vieux cuir sale et poilu, il ne voulait plus faire s'il vous plaît et merci et pardon. C'était malheureux. Avec quoi allais-je ramper, à l'avenir?" (p. 104). He has no better luck with speech: "J'essayais de gémir, Au secours! Mais le ton qui sortait était celui de la conversation courante. Je ne pouvais plus gémir" (p. 104). Stressing the mask-like quality of language, he goes on: "La dernière fois qu'il m'avait fallu gémir je l'avais fait, bien, comme toujours, et cela en l'absence de tout coeur à fendre" (p. 105). Invented with others in mind, language is always interpersonal. Even when it is evidence of a sincere feeling, its role as a facility to communication, and especially to hypocritical communication, becomes clear. Further, the sincere expression is the most likely to be misunderstood. Thus, when Weir informs the hero that he can never be readmitted to the asylum (which he is about to leave), that his expulsion is final, the unhappy wretch responds in a way that his interlocutor finds difficult to comprehend: "Exelmans! m'écriai-je. Allons, allons, dit-il, d'ailleurs on ne comprends pas le dixième de ce que vous dites" (p. 82). Communication becomes less possible in the trilogy. In order to 'speak' with his mother, Molloy resorts to blows: "Je me mettais en communication avec elle en lui tapotant le crâne" (*Molloy*, p. 24). Similarly, when Malone's Louis tells a story, his words fail to adequately express his meaning and are not understood by his listener, Sapo: "Ils étaient là, en face l'un de l'autre, dans l'obscurité, l'un parlant, l'autre écoutant, et loin, l'un de ce qu'il disait, l'autre de ce qu'il entendait, et loin l'un de l'autre" (*Malone*, p. 70). Confined in his jar, the Unnamable makes violent efforts to communicate with his patroness, but all to no avail: "J'ai essayé de lui faire comprendre, en cognant ma tête avec rage contre les parois du goulot, au moment où, la niege ayant diminué, elle me découvrait, que j'aimerais être occulté plus souvent. En même temps je jetais de la bave, en signe de mécontentement. Elle n'a rien compris. Je me demande quelle explication elle a bien pu trouver à cette conduite" (*L'Innommable*, p. 86). Even the narrator of *Comment c'est*, who as tormentor seems relatively successful in making himself understood by means of blows and scratches, encounters problems in his attempt to derive information from Pim. For instance, when he indicates that he wishes to know about Pim's former life, the result is "confusion complète" (p. 91).

A foreign collection of concepts and sounds, language is particularly unsuited to the task of laying bare the truth – be it that of the human condition or that of the individual self. Language cannot serve as a tool for discovery of new knowledge because it is nothing but a fabric created by old ideas and by habit. Referring always to the familiar, it cannot throw light on the not yet seen. As Mme Bernal explains, "S'approprier le langage, c'est écrire dans l'éclairage des mots."[18] A closed system of nuance and logic, language once adopted insinuates itself into the writer's thought where it distorts all that is original and masks the unheard of with its prosaic sameness. "Qui parle est entraîné par la logique du langage et de ses articulations", observes Claude Mauriac; "aussi l'écrivain affronté à l'indicible doit-il ruser pour ne pas dire ce que les mots lui font dire malgré lui, mais pour exprimer au contraire ce que leur raison d'être est précisément de taire: l'incertain, le contradictoire, l'impensable. L'innommable."[19] Constantly aware of the limits which language imposes in this way on expression, the author-hero when commenting on his creative efforts stresses the difficulties he encounters with an inflexible set of formulae. In *Premier amour*, for example, the hero complains: "c'est toujours le même ciel et ce n'est jamais le même ciel, comment exprimer cette chose, je ne l'exprimerai pas, voilà" (p. 36). Similarly, in *Mercier et Camier*, language fails Mercier: "Les paroles me manquent, dit-il pour exprimer ce que je ressens" (p. 63). Molloy, too, has difficulties with the idiom, which for him does not have enough different tenses: "Ma vie, ma vie, tantôt j'en parle comme d'une chose finie, tantôt comme d'une plaisanterie qui dure encore, et j'ai tort, car elle est finie et elle dure à la fois, mais par quel temps du verbe exprimer cela?" (*Molloy*, p. 53). Calling attention to the inadequacy of words, Malone describes his impression of a visitor's

[18]   Bernal, *Langage et fiction*, 149.
[19]   Mauriac, "Samuel Beckett", 83.

yellow shoes as "un effet dont les mots sont impuissants à donner la plus faible idée" (*Malone*, p. 185). But it is the Unnamable who pronounces final judgment upon language. "Les mots se bousculent, comme des fourmis", he says, "pressés, indifférents, n'apportant rien, n'emportant rien, trop faibles pour creuser" (*L'Innommable*, p. 139). Declaring language unfit for excavation, he condemns it as a tool for the artist, whose principal task is the inner descent, the endless penetration deep into being. Language is totally inadequate in the search for self, and the writer who is compelled to use it will never fulfill his expiation. As Janvier explains it: "La parole se conteste au fur et à mesure qu'elle se dévide, parce que le langage est constitué quand je le saisis, et que si je veux avec cette vieille arme me dire, moi, je reste introuvable et trompé." Thus, "il y a illusion à vouloir parler à neuf parce que le langage est fait avant moi".[20] More, "se raconter est encore une naïveté insupportable au regard de ce que ces racontars veulent livrer, tendent passionnément à dévoiler". Through language, the author-hero can only suggest what he would say. "C'est pourquoi", continues Janvier, "le racontar, en se désignant, se condamne comme tel, et renvoie toujours à ce moi en creux, connaissant l'impossibilité de le faire apparaître en relief."[21]

Condemnation of language in the *Textes* stresses the weakness of words. One hero compares them to smoke (p. 131) and declares: "plus peur des grands mots, ils ne sont pas grands" (p. 133). Another admires their negative quality but at the same time regrets how easily negations themselves are negated: "la beauté toute négative de la parole, dont malheureusement les négations subissent le même sort, en voilà la laideur" (p. 186). Still another uses negations to show how concepts and things have been devoured by the words that name them and have thus lost all their significance: "Non, pas d'âmes, pas de corps, ni de naissance, ni de vie, ni de mort, il faut continuer sans rien de tout cela, tout cela est mort de mots, tout cela est trop de mots, ils ne savent pas dire autre chose, ils disent qu'il n'y a pas autre chose, qu'ici ce n'est pas autre chose, mais ils ne le diront plus, ils ne le diront pas toujours, ils trouveront autre chose, peu importe quoi, et je pourrai continuer" (p. 200). In the end the narrator is left with nothing but lifeless words: "rien à tout jamais que mots morts" (p. 214). The motif of dead language appears as early as *Murphy*, where Celia "felt so often with Murphy, spattered with words that went dead as soon as they sounded; each word obliterated, before it had time to make sense, by the word that came next; so that in the end she did not know

[20]   Janvier, *Pour Samuel Beckett*, 77.
[21]   Janvier, 78.

what had been said" (p. 40). In *All That Fall*, Mrs. Rooney finds language
lifeless and unbearably difficult to deal with; and her husband, who takes
note of her problem, admits that he has experienced similar trouble: "Do
you know, Maddy", he says, "sometimes one would think you were strug-
gling with a dead language." "Yes indeed, Dan", she replies, "I know full
well what you mean, I often have that feeling, it is unspeakably excruciat-
ing." "I confess I have it sometimes myself", Mr. Rooney rejoins, "when
I happen to overhear what I am saying" (p. 80). For the creator, then,
"all speech [is] a struggle with dying idioms",[22] with feeble words that
cannot help him in his plight, that, in fact, contribute to the agony of his
dilemma. Perhaps the final note here should be an observation on the kind
of character for whom language does not pose a problem. Blindly self-
confident, the creature of habit depends so completely upon the clichés
and pat answers which language provides that the utter impotence of
words never strikes him. Commenting sardonically upon just such a con-
tented soul, the narrator in *Murphy* writes: "But words never failed Dr.
Killiecrankie, that for him would have been tantamount to loose thinking" (p. 262).

Demonstrating the inadequacy of language to the task of creation and
self-exploration, each novel reveals "la parole toujours plus dépouillée,
démunie, mise à nu".[23] Communication and expression are equally impossible. As Claude Mauriac notes, "ou nous parlons pour ne rien dire,
ou nous disons tous la même chose".[24] In the final analysis, "tous les
mots se valent et... ils disent tous la même chose,... ils répètent inlassablement le même appel au secours".[25] Yet the author-hero has no other
equipment with which to undertake his creation, his excavation. As Ruby
Cohn puts it, "we have nothing but language, at once our only tool and
our impenetrable barrier to understanding".[26] Language bars the way to
truth, but one cannot go on, as he must, without it. "Quand tout est
perdu", writes Onimus, "il reste la Parole. Elle se dresse toute seule aux
frontières du néant, ultime témoignage de présence humaine et si jamais
elle s'arrêtait, alors il n'y aurait vraiment plus rien."[27] "L'homme qui
perd sa trace, qui perd son paysage, et qui est en train de perdre son corps,
que lui reste-il", asks Domenach, "sinon la parole?"[28] Clinging to lan-

[22] Kenner, *A Critical Study*, 172.
[23] Janvier, "Les difficultés d'un séjour", 323.
[24] Mauriac, "Samuel Beckett", 78.
[25] Mauriac, 81.
[26] Cohn, *The Comic Gamut*, 155.
[27] Onimus, *Beckett*, 14.
[28] Domenach, *Le Retour du tragique*, 271.

guage as a tranquillizer and a refuge, the author-hero must embrace it, too, as the only means by which he can attempt to find and reveal the truth of himself. Although language, as we have seen, neither diverts him satisfactorily nor facilitates his search, outside of words, in the silence, he ceases to have any existence at all. As Klawitter observes: "Beckett's hero is desperately aware of the inadequacy of language, this tool of the spatializing intellect, to grasp the reality of temporal being. Yet ...this hero cannot simply live in himself without language because language is after all his world. His being is verbal, his silence unreal." [29] The paradox for the writer is, again, one of compulsion and impotence. Compelled to use language, he is at the same time incapable of making it work for him. Bound to the wheel of words, which circumscribe his surface personality, he can never reach the hub of the self. As Janvier describes the situation: "Qui est-on? Dans l'angoisse et l'impossibilité de toucher le fond toujours fuyant sous la parole qui le cherche, la seule trace de l'existant, ce seront ces mots qui à la fois lui appartiennent et ne sont pas à lui, le situent hors le monde et sont son seul monde, le disent et le mentent, le poursuivent par tous les détours et jamais ne le rattrapent." [30] The hero's only vital sign, words act at the same time to disperse his being, to decompose him, to draw him away from himself. According to Domenach, "les mots qui sont les seuls points fixes, se dissipent aussitôt prononcés, et le langage, qui assure qu'on n'est pas tout à fait mort, puisqu'on parle et qu'on entend, est en même temps ce qui nous évapore et nous étouffe, ce qui nous tue". [31] Stripped and starved like the hero himself, language might be forced to convey some part of the truth, "une parcelle du véritable moi, un mot au-delà les mots, une combinaison qui n'était jamais encore apparue à travers les millions de combinaisons usitées". [32] But this point of view is perhaps too optimistic. What is needed is an entirely new language, one which the self creates in order to make itself manifest. The discovery of such an idiom, however, remains to be made, and the creator is trapped as ever by his dilemma. Referring specifically to the Unnamable, Chambers writes: "To speak the language of the self, it will have to invent a new language, of timelessness and spacelessness. But meanwhile, knowing no words but the useless ones of the common tongue, it can only struggle on, performing its 'pensum," its absurd but unavoidable task, condemned to name itself with a language that cannot name it, and condemned not to

[29]   Klawitter, "Being and Time", 7320.
[30]   Janvier, *Pour Samuel Beckett*, 78-79.
[31]   Domenach, *Le Retour du tragique*, 274.
[32]   Domenach, 272.

cease trying to name itself until it has done so, condemned therefore to an endless 'wordy-gurdy' from which there is no escape." [33] The hero is unable to forge a new language, since "les formes linguistiques ne s'inventent pas; elles sont en dehors du pouvoir d'un homme isolé". [34] At the same time, conventional speech will never serve his purpose. What remains is the unbearable tension he feels "dans cet espace du non-être entre le langage public refusé et le langage privé infaisable". [35] Because he is bound to language, his fate is sealed, "for all speech is lying, and there is no end to creation, that impossible 'pensum': only by arriving at a truth at last could one earn the right to be silent." [36] But armed only with the dull tool of words, the creator cannot even approach the deep realm of truth at the center of being.

Thus, the desperate struggle to achieve fullness of identity remains forever ineffectual. Having to speak of the self and being unable to find adequate words, the narrator-hero unmasks language as "aimless search and constant deception". [37] Still, his dependence on words goes on eternally as a part of his very existence. "L'écrivain ...ne peut échapper à la condition du langage", writes Mme Bernal; "il ne peut écrire une phrase, un mot sans être entraîné dans les significations, sans retomber dans le déjà représenté. L'écrivain ne peut pas avoir recours à l'expédient de la page blanche, il doit parler et il est contraint aux mots. La page blanche n'est pas pour l'écrivain un silence communiqué tel le tableau blanc, mais menace d'inexistence. L'écrivain est captif du langage comme ne l'est aucun autre artiste de la matière qu'il travaille." [38] Compelled to create, he is, then, imprisoned by the disguises of his fictions which divert him from himself and by the mask of language which betrays him. Yet these obstacles to expiation are not the sole source of his difficulty. The obligation to express cannot be met in part because of the artist's very nature.

Traditionally, the artist is dual, and the nature of his duality has received considerable attention. In his study of the creative process, Beebe recalls that, according to tradition, a force greater than himself, a divine afflatus, descends upon the artist. Noting that this compulsion to create arises from within, Beebe identifies it as "the *persona*, the second self... implicit in the archetype of the artist". [39] Moreover, he describes the motive force as

[33] Chambers, "Beckett's Brinkmanship", 155-156.
[34] Bernal, *Langage et fiction*, 150.
[35] Bernal, 151.
[36] Mayoux, "Samuel Beckett and Universal Parody", 81.
[37] Wellershoff, "Failure of an Attempt at De-Mythologization", 105.
[38] Bernal, *Langage et fiction*, 90.
[39] Beebe, *Ivory Towers and Sacred Founts*, 310.

"that creative spirit which joins the maker with the creation" and suggests that "the best criticism of the future may be that which emphasizes neither the maker nor the work, but finds a link between them in that *persona* of the artist which functions like a Holy Ghost".[40] To define the means by which the inspirational force acts upon the creator, Beebe gives the example of Conrad who "liked to insist that he was but an agent for still another Conrad, a creative force that operated through him, making use of the physical energy of the mortal Conrad but remaining apart from the man".[41] Neither the man nor the writer, this inner force is above all essential to creation. It finds concrete representation in Joyce's character Shem of *Finnegans Wake*, who according to Beebe is "static and solipsistic, the nonconformist, the exile and the true artist".[42] Still, alone the creative urge can do little; it must have an agent. "Shem may write the manifesto". continues Beebe, "but he needs his brother to communicate it to the world, for the second self must always find a mortal body through whom to act."[43]

Clearly compelled to create by a force from within, the Beckettian artist is characterized by a marked duality. He is both the inner voice and the ear which hearkens to that voice. "Je suis Mathieu et je suis l'ange", declares the Unnamable (*L'Innommable*, p. 28). Combining in himself both divine inspiration and the means for its operation, the author-hero experiences constant tension between the commanding part of himself and that 'lower' part which must respond though it cannot. An example of the lack of cooperation between the two selves appears in *Words and Music*, where the aged Croak announces themes to be orchestrated and developed by his servants Words and Music. Not only does he have difficulties in making his commands understood, his agents themselves do not work well together; and as a result he is scarcely satisfied with their performance.[44] Here Croak plays the role of artistic inspiration while the other two characters portray the artist's inadequate and reluctant faculties in need of constant prodding. The experience of being spoken through, which we first encountered in the image of Neary compared to Saint Matthew (*Murphy*, p. 215), dominates the heroes of the later fiction. Describing them, Domenach writes: "ce qu'ils disent semble souvent passer à travers eux comme s'ils n'étaient que des haut-parleurs pour des

---

[40] Beebe, 301, 300.
[41] Beebe, 302.
[42] Beebe, 311.
[43] *Ibid.*
[44] *Words and Music*, 24-25.

émetteurs – eux-mêmes peut-être – très lointains."[45] Recalling the image
of the angel perched on the saint's shoulder (*Murphy*, p. 215), the narrator
of one later piece compares the voice he hears to "un ouistiti à la queue
touffue assis sur mon épaule à me tenir compagnie" (*Têtes*, p. 18). The
Unnamable, suggesting that he has no control over his words, compares
himself to a parrot: "Un perroquet, ils sont tombés sur un bec de perroquet" (*L'Innommable*, p. 99). In similar terms, one of the heroes in the
Textes menaces the voice which compels him to speak: "assez, sale perroquet, je te tuerai" (p. 177). But for the inner voice to be effective, it must
have a receptive ear. Consequently, the Unnamable finds at one point
that he is nothing more than "une pure oreille" (*L'Innommable*, p. 137)
The ear receives the words of the voice in order to convey them to the pen
or mouth for expression. The entire process, then, takes on the characteristics of continuous dictation, a motif which reappears in one work after
another. For example, the Unnamable says: "je dis ce que j'entends"
(*L'Innommable*, p. 257); and a hero from the *Textes* declares: "je le dis
comme je l'entends" (p. 163). But, since it is relatively more permanent,
the written word is preferable to speech for some. Thus, one narrator imagines that "d'autres doigts encore, d'autres tentacules, voilà, d'autres
bonnes ventouses... consignent mes déclarations" (*Textes*, p. 199). Another likes to think of a hand or at least of "quelque chose, quelque part,
qui laisse des traces, de ce qui se passe, de ce qui se dit" (*Textes*, pp. 215-
216).

The roles of the inner voice and its agent are perhaps best illustrated in
Comment c'est, where from the outset there is reference to dictation from
an unceasing voice – "je le dis comme je l'entends" (p. 9 and passim) – and
to a combination of ear and hand responding to the voice – "quelqu'un
qui écoute un autre qui note ou *le même*" (p. 10 and passim; my emphasis).
The distinct parts played by the artist's two selves become even more
clearly designated later in this novel when the narrator imagines that he is
being watched by a witness named Kram who conveys his observations to
a scribe Krim: "tout seul et le témoin penché sur moi nom Kram... et le
scribe nom Krim... tenant le greffe un peu à l'écart" (p. 98). Insisting that
this pair pursues work carried on for generations, the hero indicates the
endlessness of his situation and the constant, unrelenting agony of the artist's dilemma. Later he refers again to the two parts of himself, but suggests significantly that they are actually combined in one person: "Kram
qui écoute Krim qui note ou Kram seul un seul suffit Kram seul *témoin*

---

[45]   Domenach, *Le Retour du tragique*, 263.

et scribe ses feux qui m'éclairent Kram avec moi penché sur moi jusqu'à la limite d'âge puis son fils son petit-fils de suite" (p. 161; my emphasis). With the inner eye of self-perception fixed eternally upon him and compelling him to note unceasingly his own misery, the hero feels continuously watched and constantly forced to utter words at the dictate of his inner voice. Combined within himself, the witness and the scribe never leave their posts, never allow him a moment's rest.

In his essay on Proust, Beckett states unequivocally the dual nature of the artist and defines the kind of interaction which takes place between the inner force and its agent: "The artist has acquired his text: the artisan translates it" (*Proust*, p. 64). The inspired perception which the inner eye and voice convey must be processed by the conceptual faculties, must be given some tangible form. Stressing the duality of the author, whose task it is to give verbal form to his inner vision, Beckett quotes Proust: "The duty and the task of a writer (not an artist, a writer) are those of a translator" (p. 64).[46] The creator is, then, artist and artisan, inspired visionary and writer, he who perceives the yet unseen and he who makes that invisible perception visible, divine seer and interpreter. But, as shown in Chapter 1, the task of giving adequate form to one's inner vision is a most difficult and trying one. The effort must go on forever because the ideal image is never found. Once again the artist appears in the anguish of his dilemma, faced "on one hand [by] the ineluctable necessity of consciousness to express itself... and on the other [by] the impossibility of expression, since consciousness is by nature unique and uniqueness is by definition incommunicable".[47] Having its source deep within, the inner vision has nothing to do with the realm of words and so does not lend itself to verbal translation. Explaining the unique nature of the only art he considers valid, Proust calls attention to the problem of interpretation: "Seul il [l'art] exprime pour les autres et nous fait voir à nous-même notre propre vie, cette vie qui ne peut pas s' 'observer,' dont les apparences qu'on observe ont besoin d'être traduites, et souvent lues à rebours, et péniblement déchiffrées."[48] The creator, then, performs a double task; first, he strips existence to its essence, and then he gives an outward form to his essential vision. What the writer must translate is "the spiritual assimilation of the immaterial as provided by the artist, as extracted by him from life" (*Proust*, p. 48). But a simple translation is not enough. The image

---

[46] Cf. Proust, *Le Temps retrouvé, Œuvres complètes*, 7, pt. 2, (Paris: Nouvelle Revue Française, 1932), 40: "Le devoir et la tâche d'un écrivain sont ceux d'un traducteur".
[47] Morse, "The Ideal Core of the Onion", 23.
[48] Proust, *Le Temps retrouvé*, 48.

chosen to represent the inner vision must coincide precisely with that vision. As Beckett writes of form and content, "The one is a concretion of the other, the revelation of a world" (p. 67). Only perfect coincidence between image and idea will satisfy the inner voice, the artist within the writer. Only the most tangible transcription will reveal fully the most intangible inner world. Thus, the artisan must struggle again and again to approach the perfect image, to capture in its totality the inspired vision. It is his duty to find a form worthy of the compulsion itself, one which can translate, if nothing else, "l'urgence et la primauté de la vision intérieure".[49] The task is an impossible one, for the experience of the essential "resists interpretation by intellect";[50] the mind deforms authentic perception. Habit and language block the path to a satisfactory formal realization of the artist's vision. As seen in Chapter 2, authentic perception in itself is made difficult by constant conceptualization and rationalization. Memory and language obstruct the way to truth and its expression. As Ruby Cohn explains: "Since facts are empirical, and logic is tautological, knowledge of the world can be obtained only through the forms of a language which is filtered through a configuration of experience that may be called 'I'."[51] The writer must be on guard in conceiving and expressing his vision lest he be misled by habit and language.

Fully aware of the dangers inherent in mental processes, "all the narrators seek to convey the immediacy of experience before the rational intelligence tampers with it".[52] Camier, for example, distrusts the voice which whispers to him, because he knows the course it has had to run to reach him: "Mais elle est contaminée avant de nous parvenir, dit Camier. Ne sois pas puéril, Mercier. Pense un peu aux miasmes qu'elle a dû traverser" (*Mercier et Camier*, p. 97). Still ,the creator must possess both penetrating perception and the conceptual means to give his interior vision a corresponding artistic image. As Lascelles Abercrombie describes it: "The art of poetry is divisible into: (i) *Conception* or Internal Expression: the private expression of the inspiration in the poet's own mind, by the completion of the imaginative process into a stable, isolated and self-contained whole (which may be referred to as the Image [we call it the vision])... [and] (ii) *Technique* or External Expression: the publication of the Image [vision] in language."[53] Forever alien to the realm of language,

---

49 Beckett, "La Peinture des van Velde", 354.
50 Cohn, *The Comic Gamut*, 103.
51 Cohn, "Philosophical Fragments", 175.
52 Cohn, *The Comic Gamut*, 117.
53 L. Abercrombie, *Principles of English Prosody, Part I: The Elements* (London: M. Secker, 1923), 13-14.

the vision "is not itself communicable, since it does not and cannot exist in words, but it is a formalized experience. External expression in language cannot therefore be other than symbolic.... Technique has to provide an *imitation in words* of the Image [vision]; it cannot give the Image direct." [54] Perfect correspondence can never be achieved, then. Yet the creator must press on, must struggle on, though the result be but "the meagre 'precipitate'... of a long and difficult grappling with the incoercible raw materials of brute data".[55] In the novels, as we have seen, the author-heroes strive to create in spite of their impotence; and often their duality is at the source of their difficulties. Moran, for instance, must make an enormous and prolonged effort to understand the voice he hears: "J'ai parlé d'une voix qui me disait ceci et cela. Je commençais à m'accorder avec elle à cette époque, à comprendre ce qu'elle voulait. Elle ne se servait pas des mots qu'on avait appris au petit Moran, que lui à son tour a appris à son petit. De sorte que je ne savais pas d'abord ce qu'elle voulait. Mais j'ai fini par comprendre ce langage. Je l'ai compris, je le comprends, de travers peut-être. La question n'est pas là. C'est elle qui m'a dit de faire le rapport" (*Molloy*, p. 272). To speak the language of the self, one must first learn to understand it, and for Moran the lesson is hard. Even the heroes of the *Textes* do not master it. For example, one says of his attempt to transcribe the utterances of the inner voice: "C'est là-dedans ce soir les assises, au fond de cette nuit voûtée, c'est là où je tiens le greffe, ne comprenant pas ce que j'entends, ne sachant pas ce que j'écris" (p. 165). Confronted with essential perception, the intelligence is always at a loss. The artisan can never even know how close his image comes to correspondence with vision. Still, were he to achieve the most nearly perfect expression possible, the artist within him would sense it. As Beckett writes of the anti-intellectual artist, "Entendons-nous. Il sait chaque fois que ça y est, à la façon d'un poisson de haute mer qui s'arrête à la bonne profondeur, mais les raisons lui en sont épargnées." [56] Irrational, nonintellectual, the creative impulse is at the same time incomprehensible and irresistible. Responding to the deepest needs of his being, to see and know the self and to give form to this vision, the artist-artisan performs over and over the act which is for him existence itself. The difficulty of his work, however, cannot be underestimated, for it involves a making visible of the invisible, of the never yet seen. Stressing the value of this essential revelation, Sir Herbert Read

---

54   Abercrombie, *Principles of English Prosody, Part I: The Elements*, 14-15; Abercrombie's emphasis.
55   Fletcher, "The Private Pain and the Whey of Words", 24.
56   "La Peinture des van Velde", 356.

writes: "we must always distinguish (as Burckhardt does) between the craftsmen and the visionaries. 'To give tangible form to that which is inward, to represent it in such a way that we see it as the outward image of inward things – that is a most rare power. To recreate the external in external form – that is within the power of many.'"[57]

In the Beckettian universe, the lot of the artist is truly a miserable one – a life of agony, of constant tension between obligation and impotence – with no hope of satisfaction or respite. In fact, as surely as to be a man is to die, just so for the Beckettian hero "to be an artist is to fail".[58] The theme of failure appears in the earliest fiction where the hero Belacqua Shuah bears in his very name the stamp of inevitable failure (*Shuah* being derived most probably from the French verb *échouer* 'to fail'). Representing the human condition itself, this bungling hero seems to illustrate Bram van Velde's words: "Il faut comprendre: ce que fait l'homme n'a aucune valeur."[59] The inevitability of failure applies particularly to attempts to express or understand. In *Murphy*, for instance, the narrator describes silence as "that frail partition between the ill-concealed and the ill-revealed, the clumsily false and the unavoidably so" (p. 257). Declaring the uncertainty of all knowledge, Arsene in *Watt* insists upon the total impossibility of comprehension and meaningful expression: "what we know partakes in no small measure of the nature of what has so happily been called the unutterable or ineffable, so that any attempt to utter or eff it is doomed to fail, doomed, doomed to fail" (p. 62). Although more acutely aware of the disappointment of failure, the narrator-heroes grow accustomed to it even as they suffer from it. The Unnamable, for example wearily observes: "Je fais de mon mieux, je suis en train d'échouer, encore une fois. Ça ne me fait rien d'échouer, j'aime bien ça, seulement je voudrais me taire" (*L'Innommable*, p. 46). Indeed, the creator comes to regard his task as utterly beyond possibility and only hopes that it will soon come to an end: "que l'infaisable finisse et se taise le silence" (*Textes*, pp. 218-219). For the Beckettian artist, then, "creation always and inevitably spells failure".[60] As Germaine Brée says: "En marge de la comédie humaine se joue alors dans une sorte d'angoisse, le drame d'une création toujours en voie d'avortement, entreprise manquée, se situant quelque part entre l'obscurité et la lumière, toujours à reprendre."[61] Recogni-

---

[57] Read, "The Necessity of Art", 25.
[58] Beckett and G. Duthuit, "Three Dialogues", 21.
[59] "Paroles de Bram van Velde", *Derrière le Miroir* 11-12, 13.
[60] Fletcher, *Samuel Beckett's Art*, 21-22.
[61] Brée, "L'Etrange monde des 'grands articulés'", 91.

tion of his fate and total acceptance of it characterize the lucid artist, as Beckett describes him in the "Three Dialogues". Those who refuse to confront the truth of their dilemma suffer from "the malady of wanting to know what to do and the malady of wanting to be able to do it"[62] (an Apollonian affliction). But the lucid artist, like Bram van Velde, realizes "that expression is an impossible act"[63] and accepts the impossibility of his task without allowing that certitude to keep him from his work. Hailing van Velde as the first to demonstrate such lucidity, Beckett goes on to designate him as "the first to admit that to be an artist is to fail, as no other dare fail, that failure is his world and the shrink from it desertion, art and craft, good housekeeping, living." Further, in spite of "this submission, this admission, this fidelity to failure", the painter persists in his creative act, "the act which, unable to act, obliged to act, he makes".[64] Compelled to paint, he paints though he is totally bereft of the means and desire to do so. Although he knows that the result will only disappoint him, he must keep trying all the same.

Thus, the lucid artist's fidelity to failure does not stem from the choice of failure as an artistic goal, as some critics would lead us to believe.[65] To be an artist is to fail because to be an artist is to require of oneself the impossible expression of incommunicable perception. Beckett has not "deliberately chosen failure as an artistic goal";[66] he has rather shown over and over again how, for the self-conscious artist compelled to define himself through creation, there can be no other fate. The project being at once obligatory and impossible, the creator has no choice but to make repeatedly the same futile efforts, in short, to fail. Indeed, the novels are about the author-hero's endless unsuccessful attempts to reach the self through words, to be done with his endless series of self-portraits. Constantly reflecting his own impotence in his works, the lucid creator exemplifies, too, the futility of all human activity. Attuned to the state of human affairs as well as to his own anguish, the artist must reveal the truth of existence in general. As Beckett remarked in an interview, "One can only speak of what is in front of him, and that now is simply the mess."[67] Having renounced the blinders of habit and conventional ways of thinking the artist suffers from acute awareness both of his own inadequacy and of

---

[62] "Three Dialogues", 17.
[63] "Three Dialogues", 20.
[64] "Three Dialogues", 21.
[65] See Federman, *Journey to Chaos*, 9, 118, 203, and 204, and Leo Bersani, "No Exit for Beckett", *Partisan Review*, 33, 264.
[66] Federman, *Journey to Chaos*, 204.
[67] Driver, "Beckett by the Madeleine", 23.

the universal pitifulness of all mankind. As a revelation of the way things really are, responsible art refuses to compromise with our desire to be protected from the painful truth. In the end, "it is a failure because the human condition it reflects willy-nilly is a failure".[68]

Still, Beckett is most pessimistic not about life but about literature.[69] Merciless in its self-consciousness, his work as a whole moves "towards an impatience with 'literature' that is so severe as finally to make the art of fiction, as in *L'Innommable*, an art of unintelligibly orchestrating the ultimate Silence".[70] But a pronounced dissatisfaction with his creative efforts characterizes the narrator-hero even in the early fiction. Speaking of his writings, the hero of *Premier amour*, for example, declares that all but his epitaph "n'ont pas le temps de sécher qu'ils me dégoûtent déjà" (p. 9). Expressing himself much more forcibly, the narrator in *Mercier et Camier* has this to say of the writer's lot: "on sait à quoi on s'engage lorsqu'on fait de la littérature, à des déceptions qui feraient insérer au peintre ses pinceaux dans le cul".[71] Certainly this irrefutably strong statement reveals without doubt that the artist would prefer to succeed in his efforts but that he is compelled to fail. Molloy, too, uses unequivocally forceful language to express his opinion of the author's plight. "On ferait mieux, enfin aussi bien", he declares, "d'effacer les textes que de noircir les marges, de les boucher jusqu'à ce que tout soit blanc et lisse et que la connerie prenne son vrai visage, un non-sens cul et sans issue" (*Molloy*, p. 17). Resigned to his fate, the Unnamable refers to the artistic tendency simply as "le funeste penchant à l'expression" (*L'Innommable*, p. 212). Failure is inevitable for the writer, as for the artist in general, since the impossible is required of him. He must try to fulfill his obligation to express though "there is nothing to express, nothing with which to express, nothing from which to express, no power to express, no desire to express".[72] "Art", explains Harvey, "has been moved out of the 'domain of the feasible' where expression more or less adequate was possible."[73] Now the artist must discover an inexistent language if he is to speak of the self. Now he must get below the surface, wrench off the masks his fictions impose upon him. Yet "even the attempt to reach the truth by a gradual dis-

---

[68]   Fletcher, *Samuel Beckett's Art*, 145.
[69]   *Ibid.*
[70]   Scott, *Samuel Beckett*, 60.
[71]   Fletcher, "Sur un roman inédit", 148; cited from a copy of the original typescript, this passage does not appear in the edition of the novel published in 1970 by Editions de Minuit.
[72]   Beckett, "Three Dialogues", 17.
[73]   Harvey, "Life, Art, and Criticism", 555.

mantling of fictions is no more than another fiction";[74] and the creative
act appears once again "as the continuous failure of a quest for truth".[75]
Aspiring toward the impossible, the Beckettian artist will always be the
victim of a hopeless endeavor. Thus, "it is not as though the end of the
quest were joy and fulfillment".[76] On the contrary, the creator like all
humanity is condemned to frustration. Because, as Harvey says, "his
imperious need to know can never really be fulfilled", he is by definition
"a creature deprived, doomed to the eternal pursuit of an ever receding
goal".[77] Seeking always to be at one with himself through his creation, he
finds himself separated forever from the self by his fictions and by language.
Still the implacable compulsion, the persistent inner demand for expiation,
forces him to continue his efforts though they are doomed to fail from the
outset. Aware of his limitations and of the enormity of his task, the lucid
creator can only accept his fate, his failure. As Ruby Cohn interprets it,
"In the fiction Beckett pushes to the frontiers of art and being, knowledge
and being – beyond the illogical, paradoxical comedy of an absurd world,
to the cruel savage comedy of the necessary failure of creation and
creator." [78]

   The dilemma of the self-conscious artist is, then, without solution. His
agony must go on indefinitely, since he can never find the words which
would at last coincide precisely with the essence of his self. He is compelled
to recount over and over again the anguish of his plight, in an effort to
give it verbal form; but there is no language suited to his purpose, and he
can only go on with the hope of someday discovering that idiom which
would set him free. Paradoxically, however, as he pursues himself, as he
penetrates more and more deeply into the bottomless self, as he removes
mask after mask, he finds that he has less and less to go on with. In each
successive novel, the creator-hero is more deprived than ever, not only of
the physical means necessary to creation, but also of material for his
monologue. He becomes in the end frantic for something to say; and even
though he is eager for the peace of silence, he fears the nothingness which
silence represents. Further, realizing his utter inadequacy more clearly
with each renewed attempt at self-discovery, the author-hero, who must
reflect his present creative effort in his work, finds an ever diminishing
source of material in himself. Each new self-portrait limits the field of

[74] Wellershoff, "Failure of an Attempt at De-Mythologization", 106.
[75] *Ibid.*
[76] Harvey, "Life, Art, and Criticism", 549.
[77] *Ibid.*
[78] Cohn, "The Comedy of Samuel Beckett", 16.

possibility for the next. Growing self-consciousness, which gnaws away at
the protective, diverting veils of language and fiction, brings the hero ever
nearer to complete paralysis and silence. A reflection of his impotence, the
creation he can produce becomes more and more minimal, being the
meagre result of his ever more feeble efforts. As Beckett himself avows
in an interview: "For some authors writing gets easier the more they
write. For me it gets more and more difficult. For me the area of possibili-
ties gets smaller and smaller."[79] Taking *L'Innommable* as an example,
he continues: "At the end of my work there's nothing but dust – the
nameable. In the last book – 'L'Innommable' – there's complete disintegration. No 'I,' no 'have,' no 'being.' No nominative, no accusative, no
verb. There's no way to go on. The very last thing I wrote – 'Textes pour
Rien' – was an attempt to get out of the attitude of disintegration, but it
failed."[80] Perfectly aware of his plight, the artist who depicts his own
misery only finds himself more and more bound up by his inadequacy.
Writing of Bram van Velde (who has said, "Je peins ma misère"),[81]
Beckett describes the inevitable cul-de-sac situation into which the lucid
artist drives himself: "l'ensevelissement dans l'unique, dans un lieu d'impénétrables proximités, cellule peinte sur la pierre de la cellule, art d'in-
carcération".[82] Coming to a realization of his ultimate impotence, the
artist virtually paralyses himself by the mirror-image of his issueless plight.
Penetrating ever more deeply into the labyrinth of the inner self, he finds
himself imprisoned, buried, by his inability to give expression to the dreadful truth of his condition. Describing this kind of paralysis to Harvey,
Beckett speaks of "one on his knees, head against a wall – more like a
cliff – with someone saying 'go on'".[83] Ever compelled to express, the
artist incapable of expression endures a ceaseless agony. Ever more acute
self-perception threatens to bring about in the end the dreadful paralysis
of complete silence. Thus, the Beckettian quest leads the "the protean
hero in an ever-diminishing spiral toward total immobility and contain-
ment",[84] toward "the paralysis of identity".[85] Moreover, the artist compelled to create by intense self-consciousness experiences a sickening ver-
tigo brought on by the self-consuming activity of his consciousness. As
Onimus explains it: "La conscience n'est heureuse que dans l'action quand

[79] Shenker, "Moody Man of Letters", 1.
[80] Shenker, 1-3.
[81] "Paroles de Bram van Velde", 13.
[82] "Peintres de l'empêchement", 7.
[83] Harvey, "Life, Art, and Criticism", 556.
[84] Macksey, "The Artist in the Labyrinth", 250.
[85] *Ibid.*

elle s'accomplit au dehors, lorsqu'elle peut aimer, agir, espérer, se donner. Mais, lorsqu'elle se réverbère sur soi, un jeu de miroirs s'instaure dont le vertige est nauséeux. Invasion sournoise de l'être intérieur: on se trouve englué, pris au piège. La rupture avec le monde ne mène nullement au repos, au silence, mais à une effervescence morbide, à la frénésie d'une pensée qui, littéralement, se dévore elle-même."[86] It is against this delirium that the artist-hero struggles, but, ironically, he cannot escape from himself. Impotent and weary, he must try to keep on creating though his self-perception reveals constantly the impossibility of creation. He will fail inevitably, for his task is truly beyond his powers. But he will not cease making the impossible creative act; he must not stop, for his existence depends upon the endless self-portrait he creates. Though his path leads ever more painfully toward immobility and silence, he must continue to express in order to hold off the "glacial, aboriginal sleep"[87] which would come with his last word.

[86] Onimus, *Beckett*, 44.
[87] Hassan, *The Literature of Silence*, 114.

A SELECTED BIBLIOGRAPHY

WORKS BY SAMUEL BECKETT

Critical Essays

1929 "Dante ... Bruno . Vico .. Joyce", *Our Exagmination Round His Factification for Incamination of Work in Progress*, ed. by Sylvia Beach (Paris: Shakespeare and Co.), 3-22.

1931 *Proust* (London: Chatto and Windus); rpt. (New York: Grove Press, 1957).

1938 "Denis Devlin", *Transition*, 27, 289-294.

1945 "La Peinture des van Velde ou le monde et le pantalon", *Cahiers d'Art* 20-21, 349-354 and 356.

1948 "Peintres de l'empêchement", *Derrière le Miroir* 11-12, 3, 4, and 7.

1949 "Three Dialogues" (with Georges Duthuit), *Translation Forty-nine* 5, 97-103; rpt. in *Samuel Beckett: A Collection of Critical Essays*, ed. by Martin Esslin (= Twentieth Century Views) (Englewood Cliffs, N.J.: Prentice -Hall,1965), 16-22.

1958 *Bram van Velde* (with Georges Duthuit and Jacques Putnam) (Paris: Georges Fall). Deluxe edition (Turin: Fratelli Pozzo, 1961); American edition (New York: Harry N. Abrams, 1962?).

Narrative Prose

1934 *More Pricks Than Kicks* (London: Chatto and Windus). Mimeographed reedition (London: Calder and Boyars, 1966).

1938 *Murphy* (London: Routledge); rpt. (New York: Grove Press, 1957). French translation* (Paris: Bordas, 1947); rpt. (Paris: Editions de Minuit, 1965).

1951 *Molloy* (Paris: Editions de Minuit); rpt. 1965. English translation by Patrick Bowles in collaboration with the author (Paris: Olympia Press and New York: Grove Press, 1955) rpt. in *Three Novels* (New York: Grove Press, 1965), 7-176.

1951 *Malone meurt* (Paris: Editions de Minuit); rpt. 1963. English trans. *Malone Dies* (New York: Grove Press, 1956); rpt. in *Three Novels*, 1965, 179-288.

1953 *L'Innommable* (Paris: Editions de Minuit); rpt. 1969. English trans. *The Unnamable* (New York: Grove Press, 1958); rpt. in *Three Novels*, 1965, 291-414.

1953 *Watt* (Paris: Olympia Press); third edition (New York: Grove Press, 1959). French trans. by Ludovic and Agnès Janvier in collaboration with the author (Paris: Editions de Minuit, 1968).

1955 *Nouvelles et Textes pour rien* (Paris: Editions de Minuit; third edition, 1965. English trans. *Stories and Texts for Nothing* by Richard Seaver and Anthony Bonner in collaboration with the author (New York: Grove Press, 1967).

1956 "From an Abandoned Work", *Trinity News* 3, 4; rpt. in *No's Knife: Collected*

* Translations are by Beckett unless otherwise indicated.

Shorter Prose 1945-1966 (London: Calder and Boyars, 1967), 139-149. French trans. "D'un ouvrage abandonné", by Ludovic and Agnès Janvier in collaboration with the author (Paris: Editions de Minuit, 1967); rpt. in *Têtes-mortes* (Paris: Editions de Minuit, 1967), 7-30.

1959 "L'Image", *X, A Quarterly Review* 1, 35-37.

1961 *Comment c'est* (Paris: Editions de Minuit); rpt. 1969. English trans. *How It Is* (New York: Grove Press, 1964).

1965 "Imagination morte imaginez" (Paris: Editions de Minuit); rpt. in *Têtes-mortes*, 1967, 51-57. English trans. "Imagination Dead Imagine" (London: Calder and Boyars, 1965); rpt. in *No's Knife*, 1967, 161-164.

1966 "Assez" (Paris: Editions de Minuit); rpt. in *Têtes-mortes*, 1967, 33-47. English trans. "Enough" in *No's Knife*, 1967, 153-159.

1966 "Bing" (Paris: Editions de Minuit); rpt. in *Têtes-mortes*, 1967, 61-66. English trans. "Ping" in *No's Knife*, 1967, 165-168.

1967 "Dans le cylindre", *Livres de France* 18, 23-24.

1970 *Mercier et Camier* (Paris: Editions de Minuit).

1970 *Premier amour* (Paris: Editions de Minuit).

1970 "Lessness", *Evergreen Review* 14, 35-36.

Plays

1952 *En attendant Godot* (Paris: Editions de Minuit); rpt. 1963. English trans. *Waiting for Godot* (New York: Grove Press, 1954).

1957 *Fin de partie, suivi de Acte sans paroles* (Paris: Editions de Minuit); rpt. 1965. English trans. *Endgame, Followed by Act Without Words* (New York: Grove Press, 1958).

1957 *All That Fall* (New York: Grove Press); rpt. in *Krapp's Last Tape and Other Dramatic Pieces* (New York: Grove Press, 1960), 31-91. French trans. *Tous ceux qui tombent* by Robert Pinget and the author (Paris: Editions de Minuit, 1957); rpt. 1968.

1958 *Krapp's Last Tape, Evergreen Review* 2, 13-24; rpt. in *Krapp's Last Tape and Other Dramatic Pieces*, 1960, 9-28. French trans. *La Dernière bande* by Pierre Leyris and the author, *Lettres Nouvelles* 1, 5-13; rpt. in *La Dernière bande, suivi de Cendres* (Paris: Editions de Minuit, 1960); rpt. 1968, 5-33.

1959 *Embers, Evergreen Review* 3, 28-41; rpt. in *Krapp's Last Tape and Other Dramatic Pieces*, 1960, 93-121. French trans. *Cendres* by Robert Pinget and the author, *Lettres Nouvelles* 36, 3-14; rpt in *La Dernière bande, suivi de Cendres*, 1960, 35-72.

1961 *Happy Days* (New York: Grove Press). French trans. *Oh les beaux jours* (Paris: Editions de Minuit, 1963); rpt. 1969.

1962 *Words and Music, Evergreen Review* 6, 34-43; rpt. in *Cascando and Other Short Dramatic Pieces* (New York: Grove Press, 1967), 23-32. French trans. *Paroles et musique* in *Comédie et actes divers* (Paris: Editions de Minuit, 1966); rpt. 1969, 63-78.

1963 *Acte sans paroles II, Dramatische Dichtungen* 1 (Frankfort: Suhrkamp Verlag), 330-337; rpt in *Comédie et actes divers*, 1969, 95-99. English trans. *Act Without Words II* in *Krapp's Last Tape and Other Dramatic Pieces*, 1960, 137-141.

1963 *Cascando, Dramatische Dichtungen* 1, 338-361; rpt. in *Comédie et actes divers*, 1969, 47-60. English trans. in *Cascando and Other Short Dramatic Pieces*, 1967, 9-19.

1964 *Play* (London: Faber and Faber); rpt. in *Cascando and Other Short Dramatic Pieces*, 1967, 45-63. French trans. *Comédie* in *Comédie et actes divers*, 1969, 9-35.

1967 *Eh Joe* in *Eh Joe and Other Writings* (London: Faber and Faber); rpt. in *Cascando and Other Short Dramatic Pieces*, 1967, 35-41. French trans. *Dis Joe* in *Comédie et actes divers*, 1969, 81-91.

1967 *Come and Go* (London: Calder and Boyars); rpt. in *Cascando and Other Short Dramatic Pieces*, 1967, 67-71. French trans. *Va et vient* in *Comédie et actes divers*, 1969, 39-44.

1967 *Film* in *Cascando and Other Short Dramatic Pieces*, 75-88; rpt. in *Film* (New York: Grove Press, 1969).

1970 *Breath*, produced by the British Broadcasting Co. for television, presented by the National Broadcasting Co. on its program "First Tuesday", April 7, 1970.

CRITICISM AVAILABLE IN BOOK FORM

Bauer, George H.
  1969 *Sartre and the Artist* (Chicago: University of Chicago Press).
Beebe, Maurice
  1964 *Ivory Towers and Sacred Founts: The Artist as Hero in Fiction from Goethe to Joyce* (New York: New York University Press).
Bernal, Olga
  1969 *Langage et fiction dans le roman de Beckett* (Paris: Gallimard).
Calder, John ed.
  1967 *Beckett at 60: A Festschrift* (London: Calder and Boyars).
Cohn, Ruby
  1962 *Samuel Beckett: The Comic Gamut* (New Brunswick, N.J.: Rutgers University Press).
Cohn, Ruby ed.
  1959 *Perspective* 11, 119-196.
  1966 *Modern Drama* 9, 237-346.
  1967 *Casebook on "Waiting for Godot"* (New York: Grove Press).
Deyle, Huguette
  1960 *Samuel Beckett, ou la philosophie de l'absurde* (Aix-en-Provence: La Pensée Universitaire).
Domenach, Jean-Marie
  1967 *Le Retour du tragique* (Paris: Editions du Seuil).
Esslin, Martin
  1961 *The Theatre of the Absurd* (Garden City, New York: Doubleday).
Esslin, Martin ed.
  1965 *Samuel Beckett: A Collection of Critical Essays* (= Twentieth Century Views) Englewood Cliffs, N.J.: Prentice-Hall).
Federman, Raymond
  1965 *Journey to Chaos: Samuel Beckett's Early Fiction* (Berkeley: University of California Press).
Federman, Raymond and John Fletcher
  1970 *Samuel Beckett: His Works and His Critics* (Berkeley: University of California Press).
Fletcher, John
  1964 *The Novels of Samuel Beckett* (London: Chatto and Windus).
  1967 *Samuel Beckett's Art* (London: Chatto and Windus).
Friedman, Melvin J. ed.
  1964 *Samuel Beckett: Configuration critique* (Paris: M. J. Minard).
Grossvogel, David I.
  1958 *The Self-Conscious Stage in Modern French Drama* (New York: Columbia University Press).
  1962 *Four Playwrights and a Postscript: Brecht, Ionesco, Beckett, Genêt* (Ithaca, N.Y.: Cornell University Press).

Hassan, Ihab
1967 *The Literature of Silence: Henry Miller and Samuel Beckett* (New York: Knopf).
Hayman, Ronald
1968 *Samuel Beckett* (London: Heinemann).
Hoffman, Frederick J.
1964 *Samuel Beckett: The Language of Self* (New York: Dutton).
Janvier, Ludovic
1966 *Pour Samuel Beckett* (Paris: Editions de Minuit).
Kenner, Hugh
1961 *Samuel Beckett: A Critical Study* (Berkeley: University of California Press); revised ed., 1968.
1962 *Flaubert, Joyce and Beckett: The Stoic Comedians* (Boston: Beacon Press).
Mercier, Vivian
1962 *The Irish Comic Tradition* (Oxford: Clarendon Press).
Onimus, Jean
1968 *Beckett* (= Les écrivains devant Dieu, 16) (Bruges, Belgium: Desclée de Brouwer).
Pronko, Leonard C.
1962 *Avant-garde: The Experimental Theater in France* (Berkeley: University of California Press).
Scott, Nathan A.
1965 *Samuel Beckett* (London: Bowes and Bowes).
Sypher, Wylie
1962 *Loss of the Self in Modern Literature and Art* (New York: Random House).
Tindall, William York
1964 *Samuel Beckett* (= Columbia Essays on Modern Writers, 4) (New York: Columbia University Press).

CRITICAL ESSAYS AND ARTICLES IN PERIODICALS

Abirached, Robert
1964 "La Voix tragique de Samuel Beckett", *Etudes* 320, 85-88.
Bajomée, Danielle
1969 "Lumière, ténèbres et chaos dans *L'Innommable* de Samuel Beckett", *Lettres Romanes* 23, 139-158.
Bataille, Georges
1951 "Le Silence de Molloy", *Critique* 7, 387-396.
Bishop, Tom
1969 "Samuel Beckett", *Saturday Review*, 15 November, 26-27 and 59.
Boisdeffre, Pierre de
1959 "Samuel Beckett ou l'au-delà", in his *Une Histoire vivante de la littérature d'aujourd'hui, 1939-1959* (Paris: Le Livre contemporain).
Booth, Wayne C.
1957 "The Self-Conscious Narrator in Comic Fiction Before *Tristram Shandy*", *PMLA* 67, pt. 1, 163-185.
Bowles, Patrick
1958 "How Samuel Beckett Sees the Universe", *The Listener* 59, no. 1525, 1011-1012.
Brée, Germaine
1964 "L'Etrange monde des 'grands articulés'", *Samuel Beckett: Configuration critique*, ed. by Melvin J. Friedman (Paris: M. J. Minard), 83-97.

Brick, Allan
    1959   "The Madman in His Cell: Joyce, Beckett, Nabokov and the Stereotypes",
           The Massachusetts Review 1, 40-55.
Butler, Michael
    1961   "Anatomy of Despair", *Encore* 8, 17-24.
Chambers, Ross
    1965   "Beckett's Brinkmanship", *Samuel Beckett: A Collection of Critical Essays*,
           ed. by Martin Esslin (= Twentieth Century Views) (Englewood Cliffs, N.J.:
           Prentice-Hall), 152-168.
    1967   "Vers une interprétation de 'Fin de Partie'", *Studi Francesi* 11, 90-96.
Cixous, Hélène
    1969   "Le maître du texte pour rien", *Le Monde* 1096, 13.
Cmrada, Geraldine
    1960   "*Malone Dies*: A Round of Consciousness", *Symposium* 14, 199-212.
Coe, Richard N.
    1963   "Le Dieu de Samuel Beckett", *Cahiers de la Compagnie Madeleine Renaud –
           Jean-Louis Barrault* 44, 6-36.
Cohn, Ruby
    1959   "The Comedy of Samuel Beckett: 'Something old, something new...'", *Yale
           French Studies* 23, 11-17.
    1959   "Still Novel", *Yale French Studies* 24, 48-53.
    1961   "*Watt* in the Light of *The Castle*", *Comparative Literature* 13, 154-166.
    1962   "Play and Player in the Plays of Samuel Beckett", *Yale French Studies* 29,
           43-48.
    1965   "Philosophical Fragments in the Works of Samuel Beckett", *Samuel Beckett:
           A Collection of Critical Essays*, ed. by Martin Esslin (= Twentieth Century
           Views) (Englewood Cliffs, N.J.: Prentice-Hall), 169-177.
    1966   "Acting for Beckett", *Modern Drama* 9, 237.
Davin, Dan
    1956   "Mr. Beckett's Everymen", *Irish Writing* 34, 36-39.
Driver, Tom F.
    1961   "Beckett by the Madeleine", *Columbia University Forum* 4, 21-25.
Dukore, Bernard F.
    1965   "Beckett's Play, *Play*" *Educational Theatre Journal* 17, 19-23.
Easthope, Anthony
    1968   "Hamm, Clov, and Dramatic Method in *Endgame*", *Modern Drama* 10, 424-
           433.
Erickson, John D.
    1967   "Objects and Systems in the Novels of Samuel Beckett", *L'Esprit Créateur* 7,
           113-122.
Esslin, Martin
    1962   "Looking for Beckett", *The Listener* 68, no. 1757, 923.
    1962   "Samuel Beckett", *The Novelist as Philosopher*, ed, by John Cruickshank
           (London and New York: Oxford University Press), 128-146.
    1963   "Godot and His Children: The Theatre of Samuel Beckett and Harold Pinter",
           Experimental Drama, ed. by William A. Armstrong (London: G. Bell), 128-
           146.
    1965   "Introduction", in his *Samuel Beckett: A Collection of Critical Essays* (=
           Twentieth Century Views) (Englewood Cliffs, N.J.: Prentice-Hall), 1-15.
    1967   "Samuel Beckett's Poems", *Beckett at 60: A Festschrift*, ed. by John Calder
           (London: Calder and Boyars), 55-60.
Federman, Raymond
    1967   "*Film*", *Film Quarterly* 20, 46-51.

Fletcher, John
1964 "Beckett et Proust", *Caliban: Annales Publiées par la Faculté des Lettres de Toulouse* 1, 89-100.
1965 "Beckett and the Fictional Tradition", *Caliban: Annales Publiées par la Faculté des Lettres et Sciences Humaines de Toulouse* n.s. 1, 147-158.
1965 "The Private Pain and the Whey of Words: A Survey of Beckett's Verse", *Samuel Beckett: A Collection of Critical Essays*, ed. by Martin Esslin (= Twentieth Century Views) (Englewood Cliffs, N.J.: Prentice-Hall), 23-32.
1965 "Sur un roman inédit de Samuel Beckett", *Littératures 12: Annales Publiées par la Faculté des Lettres et Sciences de Toulouse* n.s. 1, 139-152.
1966 "Action and Play in Beckett's Theater", *Modern Drama* 9, 242-250.
1967 "Roger Blin at Work", *Casebook on "Waiting for Godot"*, ed. by Ruby Cohn (New York: Grove Press), 21-26.
Friedman, Melvin J.
1967 "Molloy's 'Sacred' Stones", *Romance Notes* 9, 8-11.
Frye, Northrop
1960 "The Nightmare Life in Death", *Hudson Review* 13, 442-449.
Furbank, P. N.
1964 "Beckett's Purgatory", *Encounter* 22, 69-70, and 72.
Gerard, Martin
1960 "Molloy becomes Unnamable", *X, A Quarterly Review* 1, 314-319.
Glicksberg, Charles I.
1961 "Forms of Madness in Literature", *The Arizona Quarterly* 17, 43-53.
1962 "The Lost Self in Modern Literature", *Personalist* 43, 537-538.
1962 "Samuel Beckett's World of Fiction", *The Arizona Quarterly*, 18, 32-47.
Gresset, Michel
1963 "Création et cruauté chez Beckett", *Tel Quel* 15, 58-65.
Gruen, John
1969 "Nobel Prize Winner, 1969. Samuel Beckett Talks About Beckett", *Vogue* 154, 210.
Hamilton, Carol
1962 "Portrait in Old Age: The Image of Man in Beckett's Trilogy", *Western Humanities Review* 16, 157-165.
Hamilton, Kenneth
1959 "Boon or Thorn? Joyce Cary and Samuel Beckett on Human Life", *The Dalhousie Review* 38, 433-442.
Harvey, Lawrence E.
1960 "Art and the Existential in *Waiting for Godot*", *PMLA* 75, pt. 1, 137-146.
1964 "Samuel Beckett: Initiation du poète", *Samuel Beckett: Configuration critique*, ed. by Melvin J. Friedman (Paris: M. J. Minard), 153-168.
1965 "Samuel Beckett on Life, Art, and Criticism", *Modern Language Notes* 80, 545-562.
Hayman, David
1962 "Quest for Meaninglessness: The Boundless Poverty of *Molloy*", *Six Contemporary Novels*, ed. by W. O. S. Sutherland, Jr. (Austin, Texas: University of Texas Press), 90-112.
Hobson, Harold
1967 "The First Night of *Waiting for Godot*", *Beckett at 60: A Festschrift*, ed. by John Calder (London: Calder and Boyars), 25-28.
Hoefer, Jacqueline
1965 "*Watt*", *Samuel Beckett: A Collection of Critical Essays*, ed. by Martin Esslin (= Twentieth Century Views) (Englewood Cliffs, N.J.: Prentice-Hall), 62-76.

Janvier, Ludovic
  1969 "Les difficultés d'un séjour", *Critique* 25, 312-323.
Johnston, Denis
  1956 "Waiting With Beckett", *Irish Writing* 34, 23-28.
Kern, Edith
  1955 "Drama Stripped for Inaction: Beckett's *Godot*", *Yale French Studies* 14, 41-47.
  1959 "Moran-Molloy: The Hero as Author", *Perspective* 11, 183-193.
  1959 "Samuel Beckett – Dionysian Poet", *Descant* 3, 33-36.
  1962 "Beckett's Knight of Infinite Resignation", *Yale French Studies* 29, 49-56.
  1966 "Beckett and the Spirit of the Commedia Dell'Arte", *Modern Drama* 9, 260-267.
Kenner, Hugh
  1967 "Progress Report, 1962-65", *Beckett at 60: A Festschrift*, ed. by John Calder (London: Calder and Boyars), 61-77.
Klawitter, Robert L.
  1965 "Being and Time in Samuel Beckett's Novels", *Dissertation Abstracts* 26, pt. 6, 7320.
Lamont, Rosette
  1964 "La Farce métaphysique de Samuel Beckett", *Samuel Beckett: Configuration critique*, ed. by Melvin J. Friedman (Paris: M. J. Minard), 99-116.
Macksey, Richard
  1962 "The Artist in the Labyrinth: Design or *Dasein*", *Modern Language Notes* 77, 239-256.
Mauriac, Claude
  1958 "Samuel Beckett" in his *L'Allitérature contemporaine* (Paris: A. Michele), 77-92.
Mayoux, Jean-Jacques
  1959 "The Theatre of Samuel Beckett", trans. by Ruby Cohn, *Perspective* 11, 142-155.
  1965 "Samuel Beckett and Universal Parody", trans. by Barbara Bray, *Samuel Beckett: A Collection of Critical Essays*, ed. by Martin Esslin (= Twentieth Century Views) (Englewood Cliffs, N.J.: Prentice-Hall), 77-91.
  1966 "Beckett and Expressionism", trans. by Ruby Cohn, *Modern Drama* 9, 238-241.
Moore, J. R.
  1967 "Some Night Thoughts", *The Massachusetts Review* 8, 529-539.
Morrissette, Bruce
  1964 "Les Idées de Robbe-Grillet sur Beckett", *Samuel Beckett: Configuration critique*, ed. by Melvin J. Friedman (Paris: M. J. Minard), 55-67.
Morse, J. Mitchell
  1964 "The Ideal Core of the Onion: Samuel Beckett's Criticism", *French Review* 38, 23-29.
Nadeau, Maurice
  1951 "Samuel Beckett, l'humour et le néant", *Mercure de France* 1056, 693-697.
  1952 "Samuel Beckett ou le droit au silence", *Les Temps Modernes* 7, 1273-1282.
  1963 "Le chemin de la parole au silence", *Cahiers de la Compagnie Madeleine Renaud – Jean-Louis Barrault* 44, 63-66.
Oates, J. C.
  1962 "The Trilogy of Samuel Beckett", *Renascence* 14, 160-165.
Radke, Judith
  1962 "The Theater of Samuel Beckett: 'Une Durée à Animer'", *Yale French Studies* 29, 57-64.

Read, Herbert
  1969 "The Necessity of Art", *Saturday Review*, 6 December, 24-27.
Reid, Alec
  1962 "Beckett and the Drama of Unknowing", *Drama Survey* 2, 130-138.
Rexroth, Kenneth
  1959 "Samuel Beckett and the Importance of Waiting", in his *Bird in the Bush* (New York: Laughlin), 75-85.
Rickels, Milton
  1962 "Existential Themes in Beckett's *Unnamable*", *Criticism* 4, 134-147.
Schneider, Alan
  1969 "On Directing *Film*", Film (New York: Grove Press), 63-94.
Senneff, Susan F.
  1964 "Song and Music in Samuel Beckett's *Watt*", *Modern Fiction Studies* 10, 137-149.
Serreau, Geneviève
  1966 "Samuel Beckett", in her *Histoire du "Nouveau Théâtre"* (Paris: Gallimard), 83-116.
Shenker, Israel
  1956 "Moody Man of Letters", *New York Times*, 6 May, sec. 2, 1 and 3.
Steiner, George
  1968 "Of Nuance and Scruple", *The New Yorker*, 27 April, 164-174.
Tindall, William York
  1958 "Beckett's Bums", *Critique: Studies in Modern Fiction* 2, 3-15; rpt. privately (London: Shenval Press, 1960).
Todd, Robert E.
  1967 "Proust and Redemption in *Waiting for Godot*", *Modern Drama* 10, 175-181.
Torrance, Robert M.
  1967 "Modes of Being and Time in the World of *Godot*", *Modern Language Quarterly* 28, 77-95.
Updike, John
  1965 "How How It Is Was", in his *Assorted Prose* (New York- Knopf), 314-318.
Warhaft, Sidney
  1963 "Threne and Theme in *Watt*", *Wisconsin Studies in Contemporary Literature* 4, 261-278.
Wellershoff, Dieter
  1965 "Failure of an Attempt at De-Mythologization: Samuel Beckett's Novels", *Samuel Beckett: A Collection of Critical Essays*, ed. and trans. by Martin Esslin (= Twentieth Century Views) (Englewood Cliffs, N.J.: Prentice-Hall) 92-107.
Wellwarth, G. E.
  1961 "Life in the Void: Samuel Beckett", *University of Kansas City Review* 28, 25-33
Wilson, Robert N.
  1964 "Samuel Beckett: The Social Psychology of Emptiness", *Journal of Social Issues* 20-21, 62-70.

INDEX

de proprietatibus litterarum

Dfl.

de proprietatibus litterarum

Dfl.

de proprietatibus litterarum